Arts Entrepreneurship

Arts Entrepreneurship: Creating a New Venture in the Arts provides the essential tools, techniques, and concepts needed to invent, launch, and sustain a business in the creative sector.

Building on the reader's artistic talents and interests, the book provides a practical, action-oriented introduction to the business of art, focusing on product design, organizational planning and assessment, customer identification and marketing, fundraising, legal issues, money management, cultural policy, and career development. It also offers examples, exercises, and references that guide entrepreneurs through the key stages of concept creation, business development, and growth. Special attention is paid to topics such as cultural ventures seeking social impact, the emergence of creative placemaking, the opportunities afforded by novel corporate forms, and the role of contemporary technologies in marketing, fundraising, and operations.

A hands-on guide to entrepreneurial success, this book is a valuable resource for students of Arts Entrepreneurship programs, courses, and workshops, as well as for early-stage business founders in the creative sector looking for guidance on how to create and sustain their own successful venture.

Richard S. Andrews teaches Arts Entrepreneurship at UC Berkeley and other universities in the US and abroad. He is the Associate Director of the UC Berkeley Center for New Music and Audio Technologies (CNMAT) and Executive Director of the Eco Ensemble. He has been working in arts management for over twenty years.

Arts Entrepreneurship
Creating a New Venture in the Arts

Richard S. Andrews

 Routledge
Taylor & Francis Group

NEW YORK AND LONDON

First published 2020
by Routledge
52 Vanderbilt Avenue, New York, NY 10017

and by Routledge
2 Park Square, Milton Park, Abingdon, Oxon, OX14 4RN

Routledge is an imprint of the Taylor & Francis Group, an informa business

Library of Congress Cataloging-in-Publication Data
Names: Andrews, Richard S., author.
Title: Arts entrepreneurship : creating a new venture in the arts / Richard S. Andrews.
Description: New York : Routledge, 2020. | Includes index.
Identifiers: LCCN 2019020579 | ISBN 9781138889767 (hardback) |
ISBN 9781138889743 (paperback) | ISBN 9781315712635 (ebook)
Subjects: LCSH: Arts—Management. | Arts—Economic aspects.
Classification: LCC NX760 .A53 2020 | DDC 706—dc23
LC record available at https://lccn.loc.gov/2019020579

ISBN: 978-1-138-88976-7 (hbk)
ISBN: 978-1-138-88974-3 (pbk)
ISBN: 978-1-315-71263-5 (ebk)

Typeset in Univers
by codeMantra

Contents

List of Illustrations ix

Preface x

Acknowledgments xiv

Chapter 1 *What Is Arts Entrepreneurship?* 1
Definitions of Entrepreneurship 1
Developing a Business Idea 3
Marketing the Business 8
Building the Business 9
Design of the Business Launch 11
Arts Entrepreneurship 15
Collaborating 28
Launching a New Business 30
Chapter Summary 31
Discussion Questions 33
Notes 34

Chapter 2 *Planning and Assessment* 35
Planning for Artists and Arts Organizations 35
Defining the Vision, Mission, and Goals of the Organization 36
Strategic Planning 40
Evaluation and Assessment 55
Chapter Summary 65
Discussion Questions 66
Notes 66

Chapter 3 *Marketing* 67
The Role of Marketing in Shaping Your Image: Educating
Your Audience and Inviting Participation 68
The Exchange Model of Interaction Between Producers and
Consumers 70
Market Research and Competitive Analysis: Understanding
Customers and the Marketing Landscape 71

Promoting and Growing a New Business   73
Strategic Marketing Plans   77
Internal Databases, Software, Tools, and Techniques for the
   Planning, Execution, and Evaluation of Marketing   82
Integrated Digital Marketing   90
Connecting Your Products and Services with the Needs and
   Wants of the People in Your Market   100
Create Your Marketing Plan   101
Chapter Summary   103
Discussion Questions   103
Notes   104
Further Reading   104

Chapter 4 *Fundraising*   106
Why Is Fundraising So Important for a Nonprofit
   Arts Organization?   106
Developing Fundraising Materials   108
Evaluating Funding Methods   114
Crowdfunding   118
Fundraising Via Email, Websites, Social Media, and
   Text/IM Channels   123
Special Events   126
Understanding Why and How People Give   127
Researching Funding Sources   128
The Fundraising Strategy   134
Creating and Implementing Your Fundraising Plan   137
Data Management   141
Chapter Summary   142
Discussion Questions   143
Notes   143
Further Reading   144

Chapter 5 *Legal Issues*   145
Disclaimer   145
Choosing a Corporate Form   146
Legal Structures for Arts Organizations: Not-for-Profit   146
Legal Structures for Arts Organizations: For-Profit   148
Evaluating the Many Choices of Legal Forms for
   Your Arts Venture   153
Artists' Rights Under the Law   154
Tax Planning   159
Limiting Liability: Insurance and Risk Management   161
Corporate Organizational Structure   164
Developing a Board of Directors   168
Structure, Management, and Resource Allocation   170
Articles of Incorporation   172

Bylaws, Operating Agreements, Memorandums
   of Understanding   172
Other Business Requirements   173
Chapter Summary   174
Discussion Questions   176
Notes   176

Chapter 6   *Money Management and Entrepreneurial
Finance*   178
Financial Vision and Goals   179
Personal Expenses   179
Personal Budget   179
Business Budget   181
Other Financial Documents   186
Using Financial Reports to Keep Your Business on Track   194
Banking   197
Bookkeeping, Accounting, and Taxes   204
Record-Keeping, Archives, Filing Documents, Searchable
   Financial History   205
Chapter Summary   205
Discussion Questions   206
Notes   206
Further Reading   207

Chapter 7   *Cultural Policy and the Arts Entrepreneur*   208
The Origins of Cultural Policy   208
History of Cultural Policy in Other Countries   209
History of Cultural Policy in the US   211
US Government Grants and Loans for Culture and Art   214
Exploring Arts Agencies and Making Connections   217
Cultural Policy and the Law   221
Taxes, Including Charitable Deductions and 501(C)(3) Status   223
More Examples of Government Policies and Regulations
   that Can Have an Impact on an Arts Venture   226
Outsourcing   232
International Organizations and Foreign Ownership   234
Labor Laws for Employees, Owners, Contractors   234
Censorship   234
Chapter Summary   236
Discussion Questions   237
Notes   238

Chapter 8   *Organizational Design, Career
Development, and Future Trends*   240
Organizational Design   240
Use an Organizational Chart to Define the Roles and
   Communicate the Organizational Structure   242

Communication   243
Documentation and Records Retention   246
Assigning Responsibilities and Managing People   246
Career Development   253
Future Trends in Arts Entrepreneurship   262
Chapter Summary   270
Discussion Questions   272
Notes   273

Index   275

Illustrations

Figures

2.1 Strategic planning spreadsheet   46

6.1 Simple business budget   185

6.2 Complex business budget   185

6.3 Business budget vs. actuals   187

6.4 Cash flow projection   188

6.5 Break-even analysis   189

6.6 Profit and loss statement   191

6.7 Profit and loss statement with contributed income   192

6.8 Balance sheet   193

Table

4.1 Different funding sources for not-for-profit performing
arts groups and museums, 2012   135

Preface

A student filmmaker launches her own production company. An independent musician develops a career with multiple income streams. An arts educator creates an organization that encourages young learners from underserved communities to stay engaged in school. An art and technology major is hired to work for a company that helps connect visual artists with active collectors.

These are just a few examples of students who have made arts entrepreneurship part of their education and, eventually, their professional lives. Based on my experience teaching courses and workshops on arts entrepreneurship at UC Berkeley and elsewhere, this book aims to provide students with the knowledge, inspiration, and guidance to build their own company – or design their own career path – upon the foundation of their artistic talents and interests.

"Artists are the ultimate entrepreneurs."[1] As an area of study, arts entrepreneurship covers a wide range of topics, from business concept development to cultural policy issues, marketing strategies, fundraising techniques, legal areas, and financial management tools. *Arts Entrepreneurship: New Venture Creation for Artists* is designed to offer a useful, engaging introduction to each of these areas. The chapters present basic concepts, working methods, and valid business techniques while opening pathways for further exploration.

The contents for each topic are presented in a practical, straightforward manner. Many students prefer practical training in arts entrepreneurship because of the way this type of instruction contrasts with their other coursework. Other students prefer practical learning in order to immediately put their new knowledge and skills to work in the formation of a creative business, or in the building of a career in the arts.

This is not to say that theoretical discourse about arts entrepreneurship is less useful or necessary. On the contrary, there are number of good resources that investigate this area, especially those found in *Artivate: A Journal of Entrepreneurship in the Arts*[2] and the *International Journal of Arts and Entrepreneurship*.[3] The practical approach to arts entrepreneurship found in this book offers a complementary perspective to these and other texts focused on theory and conceptual interrogations. There are many facets of arts entrepreneurship worth studying – students should explore all of those that align with their needs and interests.

Each of the chapters in this text can be studied in any order that works with the reader's instructional program, although starting with *Chapter 1: What Is Arts Entrepreneurship?* is highly recommended because it addresses the fundamental issues around connecting the founder's personal values and goals with a viable business concept. The *Planning and Assessment* chapter (Chapter 2) emphasizes the many benefits realized through the careful design and objective analysis of an arts venture. It also lays out the basics for creating your own Business Plan, which is a project you can go back to and develop after reading the other chapters. Creating an engaging, comprehensive Business Plan can be a key goal for Arts Entrepreneurship students aiming to apply their knowledge in the formation of their own creative business.

The *Marketing* chapter (Chapter 3) introduces both market research and the development and execution of strategic marketing plans. The rapidly evolving area of digital marketing (via websites, social media, email, and text/SMS) is explored, while readers are encouraged to develop links between their unique product or service and their target consumer. Chapter 4 on *Fundraising* focuses on contributed income for the nonprofit arts organization, while the *Money Management and Entrepreneurial Finance* chapter (Chapter 6) discusses how to attract investments, manage budgets, and produce essential financial reports. Chapter 5, *Legal Issues*, covers a wide range of topics such as corporate formation, intellectual property and risk management.

Chapter 7 on *Cultural Policy* will be especially useful for business founders looking to establish an international venture, or one that operates in multiple countries. Like social entrepreneurship, international arts entrepreneurship is an area that interests many students. Results from an online survey published in D'Art Report 48[4] by the International Federation of Arts Councils and Culture Agencies (IFACCA) offer some intriguing data on "sectors of arts and creative industries that are most suitable for starting up entrepreneurial ventures."[5]

Respondents to the survey ranked sectors as follows:

music and sound recording (73 percent)
visual and applied arts (72 percent)
performing arts (62 percent)
crafts (62 percent)
design (61 percent)
cultural heritage (60 percent)
fashion (50 percent)
film (45 percent)

video (34 percent)
publishing (33 percent)
multimedia art (33 percent)
animation (28 percent)
computer games (27 percent)
architecture (22 percent)
others (11 percent)[6]

The final chapter on *Organizational Design, Career Development, and Future Trends* (Chapter 8) presents a number of ideas for organizational development and job seeking, along with suggestions about where arts entrepreneurship might be headed in the future.

With a dynamic, quickly developing area such as arts entrepreneurship, it is challenging to identify and incorporate the "best" or "optimal" strategies and resources for designing, launching, and sustaining a new venture. Web links become broken, technologies are replaced by new inventions, and news articles, interviews, and case studies emerge that reshape our understanding of – and approach to – entrepreneurial endeavors in the creative sector. This is the reason why each chapter's Notes section contains a (mostly) modest number of citations, while readers are encouraged in the main body of the text to undertake their *own* online research using suggested search terms, or others they can imagine. To develop a more fully rounded picture of each topic, online research should be combined with in-person interviews, site visits, and further study. The wealth of new ideas, tools, and materials for arts entrepreneurship will continue to grow and change – students should discover how to conduct their own research at an early stage so they can keep learning and developing along with the field. That said, the sources listed in the Further Reading and Notes sections at the end of the chapters include a number of key texts that should be consulted when undertaking a thorough exploration of arts entrepreneurship's main elements.

Business founders and arts managers have a number of interests in common: they need to understand concept development, marketing, fundraising, legal issues, financial management, organizational structure, and human resources in order to successfully manage their responsibilities and keep their business on track. The overlap between Arts Entrepreneurship and Arts Management as topics of study means that there will necessarily be some areas in this book that will also be useful for aspiring arts managers. This is in fact a necessary – and desirable – situation, since many of my Arts Entrepreneurship students have used the training found in this text to start their careers by working for existing organizations in the arts before launching their own venture. *Arts Entrepreneurship: New Venture Creation for Artists* can help the reader develop their own creative business – it can also help students become employable in the arts as a step towards reaching that goal.

How will this book help you actually *become* an arts entrepreneur? The answer depends on the degree of effort you apply to reading, thinking about, discussing, and acting upon the information and recommendations provided in the text. Applied learning can be the most daunting – and rewarding – part of becoming a new business owner. Much of your potential for success will hinge upon the quality of your business concept and your own ability to deliver a creative product or service that addresses the genuine needs and interests of consumers in your target market. But much also depends on your ability to quickly learn from – and respond to – the success or failure of your early experiments in product design and delivery. The practical ideas, tools, and techniques presented in this book are the launch pad for your aspirations in the formation of an arts-related business – their value lies in how they are understood and *used* in the creation of your new venture.

Notes

1   See www.inc.com/samuel-bacharach/art-and-entrepreneurship.html

2   See https://artivate.hida.asu.edu/index.php/artivate/index

3   See http://ijsse.org/index.php?option=com_content&view=article&id=67&Itemid=63

4   See http://media.ifacca.org/files/DArt-Report-48-IEA.pdf

5   Ibid., p. 3.

6   Ibid., p. 3.

Acknowledgments

I would like to convey my deep appreciation for the people who made this book possible. Thanks to Professor Peter Sahlins of UC Berkeley for the opportunity to create and teach my first undergraduate course on French/ U.S. cultural policy at the UC Center Paris. Thanks to Dr. Leigh Smith, Alan Roberts, and Dr. Carl Jubran at The Institute for American Universities and *Marchutz School* of Fine Arts in Aix-en-Provence for the opportunities to present guest lectures and conduct an introductory workshop on the formation of arts-related businesses. Special thanks to Dean Anthony Cascardi of UC Berkeley for the chance to develop and teach my undergraduate course on Arts Entrepreneurship. Thanks to Stacey Walker and everyone at Taylor and Francis for their patience and support. Thanks to Robert Pimm for his expert advice and counsel. Extra special thanks to my wife, Virginia, for her continued encouragement, help, and understanding.

My parents George Donald Andrews and Jacalyn Andrews gave me the inspiration to explore and appreciate creative work and the confidence to make it a significant part of my own life. This book is dedicated to their memory.

1 What Is Arts Entrepreneurship?

The term *entrepreneurship* can be interpreted and applied in many different ways depending on the ambitions, skills, and opportunities available to the artist or founder of an arts organization. In this chapter we explore the meanings of entrepreneurship as a concept and as a set of behaviors. How can entrepreneurial thinking and action be employed to produce measurable results that link the business owner's values with the needs of the marketplace? How has entrepreneurship been understood in the past, and what are the current and future prospects for applying entrepreneurial techniques to new business concepts? How is arts entrepreneurship distinctive in its approach to business design, launch, and sustainability? How does an organization's location, size, and intended community shape the entrepreneurial activity pursued by the company's founders, supporters, investors, and other stakeholders? Conceiving of a novel business idea is a crucial starting place for launching a new venture. However, a successful entrepreneur must also develop that idea, test it in the marketplace, use customer feedback to make refinements and adjustments, and work toward creating a viable business capable of growth and sustainability.

Definitions of Entrepreneurship

The *Merriam-Webster dictionary* tells us that an entrepreneur is someone who organizes, manages, and assumes the risks of a business or enterprise.[1] Management consultant Peter F. Drucker emphasizes entrepreneurship's role in creating change and introducing new business concepts and practices that replace older models:

> Entrepreneurship rests on a theory of economy and society. The theory sees change as normal and indeed as healthy. And it sees the

major task in society – and especially in the economy – as doing something different rather than doing better what is already being done. That is basically what [French economist Jean-Baptiste Say], two hundred years ago, meant when he coined the term entrepreneur. It was intended as a manifesto and as a declaration of dissent: the entrepreneur upsets and disorganizes. As [Austrian American economist] Joseph Schumpeter formulated it, his task is "creative destruction."[2]

Texts about entrepreneurship in theory and practice will often mention *disruption* as a key component in designing and launching a new venture. This is particularly true in the tech world, with examples such as Google, Facebook, and Amazon creating enormous changes in social and economic behavior. Industry disruption often implies the introduction of entire new ways for consumers to interact with one another and make purchases that satisfy their needs. Examples include Netflix disrupting the previous market for videotape rentals, Uber, Lyft, and other ride services displacing conventional taxi companies, Airbnb capturing market share from hotels and motels, and Amazon displacing traditional "brick and mortar" retail outlets for transactions involving a wide range of products and services.

Although disruption and "creative destruction" are certainly key factors in the entrepreneurship examples listed above, they are not the only ways to think about entrepreneurship, especially for an artist or founder of an arts organization. How might a skilled musician, actor, dancer, designer, or other creative individual imagine themselves as an entrepreneur in the formulation, launch, and sustained operation of their business concept? It is not always necessary for the arts entrepreneur to embrace disruption as a key element of establishing a new venture. For example, a photographer might decide to launch a new company based on teaching digital photography techniques to young learners from the nearby community. A new online business could offer web-based sales of fine art from a collection of artists whose work examines political and social issues. A composer and performing musician might create a new organization providing original music for commercial applications such as radio, television, live events, or web broadcasting. These types of businesses can follow many of the principles of entrepreneurship without needing to displace existing organizations or cause "creative destruction" within the economy. The arts entrepreneur *does* need to organize, manage, and assume the risks of the enterprise, as presented in the Merriam-Webster definition. Beyond handling risk, however, arts entrepreneurs must also work toward connecting their own values, passions, and long-term commitments to their creative practice with measurable consumer interest in their products or services in order to establish a new venture and allow it to thrive. Art entrepreneurs have the freedom to decide what their new venture is based on, where it is located, and whom it is for. They also have the freedom to choose what type of entrepreneurship they want to pursue, either through disruption and "creative destruction" or through the introduction of a new business that finds a home in an existing marketplace alongside – and even in collaboration with – similar organizations.

Developing a Business Idea

Developing a Business Idea Based upon Personal and Professional Values

How does one define a business concept that will provide a specific product or service to a target market and ultimately achieve growth and sustainability for the long term? For the arts entrepreneur who has already found employment in the creative field of their choice, it can be a natural next step to develop a new venture based on their real-world experiences. For example, a film student who has worked as an intern or part-time employee in an established film distribution company might design their own venture around what they have learned through direct exposure to established business practices in that field. Creating a new business based on your experience as an employee of an established arts organization can turn out to be an efficient and well-conceived pathway to launching a new venture. This approach – finding employment in your area of interest with an established arts organization before launching your own business – might be worth considering for a newly graduated student looking to gain experience and mentorship as an intern, employee, or volunteer. However, not everyone has the opportunity to work for an established firm in their area of interest before developing a new business concept of their own.

In the *Business of Art* workbook by the Center for Cultural Innovation (CCI),[3] we find a series of three exercises designed to help the artist or prospective owner of an arts organization define their business concept by first exploring their personal and professional values. The aim is to create a foundation of values from one's personal and professional life that will support the creation of a new venture. For example, the values of community building, creative inspiration, and opportunity generation could form the basis for a new venture focused on teaching artistic skills to people in the business owner's immediate neighborhood. Or, the values of personal expression, international relationships, and cultural exchange might help shape the creation of a new business that brings cultural products, such as music, painting, and photography to foreign destinations. The next exercise in the *Business of Art* workbook asks us to imagine our future lives and describe in some detail where and how we might want to live in the future. The aim of this exercise is to articulate a vision for our future selves in both professional and personal terms. By writing down specific goals for our professional and personal lives, the vision exercise helps us create an actionable plan that guides decisions affecting both business development and our quality of life. The third and final step is to take the results from the exploration of values, along with the goals and ambitions identified in the vision exercise, and write a brief, clearly composed statement that is informed by the insights provided by the first two steps. This vision statement – and future versions of the statement that become increasingly relevant as we make progress toward the goals we have established – serve as a guiding light that leads us into a future where our values and ambitions shape the key decisions in our personal and professional lives.

In *The $100 Startup*, author Chris Guillebeau presents three lessons that can be applied to the entrepreneur's process for identifying a business concept and turning it into a sustainable venture:[4]

1. *Convergence*: The intersection between your passion and what others care about. This is where the arts entrepreneur seeks a connection between their creative practice and the interests of the marketplace. For example, a skilled visual artist who works with pen and ink drawings could easily spend time making art purely for the enjoyment of the process. The convergence lesson requires that an artist who seeks to build a business must find a connection between their chosen art form and the interests of the potential consumer.

2. *Skill transformation*: Turning your talents into a business concept. As the owner of an arts-related venture, you will need to make use of many different kinds of skills. The ability to develop and distribute creative products and services is just one of them. You may also need to develop skills in communications, accounting, and managing other people. This lesson emphasizes the importance of using your existing skills, or developing new skills, to serve the needs of your growing enterprise.

3. *Passion or skill plus usefulness equals success*: This lesson presents us with a formula for creating a business concept that directly links the founder's interests and abilities with the perceived value of product or service being offered to the market. Success is possible, the author tells us, when we design a business around the combination of a business owner's abilities with the customer's perception of how the company's products can improve their lives.

The planning exercises and lessons described above, along with others you can discover through research, will produce some early-stage written material. You can use the results of these experiments to produce a framework for designing a business concept – and a life that is designed intentionally around it – that are both grounded in your genuine interests and capabilities and positioned to attract customers for the long term.

Finding a Business Opportunity

There are aspiring arts entrepreneurs who begin with a thoroughly developed business idea that connects their passions and skills with a well-understood market to deliver a product or service that is likely to succeed. Others are driven by their desire to produce and distribute their own creative work, but have not yet identified the business model they will need to establish a new company. There are also those who have too many ideas for arts-related businesses they might some day want to create. In each case, the ability to identify a business opportunity and establish a new venture in that space requires a combination of experience, imagination, and willingness to learn from the data generated by customer feedback.

As mentioned earlier in this chapter, some arts entrepreneurs will develop their idea for a new business based on their current or former position working for someone else. An employee of a fine arts gallery, for example, might choose to open a gallery of their own by using the many practical lessons found working for an existing organization. Other arts entrepreneurs will launch a new venture without the benefit of previous experience as an employee in a similar business. In either case, finding a business opportunity means identifying the intersection between the founder's interests and the public's willingness to engage in the new company's products or services.

In his influential book *The Lean Startup*, author Eric Ries recommends the entrepreneur work quickly to produce what he calls a Minimum Viable Product.[5] The aim is to test this prototype, even if it has some design flaws, to see if it can capture the interest of consumers and serve as a foundation for business growth. In software development, this method can be used to build and test early-stage beta versions of an application before it is refined and ready for wide distribution. For the arts entrepreneur, the Minimum Viable Product could be a small-scale version of what might eventually become the larger vision for the business. For example, an arts education business could start with a very small number of students to experiment with instructional content and measure customer response levels. Ries describes what he calls the "build-measure-learn" feedback loop. The idea is to rapidly create a prototype without excessive planning or development, test the product with customers to understand its likelihood for success, then learn as quickly as possible what works and what doesn't. The *learning* is the key to launching and growing the sustainable business. Ries uses the term "validated learning" to describe the process of measuring and understanding the customers' needs and wants in relation to the product category and the specific value delivered by a unique product. Validated learning seeks to demonstrate empirically that a new venture has discovered some basic truths about their customers and that the business concept delivers value to those consumers.

In *The $100 Startup*, Chris Guillebeau suggests developing a product that you yourself would want to purchase. He describes the creation of value in terms of delivering what the customer actually wants, not what the business owner *thinks* the customer wants or should have. For example, the founder of a new venue for live music might want to create a nightclub featuring the latest in electronic dance music. However, the patrons in the immediate neighborhood and surrounding region might actually want an intimate concert space for world music, jazz, and acoustic singer-songwriters. Adapting to the needs and interests of the marketplace may take the arts entrepreneur into areas of business opportunity they may not have considered at the outset. Responding to customer preferences and adapting to customers are something every business owner needs to consider if the venture is to find a reliable base of support for the long term.

How does an arts entrepreneur identify and pursue a business opportunity? There are several ways to approach this question. One method is to conduct market research in the prospective business owner's immediate vicinity to map out which areas of creative enterprise are already fully covered by existing businesses. Studying your local environment for music, photography, theater, or other visual and performing art forms can help clarify opportunities for the introduction of a new venture. Another technique is to interview friends, family, and colleagues – people who have known you well for an extended amount of time – and ask them to describe how *they* perceive *your* creative interests and skills. These interviews can provide insights into your recognized artistic abilities and could provoke some interesting business ideas from your network of contacts, some of whom may end up supporting your new venture as investors or consultants. Another method is to reach out to highly experienced professionals in your field of interest and ask for their advice on where current and future opportunities for a new business might be located. For example, an arts entrepreneur looking to create a new theater company could contact managers at established venues in the region to explore opportunities in the local market. Each of these methods, or a combination of all three, can generate ideas for a new arts-related business and reveal opportunities worth exploring.

Evaluating and Managing Risk

As indicated in the Merriam-Webster definition of entrepreneurship found at the beginning of this chapter, the entrepreneur is responsible for identifying and managing all of the risks associated with the new venture. The types of risks encountered during the idea formation, business launch and growth phases of an arts-related organization will differ, depending on the nature of the company and its relationship to investors, customers, and other stakeholders.

Examples of risks managed by the arts entrepreneur include:

- *Financial risk*: Managing the money that flows into and out of the business is one of the key responsibilities of the founder and their designated accounting team. Working with investors or lenders to find money for the business development, launch, and growth cycles means taking on all of the bookkeeping and reporting requirements associated with those agreements. Receiving payments from customers or contributions from a crowdfunding campaign obliges the business owner to fulfill the expectations associated with those transactions. Entering into contracts or other agreements with suppliers, vendors, landlords, or outside service providers means paying bills on time and maintaining good credit. Attracting employees to a new business means following through on all commitments for salaries, benefits, and incentives, such as annual bonuses or stock options.
- *Reputational risk*: The act of creating a new business and introducing it to customers will produce not only brand awareness for the venture but will also establish an identity and reputation for the owner and other people associated with the organization. The reputation of a business can be very positive and contribute to the success of the venture if the product or service being offered meets or exceeds the expectations of the consumer and if the overall operation is conducted in an ethical manner. Organizations that disappoint customers with false advertising, low quality products, or any type of dishonest behavior will suffer the consequences and be replaced by a different company whose positive reputation attracts the interest of consumers and the media.
- *Legal risk*: There are many rules and regulations that must be followed to stay in compliance with the numerous legal obligations that go along with owning a business. These include tax filings, insurance, corporate reporting requirements, workplace safety, employee relations, maintaining a business license, and other responsibilities. There are also a variety of laws associated with intellectual property that must be respected. Finally, there is the possibility of a lawsuit being brought against the arts organization by a dissatisfied customer or supplier – or it may be necessary for the arts-related business to file a suit against someone else.

See Chapters 3, 5, and 6 on marketing, legal issues, and financial management, for more information on managing risk as an entrepreneur.

Developing a Unique Product or Service that Addresses Customers' Needs and Wants

Once the arts entrepreneur identifies a business idea connected with their own creative practice or interests, and after that concept has been evaluated with an understanding of opportunities within the intended marketplace, the next step is to gather customer feedback. The lean startup method described earlier encourages the entrepreneur to quickly develop a working prototype and measure customer engagement to study its potential. This can be done using focus groups, surveys, or interviews with individuals who are selected based on their likelihood of being early adopters of the new business's products or services. The learning acquired through this rapid prototype development and early testing process will increase the business owner's understanding of how the *customer* values the company's offerings. For an arts entrepreneur, prototyping and testing a new business idea can be accomplished by developing a proof of concept and inviting selected consumers to give feedback. A visual artist could invite potential customers (found through social networks and other sources) to evaluate a series of fine art products and provide comments on *their* perceptions of its value. Details should include the product's unique or noteworthy characteristics, its distinctiveness from – or resemblance to – other products in the market, and the consumer's attitudes toward pricing, availability, and exclusive access. Performing artists, or entrepreneurs launching a new venue for creative work, can experiment with their ideas by presenting them as works in progress, in a pop-up environment or in an invitation-only setting. See Chapter 3 on Marketing for more ideas on understanding and connecting with the customer's perception of value.

Marketing the Business

Using Early-Stage Market Research to Rapidly Iterate Product Attributes and Marketing Messages

As with the rapid prototyping and customer feedback techniques described above, the business owner should also try a variety of marketing messages and product descriptions to see what works best. Learning how customers perceive a product's value through focus groups and interviews can be extended to discover the most effective language and visual representations to use when communicating with a broader audience of potential consumers. Working with "early adopters" as test subjects is ideal because these individuals are familiar with the overall product category and can offer suggestions based on their own experience. For example, an aspiring commercial photographer could invite a select group of potential clients to evaluate the new company's graphic design concepts, marketing messages, web presence, and social media strategies. As with the product development iteration cycle, an arts entrepreneur can quickly learn how potential customers understand their product by testing marketing messages and refining them to produce the optimal results.

Communicating Product Benefits to Consumers

Clear statements of a product's benefits to consumers are preferred to descriptions of the product's attributes, qualities, or brand identification. Customers respond to convincing messages about how the product or service will make their life better or solve a specific problem. For example, an upcoming dance performance featuring artists from a foreign country could advertise the event as "a unique opportunity to experience dance from a rarely presented culture" as a statement of benefits for customers, rather than "an evening of music and dance" as a statement of the event's main features. Some artistic products are more challenging to describe in terms of benefits to customers than others. What are the product benefits for an oil painting or original photograph? Take a look at how galleries and museums craft their marketing messages for exhibits and special events. Often the text and graphic images will tell the story of a specific artist (or art form) in a way that captures the interest of the potential customer. The benefits of a cultural experience, such as a concert or theatrical production, can be described in terms of the emotional and intellectual impact the production will have on the customer. Motion picture advertising, for example, will claim that an upcoming feature will "make you jump out of your seat" because of the powerful special effects used and the experiences the film will create.

Building the Business

Building a Team of Experienced Advisers and Partners

Although some arts entrepreneurs operate their venture by themselves, many business owners work as part of a team of individuals with specialized skills. The founder may have the creative vision and technical know-how for the new venture, while the partners may have practical experience in financial management, marketing, or product distribution. Some of the people involved in launching a new arts organization can operate as external consultants or advisors, rather than joining the company as employees. Recruiting, training, and managing full-time or part-time employees can add to the business owner's workload and expenses, but the benefits are significant in terms of the staff's dedication to the venture and everyone's commitment to achieving success. Many startups are launched by teams that have been constructed in such a way that an outside investor or other supporter can easily understand how each team member contributes their individual strengths to create an efficient, sustainable business. To design an organizational structure and build a team of effective employees, start by creating job descriptions for the different roles needed for the business to operate. An art gallery might require a small staff of experienced sales people, while a community theater would need individuals with experience in lighting, scenery construction, sound, ticket sales, advertising, and directing or acting in a series of plays for a season of performances.

Building Brand Awareness and Market Demand Through Existing Networks

In his book *The Art of the Start*, author Gary Kawasaki suggests approaching the marketplace through a series of steps that reach out to potential customers who are defined by their readiness to try out – and become advocates for – a new product and the business responsible for it.[6]

Potential customers are described using terms first developed by Everett M. Rogers and F. Floyd Shoemaker in their book, *Communication of Innovations: A Cross-Cultural Approach*:[7]

- *Innovators*: Those who seek novelty and risk and who want to acquire new products before anyone else.
- *Early adopters*: People who sense intuitively that the new product will serve their needs and who aren't afraid to try something that hasn't been widely distributed.
- *Early majority*: These customers follow the examples set by the innovators and early adopters and acquire products that have been validated by experts, media reviews, and recommendations from their peers.
- *Late majority*: Consumers who lack the confidence to try untested products and wait until they have achieved mass acceptance.
- *Laggards*: People who are turned off by new products and only buy them when they have no choice.

An arts entrepreneur can use this framework for building brand awareness and growing customer demand by starting with known innovators and early adopters. Study your network of contacts – including social media, email, and anyone you might know socially or professionally – to identify individuals who might fit the profile of an innovator or early adopter of the product your business is developing. Be prepared to use their early-stage feedback to make adjustments to the product. You might even introduce radical changes if these valuable customers offer useful suggestions (see the *build-measure-learn* feedback loop described above). The innovators and early adopters from within your network can also be critics, columnists, reviewers, and other media figures who have a strong interest in discovering new products and telling their readers about them. In this way, your first customers can not only provide useful information about how your product is understood and valued, they can also become advocates for you and your business as you work toward approaching the early majority and late majority consumers. For example, a new film festival can invite movie critics from the local media to previews of featured films to generate interest and (hopefully) spread the word to a broad base of customers through print and online media. An app developer can contact experienced, established developers to evaluate the product and suggest improvements or add their voice to the chorus of supporters who want to help promote innovative work. A fiction writer can distribute an early draft of a new short story to friendly authors, critics, and media contacts to gather positive input (and potentially usable quotes) for their marketing efforts.

Design of the Business Launch

The introduction of a new product – and the business responsible for it – creates a unique opportunity to attract attention, especially in traditional media such as newspapers, radio, and magazines. Of course, social media channels are also very appropriate for product launch announcements or invitations to special events such as a gallery opening, the first performance of the new theatrical work, or the introduction of a new arts education program. Events attract media interest because they are considered newsworthy and therefore good candidates for exposure in editorials or other published commentary.

The arts entrepreneur should carefully design the product launch to build interest over time, especially in the weeks before the event takes place. Like the marketing messages prepared for a crowdfunding campaign (see Chapter 4 on fundraising), the business founder and other team members should brainstorm a wealth of material designed to capture the attention and interest of potential customers. This can include photos, illustrations, videos, email and e-newsletters, social media postings, and text messages. It is important to get the timing of these announcements right. When Apple is about to announce its next generation of iPhones, they keep certain design details secret while others are leaked to reviewers and online tech advocates. When Pixar rolls out a marketing campaign for its next animated feature, it positions a broad range of advertisements and sneak previews to reach its customer base. For a new arts-related business, the launch can be a simple, focused effort that attracts people to a grand opening event. Starting with a small-scale occasion for a new product is fine as long as it attracts the right kind of potential consumers, such as the innovators and early adopters described earlier. From there, the organization can build its audience and expand awareness and engagement through word-of-mouth and regular communications with its growing customer base.

Planning for Business Growth

One of the risks of attracting too many people at an early stage of the business is the possibility of disappointing customers because of problems with production, distribution, or quality control. For example, if an arts entrepreneur launches a crowdfunding campaign with the goal of finding approximately 100 supporters but ends up attracting over 1000, there may be some serious challenges in producing and distributing the project's rewards and other deliverables on time. An arts-related company that relies on overseas manufacturing can run into problems if orders for their products suddenly increase at the same moment their incoming merchandise is delayed during shipping or customs inspection. A performing arts venue that sells out all available tickets and turns away large numbers of potential customers might consider expanding to a larger venue or opening an additional nearby location to satisfy demand. Each type of business – whether providing cultural experiences, artistic products, or creative services, such as education – needs to examine their ability to *scale* their operations in a way that maintains their brand identity and preserves their customers' perception of *value* received in the transaction.

Some entrepreneurs set very ambitious goals for market share and customer engagement. In the tech sector, for example, a software company might develop plans for attracting customers initially in the hundreds, then in the thousands, and eventually in the millions. This type of venture can be very attractive to investors because of the potential for significant returns on their financial support. Arts entrepreneurs can follow this path if it is appropriate to their business model and specific product. However, many arts entrepreneurs aim to develop a business that achieves success on a smaller scale. Even in the case of an arts venture that only strives to attract customers in the dozens or hundreds, there needs to be advance planning so the business grows while meeting – or preferably, exceeding – the expectations of consumers. See Chapter 2 on planning and assessment for some ideas on business stability and growth.

Refining Business Operations to Eliminate Inefficiency and Waste

In its pre-launch phase, a new business is free to experiment with the many choices available for operational issues, such as the cost of goods, expense levels for space rental and staff salaries, budgets for marketing campaigns and fundraising efforts, and other fixed and variable costs involved in running an organization. However, once the business is up and running, there needs to be careful supervision of the income and expense details. This is especially true for an arts venture working toward early-stage growth in its first 3–5 years. One of the ways to increase efficiency and manage profitability is to use cash flow projections (see Chapter 6 on budgets and financial management) to anticipate future financial activity and implement business decisions that contribute to the ongoing viability of the business. For example, an artist making and selling limited edition fine art prints might begin the business by selling each piece for approximately twice the cost of production, including printing, framing, and delivery. Over time, the artist could negotiate with service providers for printing and framing to charge lower costs per unit for higher volume orders. As the business grows, the artist can work toward selling each piece for three to four times the cost of production, thereby increasing profitability over time.

In the performing arts, there is less likelihood that the cost of each concert, play, or dance production will be significantly reduced by the quantity of performances, although expenses for sets and costumes can be amortized over time to decrease their cost per performance. In this case, profitability can be increased through higher ticket prices, lower expenses for operational categories (such as marketing or space rental) or by increasing contributed income (from grants, gifts, and other donations) to underwrite the performances and retain more of the earned income realized from ticket sales. There can be some efficiencies and income sources to consider, such as a theater company renting out its scenery, costumes, and lighting equipment to other organizations during its off-season, or a classical music ensemble developing and rehearsing a program of music for a local performance and then touring with that same program to other locations. Even if the arts organization is a nonprofit venture, the manager must accept responsibility for keeping the business financially stable and able to produce income in excess of expenses over time.

Another approach to increasing efficiency and eliminating wasted effort and time is to follow the lean startup method for product development and testing. In the section on Finding a Business Opportunity, we considered the Minimum Viable Product (a no-frills prototype that demonstrates some essential value to potential customers) and the build-measure-learn cycle that helps the entrepreneur refine, work through and choose among different versions of the proposed product or service. This approach places the emphasis on discovering truths about consumer interest while reducing or eliminating any other expenses – including marketing, aesthetics, or even product finalization – until the business owner has learned how the customer perceives the product's value. Categorizing all other expenses as extraneous or wasteful might seem extreme, but it does focus attention on measurable, reliable data upon which to build a business. This technique might be suitable for the arts entrepreneur who is designing a product or service that needs many opportunities to evolve, change, and iterate before discovering the best ways to connect with consumers and support long-term sustainability.

Measuring the Product's Success and Likelihood of Reaching a Broader Audience and Growing the Business

How will your arts organization measure success? The answer to this question can vary greatly depending on the objectives you are trying to achieve. An arts education business might set a target of growing its customer count from 50 students in Year One to 500 students in Year Five. If this type of arts organization intends to become a nonprofit, or chooses to work through a fiscal sponsor to attract grants and other financial support, the measure of success may very well be the number of students who participate in the program and the company's overall ability to continue serving more members of its community. On the other hand, a digital marketplace that sells original photography to collectors may set specific financial targets for its first year of operation and for future years. These goals might be driven by the founder's desire for personal financial rewards, as well as the expectations of investors who support the new venture through its startup phases. In either case, reaching a broader audience and growing the business are important factors in establishing a sustainable venture.

The ingredients for creating a company that can develop a successful product and reach a growing number of customers include:

- designing a unique product or service that genuinely connects with the needs and desires of a target customer base;
- raising awareness of the product's availability and desirable features through marketing and other initiatives;
- raising funds and hiring a collaborative team to build a solid business foundation for the venture's intended growth;
- developing and adhering to a set of key values and principles that guide the organization's formation, operations and expansion.

Cash flow projections (mentioned above) can serve as a framework for evaluating an organization's current levels of success and its potential for long-term viability. Chapter 6 on budgeting and financial management describes how to incorporate data about the organization's real-time financial activity (known as *actuals*) into a budget projection. This allows the business owner to analyze the venture's financial performance and discover areas where the business has exceeded expectations ... or fallen short of the mark.

Understanding Pivots and When to Employ Them

The term *pivot* is found frequently in books and articles about entrepreneurship. It refers to a process, or decision point, where the founder realizes that the time has come to make a significant change in some aspects of the product development, marketing strategy, or, in some cases, the direction of the entire company. A pivot is not an abandonment of the company's overall values, goals, and objectives – it is a redirection of the organization's process for accomplishing those aims. A basketball player making progress toward a slam dunk suddenly realizes the defense is overwhelming at that instant, so she places one foot firmly on the court and pivots 90° to send a pass to another team player who completes the drive with a successful, point-producing jump shot. The team's overall goal of the accumulating points and winning the game is not abandoned, but the method of getting there has been flexible and responsive to the changing conditions discovered in the process. In business, a pivot serves the same purpose: perceiving and responding to existing conditions, remaining flexible, adapting to circumstances as they evolve, and keeping the overall goal of success firmly in focus. Pivots come in a variety of types: some change the nature of the product itself, while others change the definition of the intended market or the methods of reaching targeted customers. A company creating and selling custom textiles might initially offer designs featuring only the most contemporary patterns and color palettes. However, close observation of the product's performance and its market environment – including customer response research and published industry trends in sales figures – might inspire the company to try developing a product line that replicates vintage fabrics and classic designs. The company's goals of offering appealing products and attracting customers have not changed, but the steps toward reaching those goals have been adapted to the realities of the market.

How does the arts entrepreneur decide when and how to use pivots to adapt to new information or changing circumstances and keep the business on track for success? As indicated above, keeping a close eye on the organization's performance in terms of customer acceptance and overall sales is the key to evaluating if and when changes should be made to the product design, marketing program, or other aspects of business. Sales figures – calculated either daily, weekly, monthly, or quarterly – are relatively easy to study by inputting the data into the "actuals" column in the budget forecast spreadsheet. This information, along with the data for expenditures, will reveal any significant variances between the expected financial activity of the venture and its performance in the real world. Measuring customer acceptance and satisfaction requires another approach. Focus groups, in-depth interviews, surveys, and online questionnaires are some of the ways a business owner can gather data about customer attitudes toward a specific product and the overall company. Taking some time to carefully interview innovators and early adopters during your business startup phase will provide crucial information about the perceived value of your product and your customers' opinions about the entire venture. Introducing these types of data acquisition and analysis tasks into your business startup cycles allows you to identify opportunities to pivot while the organization is still in its formative stages. The type (or multiple types) of pivots to initiate will depend on what has been learned from studying the company's financial performance and customer responses. For more information on pivots, see the chapter on that topic in *The Lean Startup*, by Eric Ries.[8]

Arts Entrepreneurship

Arts Entrepreneurship: Designing a Business Based on Your Long-Term Commitment to Creative Practice

In this chapter we have explored some of the ways that arts entrepreneurship resembles other types of entrepreneurship. For example, the use of pivots (described above) is a common feature of entrepreneurial thinking and behavior for tech and other industries. Likewise, well-established entrepreneurial concepts, such as disruption and lean startup methodology, can, in some cases, be very relevant to the formation and continued success of an arts-related business. There are, however, some special features of a business built upon the skills, practices, and ambitions of a trained, dedicated artist.

For someone who has invested considerable time in discovering and developing their artistic talents in drawing, painting, music, theater, dance, and a whole range of other cultural activities, the construction of a business around their creative practice may very well lead to a long-term commitment to sustaining both the enterprise and the art-making. This commitment – to both creative practice and business ownership – suggests a unique path for the arts entrepreneur relative to the trajectory sought by their peers in other industries.

Arts Entrepreneurship with Open-Ended Ownership Versus Conventional Entrepreneurship with an Exit Strategy

Many entrepreneurs in areas besides art build an exit strategy into their planning at the very beginning. There are several good reasons for this. For one, a startup that requires angel investors or venture capital to realize its planning, launch, and growth goals will often have an ending phase known as *harvest*. This is the final stage where the founders, financial partners, and other stakeholders reap their monetary rewards as the business either goes public or gets acquired by another company. The risks and sheer amount of work required to create a successful, sustainable business are reason enough, for some entrepreneurs, to insist on a significant payout as a predetermined end goal for their entire project. Other exit strategies, besides going public or selling the venture to another company, include merging with a competitor in the same market or dissolving the company and moving on to the next venture. Individuals who repeatedly start new businesses and end up selling them or closing them down to start another one are known as *serial entrepreneurs*.

Arts entrepreneurs can also follow this path if they so choose, developing a business with a predetermined exit strategy that delivers financial returns on their investments of time, effort, and capital. However, for the arts entrepreneur who is building a business based on their *lifetime* interest in a creative practice, or who want to offer an ongoing product or service in the cultural sector, the idea of an exit strategy is the opposite of what they may have in mind. Designing and launching a sustainable venture in the arts require the same levels of time and effort as any other entrepreneurial project, but the end goal for an arts entrepreneur may be very different than growing a business so it may be eventually sold to someone else for a profit. The long-term viability of a venture for the arts entrepreneur is directly connected to their lifelong, deep-rooted connection to making and appreciating art. The relationships between a business concept in a creative field and the core personal values and beliefs of the founder are additional reasons why the arts entrepreneur may commit to an indefinite, open-ended responsibility for the organization and its continued success.

In their book *Arts Entrepreneurship: The Business of Art*, Joseph S. Roberts and Clark A. Green describe the motivations of an arts entrepreneur:[9]

- They are passionate about the art form that interests them. This interest is not at all casual, but deep and abiding.
- They have a strong desire to spend their career making a living involved with their art form.
- They have a deep commitment to being the means by which the work of the artist is available to, and purchasable by, the public. In this respect, they realize that they are in business for the long haul. Most arts businesses do not lend themselves to the exit strategy of building a business over a limited number of years, and then selling or merging the business.

As you consider the options for arts entrepreneurship in your own work and creative life, think about the differences between growing a successful company in order to eventually cash out by handing over ownership to someone else, versus designing and running your own venture built upon the foundation of your long-term interests in artistic practice, cultural engagement, and community building.

Entrepreneurship for the Arts-Related Organization Focused on Positive Social Benefits

> The primary difference between traditional entrepreneurship and social entrepreneurship is the intended mission.[10]

This chapter began with an exploration of how a business owner's personal and professional values can shape the creation of a new venture. For some arts entrepreneurs, the business concept will focus on delivering a unique product or service to a target market in order to achieve commercial success. For others, however, the goal is to address certain social problems or produce positive impacts for social conditions. The range of social conditions that an entrepreneur can choose to focus on has as much variety as the range of artistic practices that can be employed to address them. Social issues such as health, education, aging, the environment, immigration, and other important areas can be central to the ambitions of a founder launching a new arts-related organization. If, through the consideration of your personal and professional values, you discover that creating a business that delivers positive social benefits is what you want to accomplish, then social entrepreneurship may be the best way to describe your venture.

Because the term *social entrepreneurship* covers many business models and a variety of business purposes, it does not lend itself to a single precise meaning or definition. Some founders of social entrepreneurship organizations seek 501(c)(3) nonprofit status from the Internal Revenue Service (IRS) in order to gain recognition as a charitable organization and qualify for grants and gifts, while others launch for-profit companies and incorporate social benefits into their mission over time.

Some of the possibilities for a social entrepreneurship venture include:

- a for-profit business seeking commercial success first, then social impact as a secondary priority;
- a for-profit business seeking social benefits primarily and placing financial rewards second;
- a for-profit business seeking both financial rewards and social benefits in equal measure;
- a startup forming as a for-profit company, but intending to acquire nonprofit status over time. In this case, the venture will adhere to its social benefits mission while it develops and operates its programs, both as a way to stay true to its core values and as part of the process of making a convincing application to become a recognized 501(c)(3) nonprofit corporation. For-profits can seek contributed income from grants and gifts by using a *fiscal sponsor* (see Chapter 4, Fundraising) as they develop and submit their application for nonprofit status.

For the arts-related organization intending to operate as a for-profit business, there is a special designation – known as a B-Corporation or Benefit Corporation – that identifies the company as one that places high value on positive social impacts. Another business form, known as L3C, or limited liability low profit company, is available in certain states for organizations that seek social impact over profits. See Chapter 5 on legal issues for more information on these corporate forms.

The principles and mission-based operational choices found in social entrepreneurship ventures do not preclude the necessity of maintaining financial stability and complying with the many rules and regulations that apply to all businesses, regardless of their motives. In other words, the arts entrepreneur who creates a social entrepreneurship organization must also assume responsibility for all of the risks associated with any type of new company. All startups, including socially responsible ventures, must successfully work through their planning, launch and sustainability phases and maintain focus on becoming established, viable businesses.

Some examples of arts-related organizations that have a social impact mission include:

- a community-based theater company launched in a disadvantaged neighborhood that seeks to involve local residents as playwrights, actors and production workers. The goal is to develop and present new plays that tell the stories of the community within which the theater operates.
- an arts education organization dedicated to teaching creative skills to people suffering psychological or emotional difficulties as a way to help people express themselves and promote healing;
- a fine arts gallery dedicated to promoting original artwork, especially photography, around themes of contemporary environmental challenges and ways to solve them;
- a performing arts space that provides opportunities for collaboration between political activism and a variety of art forms.

Social entrepreneurship is increasing in popularity among the founders of new ventures, including those with an artistic or cultural orientation. One reason has to do with the previously described connections between the business owner's core values and the mission of the new venture. The central purpose of a new company that seeks to provide social benefits can – and should – be directly tied to the essential beliefs and ambitions of the business owners. The authenticity and purpose of an organization constructed in this way will be immediately apparent in all of its actions and statements. Another consequence of forming a social entrepreneurship venture has to do with the relationship between the company and its consumers, partners, investors, suppliers, and other stakeholders. The mission of creating positive social impact can be shared among a business and all of the individuals inside and outside of the organization. Forming a new venture, especially one dedicated to the arts, requires finding and developing connections with an audience of potential customers (and other supporters) who share the organization's values. By making positive social change a central element of a new company's mission, the founders can both establish the company's identity and attract like-minded people to engage with the venture and help make it a success.

The Role of Education in Arts Entrepreneurship Initiatives

There are many ways for education to play a role in the formation, launch, and sustainable operation of an arts organization. Educational experiences – such as research, group discussions, art-making with the support of an experienced instructor, reading and writing exercises to explore new concepts, and listening to presentations by experienced professionals – can all offer value to the customers of an arts venture. These kinds of activities can also inspire and inform the business ownership and their team. An educational program within an arts-related business might be a central feature of the organization's mission. Or, learning opportunities may be integrated into the structure of the venture as a complementary program. In either case, inviting patrons to take part in educational experiences can prove to be an effective way to develop connections between the company and its community.

Some arts entrepreneurs choose to make education the primary offering of their organization. For example, a team of founders with experience in music education might develop and launch a new business focused on providing individual and group lessons to students in a neighborhood where the public school system has reduced or eliminated its own arts classes. This same approach to finding and addressing a need for arts education within a community can involve writing, drawing, photography, theater, digital arts, and any number of other creative practices.

Opportunities for learning can also be introduced as a separate but vital component of the arts organization's main purpose. Art museums and galleries often develop educational programs for their patrons and younger visitors. Classes and lectures on art history, art-making techniques, or issues surrounding artists and the works they create can provoke insights and bring the public into a closer relationship with the institution. Performing arts organizations such as theater companies, orchestras, and chamber groups invite customers to participate in conversations with performers and originators of new works. They also offer training via classes, workshops, and community-based productions. For the arts entrepreneur developing a business idea that delivers a specific product to its community of customers, the addition of an integrated educational program should be evaluated and, if appropriate, implemented into the organization's structure.

In addition to expanding the venture's purpose and reaching a broader range of customers, an educational program can make it possible to attract financial support from foundations, corporations, and government agencies. For example, a company focused on producing high-quality digital prints for photographers, illustrators, and graphic designers could initiate a new training program on software-based techniques for aspiring visual artists. This part of the business, although separate from the main printmaking services, can grow to attract customers and qualify for funding from grant programs that support learning opportunities for digital art making. For an arts organization that does not have the nonprofit status required to qualify for grants and gifts that support education, it is possible to apply for and receive this type of financial support by working with a fiscal sponsor (see Chapter 4 on Fundraising).

There are other ways that education can become part of the arts entrepreneur's efforts to establish and grow a sustainable business. Learning about developments in one's own industry, for example, is essential in order to stay up-to-date on the latest technologies and market trends that may influence your company's prospects for future success. Business owners and their key staff should seek opportunities to study business trends, discover novel business practices and concepts, and develop new skills for operating their organization. This can be accomplished by scheduling customized training sessions, attending industry conferences and meetings, and investigating published accounts in books, magazines, specialized journals, or other media found in print and online. An arts-related business can also offer itself as a case study for students in nearby academic programs focused on business development, the creation of arts-related ventures, and strategies for career development for artists. There can be considerable value in offering your business as an instructional example for students who are eager to explore and understand how arts entrepreneurs conceive of and execute their organizational ambitions.

Creating and Selling Original Fine Art as a Business Model

What if your idea for an arts-related business is based on producing and distributing your own original artwork, such as painting, drawing, photography, musical compositions, or videos? There are a number of important considerations to evaluate when designing this kind of venture. The first question has to do with how you will produce the original artwork that you intend to eventually market. Do you have access to, or can you easily acquire, the necessary materials and skills required for generating the products you have in mind? Will quality control be an issue over time as your business becomes established and your products attract more interest? This can be a concern if your artistic product relies on access to resources such as paint, canvas, photo printing, or other supplies and services provided by others. Remember that the quality of an artistic product you create and sell under your own name will, to some extent, be dependent on the qualities of the materials and services you choose to employ in the creation of that product. Fine art is also a special case in that, as distinct from commercial art, it represents the artist's own vision, not concepts formulated by someone else. Even if you choose to outsource the production of your fine arts products, your name will be associated with the results. Take the time to investigate your suppliers to develop relationships with providers of high quality materials and services who can be depended upon for support for the long term.

Another important consideration for the fine arts entrepreneur is how their artistic vision might be received by consumers, critics, and other stakeholders in the new venture. Some fine artists discover that their work is immediately accepted by the public and consumer demand remains consistent throughout their careers. Others, however, must experiment with a variety of artistic concepts and creative approaches before finding an audience and cultivating enough interest to grow a sustainable business.

While the goal may not necessarily be to reach a mass audience and inspire purchases numbering in the hundreds and perhaps thousands, the fine arts entrepreneur should develop a vision for success that is based on realistic and appropriately scaled business development targets. As mentioned earlier in this chapter, it is perfectly acceptable to design a business that seeks to attract customers numbering in the dozens or even less, as long as the ambitions and needs of the artist/business owner are in line with the interests and desires of the target market. The arts entrepreneur has the freedom to define his or her own measures of success, both in terms of creative accomplishments and business goals.

Arts Entrepreneurship and the Nonprofit Creative Venture

A nonprofit organization is one that places value on delivering benefits to society. What types of social benefits might an arts entrepreneur focus on in order to develop a business that can eventually acquire the nonprofit designation? Working with underserved populations, or launching a venture in a disadvantaged neighborhood, are some examples of initiatives launched by creators of arts-related businesses. Other issues, such as race, gender, aging, immigration, economic disparity, or climate change, have proven to be essential, guiding concepts upon which to build an arts venture. This chapter's earlier discussion on the relationship between the founder's core values and the venture's mission can provide some practical ideas on developing an authentic connection between your commitment to producing social benefits and your dedication to creating a successful business.

Contrary to some interpretations, the term nonprofit does not mean that the owners or employees of the organization will not receive appropriate compensation for their efforts. In fact, many nonprofits provide very attractive financial rewards, along with benefits, such as health insurance, for their ownership and staff. What is unique about a recognized nonprofit organization is that there is no distribution of excess income after expenses are paid. In a nonprofit venture, this excess income is typically reinvested in the company or used to create an emergency fund for the future. See Chapter 5, Legal Issues, for an examination of the process of seeking and acquiring nonprofit status from the IRS.

Designing Experiences as a Business Product

What if the arts entrepreneur envisions a business that offers not physical objects, but rather *experiences* for their customers? These experiences can range from powerful theatrical works, music or performance art to the viewing of a film or a walk through a multimedia installation. Experiences are distinct from physical objects in many ways, especially in that they are specific to the time, place, and overall context within which they are delivered. A business that creates and sells artistic or cultural experiences, or one that offers these along with an educational component, needs to be designed in a way that recognizes the customers' intellectual and emotional engagement as a very high priority. The experience of a live theater production, for example, can include a sense of catharsis within the performance that profoundly affects the audience, draws the attention of critics, and generates positive word-of-mouth publicity. A music venue with exceptionally good sound, lighting, and seating that offers a season of unique, highly skilled performers can build its reputation and audience over time to become a successful, sustainable business. If your business concept involves providing customers with experiences, investigate some of the well-established arts organizations in your area of interest to develop an understanding of this type of business model and to research opportunities for launching your own venture.

Arts Entrepreneurship and Digital Products or Services Distributed Online

Does your business concept focus on developing and marketing a specialized app, or distributing digital products, such as music and video online? The online marketplace for digital products and services becomes more crowded with competing ventures every day. To make the best use of your time in this particular environment, it makes sense to study not only the providers of the digital products and services similar to your own, but also to investigate how their customers perceive the value that is delivered in the transaction. For some customers, the convenience associated with receiving online content (such as music and video) is worth the price associated with their conversion from a free to a paid consumer. The business model adopted by Pandora, for example, shows the pathway for converting customers from free users to paying subscribers. For others, access to highly specialized content, such as rarely available material produced by influential artists, provides the incentive to engage with the business as a paying customer. Because so much online content is now available for free, the arts entrepreneur must think carefully about how to provide value for consumers in a way that distinguishes their business from others in the marketplace and develops genuine, lasting connections with their audience.

Choosing to Create a Performing Arts Venue for Music, Theater, Dance, Education, etc.

Suppose your ambitions for an arts-related business include presenting a series of performances or other public events. This type of venture requires access to a suitable space, or an established venue such as a concert hall, theater, or other publicly accessible environment. Building a brand-new structure will likely be beyond the financial capacity of most early-stage arts entrepreneurs, although there may be some who begin their project with significant monetary resources or an existing partnership with a new building project. Most new ventures in the performing arts will seek to locate themselves in an existing space that meets their needs. Because the quality of the space is so important to the public perception of the event being presented, it makes sense to investigate a variety of the prospective venues within which to place your performance program. The level of commitment on the part of the business founder for occupying a performance space can range from occasional use of a fully outfitted theater, music venue, or other location to signing a lease on an undeveloped property and investing in all of the needed improvements such as lighting, sound, and audience amenities. Following the suggestions described earlier in the discussion of the lean startup method, an arts entrepreneur can experiment during the early stages of business concept development by finding an existing venue and renting it temporarily to test audience response to the Minimum Viable Product. If these early experiments prove successful, then a search can be conducted for an available space that can be leased for the long term and outfitted with the necessary equipment, services (such as ticket sales and concessions) and interior design details to help establish the organization and position it for success. This approach is not unlike that taken by developers in the food and beverage industry, who might experiment with a new concept in a pop-up environment first, then, depending on the level of success, identify a suitable space for a fully developed restaurant and invest the resources needed to launch an independent, sustainable operation.

Arts Entrepreneurship in the Community: Connecting with Partners, Supporters, Patrons, Suppliers, Investors, Donors, and Other Stakeholders in Your Venture

While the creation and development of a business idea can be accomplished by a single individual, the process of establishing a new venture within a community obviously requires participation by other people, especially customers. A business founder with a compelling idea for a new organization will likely find other individuals offering enthusiasm and advice. The challenge with any business is to discover and cultivate relationships with people who not only want the venture to succeed, but who want to become actively involved through direct support.

Attracting people to become involved in a new business requires different strategies depending on the roles these individuals play:

- *Partners* can join the organization at its earliest stages or get involved once the business becomes established. They contribute at the level of the founder, assuming responsibility for the risks of the venture and collaborating with other team members to accomplish the company's goals.

- *Supporters* can include contacts in print and online media who provide their readership with information about the new organization and encourage prospective customers to give the venture their attention. Other forms of support might include serving on the board of directors, providing free advice on legal or financial issues, working as a volunteer on behalf of the organization, or donating time to provide some needed service.

- *Patrons, or customers*, are the key to any successful business. Understanding and serving their needs is one of the primary goals of the business founder. See Chapter 3 on Marketing for more information on identifying and interacting with customers to build a sustainable business that addresses consumer interest.

- *Suppliers* are essential to maintaining the consistent, high-quality products that are offered by an arts venture – and expected by its customers. In some cases, suppliers are responsible for providing the raw materials an organization uses to produce its finished products, such as paper, ink, and framing materials. In other instances, suppliers provide maintenance or other support that contributes directly to the customer's perception of the organization's brand. This can include everything from keeping a performing arts venue or arts education facility clean and well organized to providing website hosting services and transaction support that is dependable and easy-to-use. Finding reliable suppliers and developing long-term relationships with them helps the arts entrepreneur design and grow a business that maintains a sense of quality and consistency both inside and outside of the organization.

- *Investors* offer their financial and other resources to the organization to help it grow and, eventually, deliver monetary and other returns on their support. Working with an individual or group willing to invest their money and time into your arts venture usually means accepting their participation and influence. Some business owners are happy to share the ownership and management of their venture with investors, while others will seek opportunities for support that do not require shared ownership and supervision.

- *Donors* provide financial and other support without the expectation of direct financial returns to themselves. However, donors share the interests of other types of stakeholders in that they are very focused on how the organization performs, both in economic terms and in the pursuit and accomplishment of its mission and goals.

The enthusiasm and commitment projected by the business founder can go a long way toward attracting other people to the venture as partners, supporters, patrons, suppliers, investors, or donors. Believing in yourself and your organization is the first step in convincing other people to become involved. However, the perceived *value* of your company's offerings is what keeps people committed to your cause and inspires them to become repeat customers or reliable supporters.

Studying Arts Entrepreneurship as Professional Development for Future Employment

Some students of arts entrepreneurship will be ready to launch their own business immediately upon graduation from their college, university, or other training program. Others may find it advantageous to seek employment first in order to gain experience, save money, and develop a network of references and industry contacts before creating their new venture. Learning about arts entrepreneurship – and developing the skills necessary to develop and run an arts-related organization – should be an ongoing process. Established business owners also need to keep learning and growing in order to keep their business concept relevant and their operational processes functioning well.

For the current or recently graduated student, academic exposure to business practices such as marketing, fundraising, accounting, and strategic planning will serve them well when applying for jobs within an existing company in their area of interest. An aspiring arts entrepreneur thinking about a business focused on the creation and distribution of fine arts photography could work for a gallery or an established, professional photographer for a period of time before launching their own company. Individuals interested in the performing arts could volunteer at a local theater, concert hall or other venue. The experience gained while employed or otherwise involved in an existing arts organization is extremely valuable. Exposure to real-world problems – and how organizations solve them – can provide many practical lessons in the day-to-day operations of a functioning business.

Students involved in an arts entrepreneurship course or program can use their coursework (such as business plans, financial projections or marketing campaigns) to convince an employer to hire them and offer the opportunity to become a valuable employee. The employer benefits from the contributions of an enthusiastic, knowledgeable employee while the student gains experience within the context of an established, ongoing enterprise. Along with the practical lessons learned while working for an existing arts-related business, there are opportunities to develop a network of references and contacts. The people you work with – and for – during your career can become your advisers and supporters once you start your own company, or can serve as references when applying for funding or negotiating leases and contracts.

For the creative business owner with years of experience, the need to develop skills in arts entrepreneurship does not diminish over time. Learning about new methods for product development and distribution, or studying emerging techniques for marketing and fundraising, can help the established arts entrepreneur stay current with industry trends and keep their organization on track for continued growth and success. If you are the creator of the artistic product your business offers to consumers, then developing and refining your artistic skills while running your business will also be a necessity. It is the unique combination of artistic skills and business acumen that allows the arts entrepreneur to invent an idea for new organization, attract interest among consumers and manage the venture's many business details.

Arts Entrepreneurs and Online Platforms for Fundraising, Marketing, and Community Building

The Internet has created many opportunities for an arts-related business to reach out to supporters and potential customers. Although some organizations may choose to establish themselves completely off-line (for example, a café/gallery located in a busy neighborhood that attracts customers purely through walk-by traffic and word-of-mouth), most new ventures will take advantage of the many ways online platforms can help their company become established and grow:

- *Fundraising* is one area where web-based services have become increasingly important. Crowdfunding platforms, such as Kickstarter, Indiegogo, GoFundMe and others, have become key ingredients in the fundraising and community building strategies used by individual artists and emerging arts organizations. Social media is another area where the arts venture can make its case for financial and other support and attract interest and contributions from its followers.

- *Marketing* is another area where a business can develop an online presence to expand awareness of its products and generate customer response. Developing and implementing a carefully structured marketing campaign that includes email, dynamic website design, social media postings, and even text/SMS activity can help the new venture connect within an expanding network of supporters and customers.

- *Community building* happens online as the individual artist or arts organization develops awareness among people whose interests align with, and are served by, the mission of the venture. As with other forms of community, not all relationships need to be transactional. A reader of your company's web blog, for example, may not choose to purchase something that you make available. Instead, they might decide to promote your business through their own network and, by advocating on your behalf, expand your network of contacts and generate a greater overall financial effect for your organization than a single transaction might have produced.

Using social media, websites, and email to communicate exclusively about opportunities for purchasing artwork, tickets to a performance, or some other form of sales can have the unintended consequence of driving individuals away from your online presence rather than attracting people to it. If your network of supporters is only receiving messages about opportunities to buy something from you, then they may, over time, become less interested in maintaining their connection with you and your business. Online platforms for fundraising, marketing, and community building should be used as vehicles for inspiring and engaging your audience so they become involved with – and supportive of – the mission and purpose of your venture. This is accomplished by introducing storytelling, short videos, and compelling anecdotes about the people and projects connected with your company. If your arts organization is concerned about environmental issues, for example, then an announcement about a donation, sponsorship, or other contribution made by your company to an environmental advocacy organization can be much more meaningful to your customers than yet another opportunity for customers to make a purchase. Consider developing a strategy for your company's Facebook and Instagram postings that incorporate personal, mission-focused messages along with communications intended to produce donations or sales.

Collaborating

Collaborating with Other Artists or Arts Organization Owners

As an arts entrepreneur studies the environment within which their new business will be located, there will likely be a number of similar organizations or individuals who are already established in that area. Examples include galleries, arts education programs, or performing arts venues that exist within the immediate vicinity or overall region of the intended new venture. The organizations and individuals who already have a presence in the marketplace could be viewed as competitors for the new company's prospective customers. However, in the arts and culture sector, we frequently find that like-minded organizations and individuals can become key allies and partners for an emerging new venture, rather than competition that needs to be challenged or overcome. Art galleries within a revitalized downtown historic district may welcome another similar business into the neighborhood and collectively market the group via open studio tours or monthly "art walk" events. A commercial photographer, solo musician, or graphic designer might refer a new client inquiry to another artist with similar or more compatible skills if their schedule is already full or if they feel the potential client can be better served by connecting with someone else. Artists, designers, and owners of businesses in the creative sector can refer customers, supporters, and service providers to one another in an effort to help each other succeed – they can also work on projects together and hire (or create partnerships with) one another to take on multidisciplinary projects. Although this may not be the typical approach for entrepreneurs in other fields, collaboration and mutual support among artists and arts organizations can be a natural – and very effective – way to create and grow a viable business.

Working with Schools, Colleges, Universities, or Other Arts Education Institutions

As mentioned above, using arts entrepreneurship training to find employment within an existing organization can be an efficient, productive approach toward eventually designing and launching your own business. Academic institutions can be included in your list of potential employers, especially those whose artistic and cultural programs align with your interests. If you hope to create a new dance company as your future arts venture, then working for (or volunteering with) the dance department of a local college or university can be an excellent way to get experience and develop connections. Many of today's well-established research universities have opportunities for student entrepreneurs, such as incubators, accelerator programs, or consulting opportunities featuring experienced investors and business startup professionals. If you are currently enrolled in a college or university that offers these types of programs, you should investigate opportunities to develop your business concept and expand your network of supporters and investors.

Beyond working for a higher education institution or participating in their entrepreneurship programs, you can identify individuals and departments within the academic world who could become clients or customers of your venture. Schools, colleges, and universities are also consumers of a range of products and services, including those in the artistic and cultural sectors. A new business offering customized web design services could look for clients in university departments and offer to produce a uniquely tailored online experience that addresses the needs of that particular client and their user base. Colleges and universities are also excellent resources for potential employees when an arts-related business is ready to increase its staff or expand its range of offerings.

Working with Overseas Partners, Including Suppliers, Manufacturers, Distributors, or Customers

Many startups have international ambitions built into their medium- and long-term plans. A venture may initially become established in a local community or region, then concentrate on replicating the business model in other domestic and foreign markets. Or, the organization may be founded on a set of relationships with partners overseas. For the arts entrepreneur, the key questions revolve around the agreements and processes needed to launch the business and grow the operation into a state of sustainability. As mentioned earlier, quality control and reliability need to be carefully monitored and managed when running an organization that spans multiple jurisdictions and crosses borders as part of its regular business operations. For companies that produce and distribute physical objects, details such as the country of origin for raw materials, shipping and customs duties, and regulations for importing and exporting finished products need to be taken into account. For an arts venture offering online services to a global community of users, issues such as language translation, international banking processes, and compliance with overseas laws are just a few of the concerns that will need to be addressed by the business founder. If your idea for a business depends on participation by foreign partners, suppliers, or customers, then developing a thorough understanding of all the issues involved in international trade will be a necessity. Consider working with experienced consultants who have extensive knowledge of the legal, financial, and cultural contexts of the locations where your business will be operating.

Launching a New Business

Launching a New Business, Managing Growth, and Planning for Succession

Each phase in the life of a new venture presents its own opportunities and challenges to the founder and others responsible for the company's development and operations:

- The *creation* and *launch* phases demand close attention to product design, customer engagement, and the overall structure of the organization. Moving your business concept from an idea to reality can be as straightforward as a test project that introduces your limited edition products to a small number of early adopters, or as complex as building an entire organizational structure to support the creation of a major arts festival.
- *Managing the growth* of an existing business can take the organization and its leadership into new areas, such as expanding the business into new markets or increasing the range of products and services being offered. A venture in its growth phase may also discover opportunities to pivot the organization and its products toward greater consumer acceptance and more efficient methods of product design and distribution.
- *Succession*, or turning over the business to new owners, can be anticipated and planned for in advance. Although the idea of paying attention to the end of the founder's relationship to their venture might seem a strange thing to do while formulating the initial concepts and

structures that will make it successful, there are reasons to look far into the future when designing, launching, and growing a viable business. Issues such as choosing the appropriate corporate structure for the organization are important when considering succession, since some corporate forms are better than others if the intention is to leave behind a thriving business for others to own and manage.

Arts Entrepreneurs as Employers: Attracting Talented Staff, Providing Training and Incentives, Encouraging a Sense of Direct Involvement in the Company's Mission

One of the incentives for the owner of a new business can be the ability to provide economic benefits to their community, including sales and property tax revenues, purchasing from local suppliers and service providers, and offering employment, internships, or volunteering opportunities. As an employer, the arts entrepreneur can build a team of skilled people who are committed to the mission of the organization and experience the benefits of employment. This can include not only a paycheck, but also a sense of contribution to the quality of life experienced by the venture's customers and community.

Along with the sustained effort required to create, test, and refine products and services that gain traction in the market, the business owner should invest resources in their employees' well-being (via health insurance, recreation, and other perks), job satisfaction (via performance reviews with supportive, open dialogue between management and staff), and professional development, such as paid training to develop the specialized skills needed to keep the organization on track for continued success. Interactions between management and staff should be frequent and varied, to include formal meetings and presentations and informal conversations about the company's mission and the important roles played by its employees. Some business owners offer incentives such as bonuses and salary increases to incentivize their employees, while others provide stock options or other forms of ownership to maintain and enhance a sense of commitment and participation among their team. As with the close attention paid to the customers of a new venture, the owner of an arts-related organization should listen closely to the ideas and concerns expressed by employees in order to continually refine and improve the organization's operational features and maintain an open platform for new or better business concepts to emerge and take shape.

Chapter Summary

Entrepreneurship is a word that can be applied to different ideas of business development and execution, from the management of risk to the creative destruction found in disruptive changes to economic and social norms. Arts entrepreneurs may choose to engage in creative destruction while designing and launching their new concept, or they may pursue a business strategy that places their venture alongside, and in collaboration with, other organizations. Building a business concept upon the core values of the founder and the shared interests of the company's team (and customers) can be an efficient and effective way to design and develop a sustainable enterprise. Business opportunities can be discovered through the examination of the existing landscape of organizations in your area of interest and consideration of areas of unmet need among your target consumers. Testing a business concept early on using a Minimum Viable Product can help generate useful consumer feedback and provide validated learning that guides the business owner toward better decisions about the company's purpose and offerings. The types of risks an arts entrepreneur manage include financial, reputational, and legal areas. Maintaining a consistent focus on customer needs and wants helps the business owner discover connection points between the perceived qualities of the proposed product and the values of the organization's target market. Descriptions of a product or service should highlight the benefits to consumers, rather than the features of the product. There are different types of potential customers who can provide early-stage feedback driving the product development cycle. Innovators and early adopters are eager to experiment with the latest innovations, while early and late majority consumers will often wait for validation from some other source. Business growth can be measured in accordance with the appropriately scaled ambitions of the organization leadership. Some arts organizations seek widespread market penetration to attract customers numbering in the many thousands, while others aim for consumer engagement measuring in the dozens or hundreds. The business founder has the freedom to decide which measurement of success works for their intentions.

Creating an organization that is profitable and efficient requires careful analysis of business activity and well-crafted projections about the future. Entrepreneurship is often characterized by its reliance on pivots, or quickly implemented changes of operational tactics that serve the overall goals and objectives of the venture. Arts entrepreneurship can sometimes be distinguished from other forms of entrepreneurship in that the founding artist, or business owner, seeks not an exit strategy as an intended outcome, but rather an ongoing engagement with the business purpose, products, and customers. Some arts entrepreneurs develop a business idea focused on creating positive social benefits in areas such as health, education, aging, the environment, immigration, and other important areas. Education can play a major role for some arts organizations, either as a key part of their core mission or as a target market for their products and services. Developing connections with a community is an essential component of establishing an arts-related business and encouraging its growth. The types of people you can work to attract to your business include partners, supporters, patrons, suppliers, and investors. Studying arts entrepreneurship can, in addition to preparing you for launching your own enterprise, provide valuable experience and knowledge as you pursue employment. In the overall plan for a new business, one should anticipate the launch, growth, and succession phases. Arts entrepreneurs can also be employers who recruit, train, and reward their staff and maintain a strong sense of connection between the business mission and the interests and ambitions of their team.

Discussion Questions

1. What are some of the ways the term *entrepreneurship* is understood in relation to business concept development and execution? How does the word apply to your own idea for an arts-related business?

2. Describe the process whereby personal and professional values can become the platform for a new business idea.

3. How does the creation and testing of a prototype, or a Minimum Viable Product, help the business owner learn from consumers and refine the business idea?

4. Outline some of the ways a business opportunity can be identified, including an analysis of the existing environment for similar businesses and an interview project where your closest advisers and friends give you feedback about your artistic abilities and how to apply them.

5. What are the types of risk that need to be understood and managed by an arts entrepreneur?

6. Describe how early-stage market research using potential customers can influence product design and the overall business approach to connecting with consumers.

7. How will you organize and execute a business launch for your new product or service?

8. How will your venture measure success? Will you seek consumer acceptance in the hundreds of thousands or even millions? Or, will your company target a smaller audience numbering in the dozens or hundreds but aim for a deeper impact on that market?

9. What does the term *pivot* mean in the development of a business concept? What kinds of pivots do startup businesses make, and why?

10. Describe an arts organization that places social benefits at the center of its core mission and attracts supporters and customers as a result of its commitment to positive social change.

Notes

1   See "entrepreneur" in www.merriam-webster.com/dictionary/ entrepreneur

2   Drucker, Peter Ferdinand, and Joseph A. Maciariello. *Innovation and entrepreneurship: practice and principles* (London: Routledge, 2015).

3   Kweskin, Amy, Nancy Hytone Leb, Yesenia Sanchez, Greg Victoroff, Nancy Walch, and Richard Walch. *Business of art: an artist's guide to profitable self-employment* (Los Angeles, CA: Center for Cultural Innovation, 2012).

4   Guillebeau, Chris. *The $100 startup: reinvent the way you make a living, do what you love, and create a new future: summary* (New York: Crown Business, 2016).

5   Ries, Eric. *The lean startup: how today's entrepreneurs use continuous innovation to create radically successful business* (New York: Crown Business, 2011).

6   Kawasaki, Guy. *The art of the start: the time-tested, battle-hardened guide for anyone starting anything* (New York: Portfolio, 2014).

7   Rogers, Everett M., and F. Floyd Shoemaker. *Communication of innovations: a cross-cultural approach* (New York: The Free Press, 1971).

8   Ries, *The lean startup.*

9   Roberts, Joseph S., and Clarke A. Greene. *Arts entrepreneurship: the business of the arts* (Bloomingdale, IL: United Press Services, Inc., 2004).

10 Spinelli, Stephen, and Robert J. Adams. *New venture creation. entrepreneurship for the 21st century* (New York: McGraw-Hill/Irwin, 2012).

2 Planning and Assessment

This chapter examines how business owners use planning to develop and operate a successful arts organization. It also introduces techniques for assessment, or the evaluation and analysis of the financial, programmatic, and operational features of the business. Starting from a foundational understanding of the venture's values, goals, and objectives, planning can be an essential ingredient in designing, launching, and running a successful company or building an individual career. Topics include:

- Developing a mission statement for a new business
- Understanding the organization's strengths, weaknesses, opportunities, and threats
- Strategic planning for the arts venture
- Creating and using a business plan
- Other types of planning for arts-related organizations
- Evaluation and assessment

Planning for Artists and Arts Organizations

Why is planning important and what kinds of results can it produce? Artists and owners of arts-related companies sometimes look at planning as an optional (or even avoidable) exercise that may or may not serve the venture's overall objectives. Although some individuals and organizations can become successful without investing time and effort in planning, it is far more common for businesses of all types to develop and follow plans. Specifically, strategic plans and business plans provide valuable insights and guidance for the founder and other stakeholders associated with the company, including internal management and staff and external supporters who provide crucial financial and other resources.

The strategic plan is valuable because it provides a process and structure for working through the many variables and challenges encountered when developing and operating a business. Strategic planning requires participation by key members of the organization's team – it can also include contributions by external advisers with deep knowledge and experience in the important issues that may confront the organization as it evolves. As described later in this chapter, the steps involved in crafting and implementing a strategic plan demand creative thinking, analysis, and focused problem-solving. However, the end result is not only a document that captures all of this collective effort, it is also a roadmap of actionable strategic steps that can be followed and, if necessary, adapted to the changing needs of the venture. An arts organization that commits to the strategic planning process will not only benefit from the reflection and detailed clarifications needed to produce a well-crafted plan, it will also have a practical, results-oriented guide to follow as it works toward creating a successful future.

Defining the Vision, Mission, and Goals of the Organization

In Chapter 1, we explored the process of identifying personal and professional values to look for overlapping areas that serve as the foundation for the business. The results of this exercise, plus an articulation of personal and professional goals for the future, produced a *vision statement* and related written material that can be used to craft the *mission* of the new venture. The vision statement serves to describe where the business intends to go as it works through its design, launch, and sustainability phases. The mission statement communicates, in very practical terms, the key elements of the organization. It answers the essential questions about the business, such as:

What do we do?

Why we do it?

How do we do it?

For whom do we do it?

What benefits do you provide?

Thinking about and writing down the answers to each of these five questions give the arts entrepreneur some early-stage text for the creation of a clear, inspiring mission statement. Combine the answers to these questions into a group of sentences that tell the story of the business in a direct, compelling statement that can be easily understood by someone who has never been introduced to your business idea in the past.

Revising the mission statement should include sharing it with your colleagues and consultants to invite feedback and discover ways to improve the understanding and function of this important communication tool. The mission statement not only expresses to others the basic purpose and intentions of the business, it also serves as a guiding principle for making key decisions about how to run the business itself. The founder and key personnel of an organization can look to the mission statement when considering opportunities or evaluating potential changes to the company's structure and operational processes. If an opportunity or structural change does not align with the venture's mission statement, then serious consideration should be given to avoiding that path in order to stay true to the company's core values and sense of purpose. For example, the mission statement of a community-based arts education organization might highlight social benefits and collective interest while explicitly rejecting the principles of unregulated capitalism. This arts organization might be offered the opportunity to receive financial support from a controversial private corporation in exchange for associating its brand with the corporation's products and services. If the mission statement of the arts venture places a high priority on serving the needs and interests of residents in its immediate neighborhood, the opportunity to collaborate with a questionable corporation might be rejected because it runs counter to the scope of the organization's community-based mission.

Some mission statements are composed of many sentences or even multiple paragraphs of text, while others are very brief and present a compact set of messages using only a sentence or two. Since the goals of the mission statement include both communicating essential business information to the outside world and providing guidance to internal business decisions as they emerge, it makes sense to compose a mission statement that is neither too vague nor overly wordy. Below is an example of how to turn an unfocused mission statement into one that clearly and convincingly delivers its messages.

Before: "The Theatrical Theatre Company produces plays that cover a wide range of styles and messages but share an underlying purpose: to recognize the creative potential of all human beings and affirm their ability to engage with one another."

After: "Founded in 1985, the Theatrical Theater Company presents exciting, challenging works for theatergoers in the greater Los Angeles area. Our mission is to inspire and entertain audiences with affordable, powerful, life-affirming theatrical productions that feature plays by emerging and established local playwrights."

Create a new folder called Planning and Assessment. Open a new document and name it Mission Statement. Using your answers to the five questions listed earlier in this section, create a first draft of the mission statement for your organization. Then, share it with three trusted consultants (such as friends or family) and revise the mission statement using their constructive feedback. Continue revising your mission statement until you and your consultants agree that it is ready for use. Then, save it and place it in your Planning and Assessment folder.

SWOT Analysis: Strengths, Weaknesses, Opportunities, and Threats

As the person responsible for designing, launching, and operating a new business, the arts entrepreneur will have a unique – but not necessarily objective – viewpoint on many aspects of the organization, including its internal attributes and its relationship to the outside world. Looking at the venture from multiple perspectives can help identify areas that will contribute to the organization's success, as well as areas that need attention in order to overcome deficiencies or challenges. One technique for developing an objective, multifaceted view of a new business is to conduct an analysis of the Strengths, Weaknesses, Opportunities, and Threats associated with the organization. Known as a SWOT analysis, this interrogation produces many useful insights that can guide the company's planning, decision processes and actions.

A SWOT analysis has four components, two internal and two external. The internal components are the company's strengths and weaknesses, while the external components are the organization's opportunities and threats:

- *Strengths* can include the venture's internal features, such as an excellent location, high-quality products and services, experienced and motivated leadership and staff, well-designed facilities and operating systems, and sufficient financial and other resources to accomplish its goals.
- Internal *weaknesses* can include inexperienced or unprepared managers and employees, inadequate working capital to support the venture through its early startup phases, lack of a distinct presence in the market or deficiencies in product design and execution.
- *Opportunities* found outside of the organization can include strong acceptance of the company's products among early-stage consumers and the media, support from the community and similar businesses in the organization's general category, availability of financial and other resources necessary for expansion and growth of the venture, and productive relationships with key partners, suppliers, and collaborators.
- External *threats* to the new venture can include near-term changes in the economic, political or a cultural landscape, direct competition

offering similar products and services at a higher quality and a lower price point, and changes in technology that could render the company's business model obsolete.

As with other analysis and planning processes undertaken by an arts organization and its leadership, it can be useful to include external advisers in the brainstorming and documentation activities that produce an effective SWOT analysis. Form a group of internal and external stakeholders whose input can contribute to the creation of a meaningful SWOT analysis. Then, schedule an exploratory meeting to investigate all of the organization's strengths, weaknesses, opportunities, and threats. Finally, write a comprehensive, objective presentation of the SWOT analysis results. This document will become an important component of the overall strategic plan for the venture, which will also describe actions the company can take in response to what is identified within the SWOT analysis. A version of the SWOT analysis – and the organization's responses to it – should also be incorporated into the business plan that is used to form the new venture.

It's worth noting that some issues identified in one part of the SWOT analysis can, over time, end up in a different category. For example, a new musical group might describe the obscurity of its brand among local nightclubs and concert venues as an internal weakness. However, this same issue can eventually be understood as an external opportunity, as the group reaches out to club owners and booking agents to attract interest and gains acceptance of its novel, unfamiliar performance style and other unique musical qualities.

Create a new document and name it SWOT Analysis. Carefully consider, either individually or with the help of a group of supporters, your organization's strengths, weaknesses, opportunities, and threats. Write down all of the issues identified in the SWOT analysis and add sections describing the conclusions and recommendations that your company will use to address them. Place the SWOT Analysis document in your Planning and Assessment folder.

In addition to studying the entire organization, a SWOT analysis can be applied to individual aspects of the venture's operations. For example, a SWOT analysis of the marketing plan for a documentary filmmaking company can be undertaken to examine and evaluate the strengths, weaknesses, opportunities, and threats associated with connecting their business to the outside world, especially in the pursuit of potential clients. A marketing SWOT analysis will reveal not only the internal capacities found within the filmmakers' organization (such as their ability to effectively communicate the unique qualities of their leadership, staff, and prior work) but will also identify the external conditions within which the company's marketing efforts will seek to raise awareness and generate interest. A SWOT analysis, whether general or specific, provides the foundation for an arts entrepreneur to create and implement a plan that addresses their company's internal and external issues and conditions.

Strategic Planning

Strategic planning is a process through which an organization articulates what it may accomplish in the future, what needs it hopes to meet, and how it plans to do so:[1]

> a strategic plan is a set of comprehensive choices that have been prioritized and documented to marshal the resources available to the arts organization for the purpose of meeting defined goals and objectives derived from clear mission, vision, and value statements.[2]

Developing and using a strategic plan can help an arts-related business stay focused, productive and results-oriented as it grows from a new startup into an established enterprise. Like the process of designing, creating, and delivering the actual product or service that forms the basis of the venture, strategic planning requires considerable time and effort to produce a quality result. The following sections introduce some of the key elements of strategic planning and provide a framework for crafting a custom-designed plan that suits your business needs.

Defining Terms and Choosing Appropriate Language

As with all of the written and spoken language used to invent and run your business, the strategic plan demands accurate use of words, phrases, and longer narrative structures in order to properly conceptualize and communicate your organization's ambitions and operational details. The following three general categories can help the strategic planning team as they brainstorm generally – and focus specifically – on the areas and issues important to your venture:

1. beliefs
2. results
3. methods

Beliefs are the values, principles, and assumptions that underlie all of the important decisions and actions undertaken by the business. They form the foundation upon which an arts-related business builds its identity and defines its functional behaviors. A company that dedicates itself to protecting the environment, either through its products' purpose or its manufacturing methods (or perhaps both), will articulate its values explicitly in its marketing messages and embed them in its documentation of business policies and procedures. Many arts organizations take a highly principled approach to answering fundamental questions such as why the business exists, who is it for, and what are the public benefits it hopes to deliver. Assumptions are another form of belief – they can include measurable data such as prior (and anticipated) financial activity and productivity measurements, as well as the given conditions inside and outside of the organization that have been identified using some objective method. A performing arts venue with a history of good relations with the local press can assume some degree of positive media coverage in the future, but will need to proactively maintain those relationships in order to continue generating favorable coverage.

Results: Imagine a rocket preparing to launch a new satellite into orbit. If beliefs are the platform, trajectory and weather conditions for the project, then results are the intended outcomes of the mission once the satellite reaches orbit and becomes operational. In business terms, results can be understood as the organization's vision, mission, goals, and objectives. In drafting a mission statement, the arts entrepreneur hopes to express the company's vision and purpose in order to briefly communicate what the venture is trying to accomplish. However, the ideas found within this abbreviated text need to be explored more fully in the examination of all the organization's planning and execution processes. How will your arts organization define success? What are the goals – in terms of financial performance, customer response, and overall impact on internal and external stakeholders – you and others involved in your venture hope to achieve? What are the near- and long-term objectives that your company is focused on?

The range of desired results identified by an arts-related business is as wide and varied as the potential products, services, and organizational structures you can choose to create. Some entrepreneurs (in the arts as well as in other fields) commit themselves to large-scale impact at the very beginning: they seek rapid expansion, significant market penetration, and dramatic financial success. Or, they aim for transformative impact on social issues and try to solve difficult problems on a large scale and around the globe. Others, however, design their businesses to serve distinct, well-defined segments of their immediate community. They seek impact on a smaller scale in terms of population, but perhaps at a much greater depth for each individual involved, including consumers and the company's staff and leadership. Arts entrepreneurs have the freedom to define results for their businesses and for themselves in any way they choose. They may also design the new venture with modest, easily achievable goals at the outset, but much grander ambitions for the future.

Methods are the strategies, actions, and assessment techniques used to propel the business forward and produce its intended results. Following our satellite launch analogy, methods include the design and fabrication of all the working parts for the project, the process of initiating the launch and achieving orbit, the initiation of the satellite's functions and the attainment of sustainability, and the regular data acquisition and analysis tasks used to assess the mission's overall success and make decisions about adjustments or changes needed in the future. Methods answer the questions about how you will run your organization in a way that allows you to achieve your goals, and how you will measure the company's activities and impacts in a way that enables it to respond to changing conditions or leverage new opportunities.

Methods can sometimes be described via *use cases*, which are examples of how people engage with the company and its offerings. Use cases allow the organization to examine all of the processes and interactions involved in its transactional activities. For example, a live music venue featuring jazz would produce use cases for different customers, including:

- highly experienced jazz fans who follow specific genres such as American jazz standards, Latin jazz, or contemporary improvisational groups and solo artists;
- adventurous listeners who are unfamiliar with most jazz forms but willing to try something new;
- young jazz musicians eager to experience (and learn from) accomplished performers in a comfortable, welcoming environment.

Each of these use cases would identify the different ways these distinct populations would learn about upcoming performances, purchase tickets, attend a concert and interact with the artists, engage with the venue's staff and management, purchase ancillary merchandise such as refreshments, posters, recordings and apparel, and consider supporting the organization as a donor or volunteer.

As you work through the process of creating a strategic plan for your arts organization, pay close attention to the terminology you choose when defining the beliefs, results, and methods associated with your venture. Be expansive and freethinking during the brainstorming processes as you unearth your company's possible concepts and operational details. But then be ready to impose rigorous editing and rewriting for your text in order to bring clarity and focus to the language – and ideas – upon which your organization will be founded and run.

The Strategic Planning Process

Although the idea generation and concept exploration aspects of strategic planning are best accomplished with freedom and open-ended dialogue around each of the topics, it is important to have structure within which the planning process takes place. The following steps will help create a productive environment and final written document for your organization's strategic planning needs.

1. Schedule a time and place that is conducive to brainstorming, effective interactions and dialogue, and progress toward an organized, clearly expressed result. The participants in your strategic planning exercises should know in advance that the process will be well managed, businesslike, and operated in a way that respects their time and efforts.

2. Allow for extended periods of deliberation and creative exploration. Some organizations plan multi-day meetings, or retreats, that provide ample time for exploratory dialogue and the pursuit of interesting ideas and proposals. Trying to conduct a thorough investigation of the company's many issues in a limited timeframe will lead to an unsatisfactory final result.

3. Budget for a comfortable rented space if necessary, plus refreshments/meals, Wi-Fi, parking, and other accommodations as appropriate. Remember that the people involved in your venture's strategic planning process should feel relaxed and focused as they engage with the numerous business details needing extended concentration. If costs are a concern, then choose a private home or apartment where distractions can be reduced to a minimum and the team can proceed with its work without interruptions.

4. Choose a planning process that suits the needs of the venture and its intended outcomes. During its start-up phase, a new company with a small team can undertake its planning with a modest amount of time and written material. An established organization with extensive data to review and many operational details to consider will require more time and participants in order to produce a useful, thoroughly developed plan.

5. Planning sessions can be designed and managed by people from within the organization, but it is often desirable to bring in an outside specialist. If your team of partners and consultants includes someone with experience in strategic planning, then that person can be approached with the opportunity to lead your group through the process. Also, hiring an outside strategic planning specialist can generate some very valuable results because they can contribute additional objectivity and experience to the effort.

6. Choose participants in the planning group to include key internal leaders of the organization, representative staff from each of the company's departments, and outside individuals who can offer objective insights and guidance. Seek a balance between experience levels, specialized professional backgrounds (such as marketing, fundraising, or legal expertise) and formal or informal approaches to their spoken/written contributions during the planning process. The inclusion of staff in the organization's strategic planning process can provide a number of benefits. Not only can the ideas and perspectives of trusted,

knowledgeable workers be incorporated into the deliberations, a sense of belonging and influence can be cultivated throughout the organization. Staff members should have the opportunity to contribute to the conversations around their specific operational issues and feel directly connected to the larger mission and purpose of the venture.

7. Prepare and distribute advance materials to the team well before the planning sessions begin. This can include financial reports and budget projections, as well as quantitative and qualitative analyses of business processes and results. The list of advance materials prepared in anticipation of a strategic planning session can include profit and loss statements from the past year or more, a current balance sheet, cash flow projections for the coming year, and individual reports focused on marketing, fundraising, legal issues, and human resources. For example, a report from the Marketing department should include quantitative analysis of the prior year's activities (such as marketing expenditures, social media engagement, website visits and purchases, and increased sales tied to specific marketing campaigns), as well as narrative descriptions covering customer feedback, marketing concepts and their actual or potential impact, and detailed plans for identifying new market segments and delivering effective marketing messages to raise awareness and inspire transactions.

8. Study the vision and mission statements upon which the business has been created. Examine whether the vision serves its purpose for all aspects of the operation and modify it if needed to incorporate the observations and understandings of all the team members. The mission statement must be agreed upon by the entire strategic planning team in order to produce meaningful strategies that are linked to the organization's purpose and intended outcomes. Examine and refine the mission statement and organizational goals, working through any conflicts or trade-offs encountered in the decision-making process.

9. Evaluate the business from a number of different angles, including the internal operations (self-reporting documents, interviews, and questionnaires) and external perceptions of the organization (through surveys, focus groups, and online forms). Honest, detailed assessments of the business are essential if the strategic planning process – and its final documentation – are worth the energy contributed by the team. The goal is to deliver actionable, focused recommendations for moving the venture forward.

10. Identify the key areas where the business needs to concentrate its efforts. After the analysis of past business performance and the projections of future activities, this section of the business plan is the most important. Rather than producing a list of hopes and wishes for the company's future, the recommendations necessary to keep the business on track must be expressed as *strategies*. Strategies are a series of steps – presented in a logical, progressive format – that address specific issues and aim to produce concrete solutions. For

example, an arts education venture might identify, through its analysis of previous financial performance, the need to increase fundraising in the coming 3–5 years. The strategies derived from considering the venture's assessment and goals could include temporarily hiring an expert fundraising consultant to identify opportunities for additional grants and donations. The recommended strategies could also incorporate commitments from the organization's leadership and board of directors to cultivate relationships with regional foundations and individual major donors. Strategies should be grounded in the mission of the organization, informed by data and narrative descriptions of where the company is and where it needs to go, and focused on specific actions that solve problems, address known issues, and leverage potential opportunities.

11. Prioritize the resulting strategies according to the mutually understood importance of each item and the availability of resources. Some strategies will be more expensive than others in terms of the money, time, and personnel needed to follow through on the tasks that are identified. In the fundraising example above, an expense line for a consultant would be added to the organization's projected budget for the coming 3–5 years, along with anticipated increases in contributed income that would be generated from additional grants and gifts. Predictions about increased income from fundraising, product sales, or other sources should be scaled appropriately to the realistic earning potential of the company and, if possible, in line with similar businesses in the organization's regional market and/or overall product category.

12. Develop a set of objectives that provide detailed answers to the "who, what, when, where and why" for each strategy. This section can be laid out on a *strategic planning spreadsheet* (Figure 2-1) with individual strategies and tasks occupying rows on the left side and columns across the top for the associated people, actions, schedule, location, and purpose of each strategy.

13. Develop budgets for the near-term and long-term execution of the organization's efforts to achieve these objectives. The strategies that have been identified for the coming years should be incorporated into the organization's overall budget projections. The financial impact of the strategic plan should be observable through both the income and expense sections of the budget projections. Income-producing strategies should be linked to their corresponding expense details. For example, a ceramics artist with the strategy of increasing sales through an expanding network of galleries should identify increased income in future years as well as increased expenses for materials, tools, marketing, and distribution.

14. Choose one individual to write a draft of the strategic plan that incorporates all of the relevant sections. Unresolved or potentially conflicting issues can remain in place so long as there is recognition of the

future work needed to reconcile any remaining problems. The draft can be circulated among the strategic planning team to elicit comments and revisions and worked on until it achieves an agreeable consensus as a finalized version.

Implementing the Plan

The value of *creating* a strategic plan lies in the process of organizing the planning sessions and working through the analysis, forecasting, and prioritization steps of each key area. The value of *using* a strategic plan lies in its actual implementation – following the recommendations and enacting strategies to accomplish the intended outcomes identified in the written document. Item 12 above suggests creating a *strategic planning spreadsheet*. Using this spreadsheet as a working template, sort the strategies according to the schedule first, then work on addressing each task according to its upcoming deadline. Implementing a strategic plan means sharing it with the people responsible for accomplishing their assigned tasks according to the schedule. Regular meetings involving managers and

Figure 2.1 Strategic planning spreadsheet.

Example: Strategic planning spreadsheet

Strategy	People	Actions	Schedule	Location	Purpose
Improve product Task 1 Task 2 Task 3					
Expand marketing Task 1 Task 2 Task 3					
Increase sales Task 1 Task 2 Task 3					
Increase fundraising Task 1 Task 2 Task 3					
Solve legal issues Task 1 Task 2 Task 3					
Improve bookkeeping Task 1 Task 2 Task 3					

staff should use the strategic planning spreadsheet to confirm strategies as they are accomplished, identify delays or operational problems that need attention and look for areas of overlap or integration where multiple tasks can be linked together or efficiently accomplished through collaboration and teamwork. As the organization proceeds through its fiscal year and uses the strategic planning spreadsheet to complete its tasks, it will also be capturing issues, concerns, and opportunities for future planning. With a shared online version of this spreadsheet, the entire company can add notes, comments, and suggestions throughout the year that can become part of the next strategic planning session and be incorporated into the regular operations of the venture.

Evaluating the Plan

Because both the process of creating a strategic plan and the experience of implementing it are intended to produce recognizable results for the organization, it helps to concentrate on each of the plan's focus areas independently in order to determine its effectiveness. The fundraising section, for example, should identify needs and opportunities in the coming year and project forward 3–5 years in the future. Capital campaigns, such as endowments or the construction of a new building, will take a number of years to produce results. By laying out near-term targets – such as creating a development board, producing a fundraising plan with scheduled financial goals, or cultivating relationships with program directors from foundations, government agencies, and corporations – the evaluation can focus on whether or not these milestones have been met and what can be done to increase the likelihood of success going forward. As with other forms of measuring and assessing your company's endeavors, attention should be paid to both quantitative data (such as increased donations and other contributions) and qualitative information (such as transcribed responses from interviews and surveys). See the sections on assessment and evaluation later in this chapter.

Create a new document and name it Organizational Strategic Plan. Follow steps 1–13 described above to create an initial draft of your planning document, then work with a colleague to edit and revise the text until a final version is produced. Place the Organizational Strategic Plan in your Planning and Assessment folder.

Strategic Planning for a Specific Project

In addition to an organization's overall strategic planning efforts, and along with plans created to further the goals of departments such as fundraising or marketing, strategic planning can be applied to individual projects. The following steps describe an abbreviated format for using strategic planning to help accomplish goals at the project level:

1. *Conduct an audit.* Assess the people, funds, workspace, and time available for the project. This step should produce a snapshot of the current conditions that will allow the project to proceed. For example, a photographer planning to launch a new website would (a) identify the person (or hired outside service) who will be assigned to the project; (b) produce a budget covering all phases of the initiative from start to finish; (c) allocate an office or desk space for the person working on the project; and (d) finalize a schedule for the design, launch, and maintenance of the new site.

2. *Define goals and organizational needs.* What are the intended outcomes of the project? How does the project's realization serve the needs of the venture? In the case of the photographer's new website, the goals might include an expanded, integrated online marketing effort that links the site to social media channels, along with the desire to find new clients. If the photographer wants to attract more clients to the business so it can be expanded and more staff can be hired, then the website serves these larger ambitions for the overall company.

3. *Identify funding and other resources for future work.* A project needs to have a budget that specifies the source of funding that will be used to complete all of its tasks. Other resources can include donated labor or services, access to space and materials, or collaborative participation by volunteers or partner organizations. The photographer's website project could include negotiating an arrangement with a local web designer: the photographer could provide free photography services for the designer as needed and the designer could help the photographer produce the new website. The photographer should also have some cash set aside for web hosting, domain name registration, and other expenses.

4. *Develop materials.* These will depend on the type of project being created. For a web design project, the required materials can include text, photography, video, and audio content.

5. *Train people.* In some cases, the organization's staff will bring existing skills and experience to serve the needs of the project. However, it can sometimes be necessary to invest in specialized training to support those individuals who are responsible for the project's design and execution. The photographer in our example may choose to send his marketing manager to a web development workshop to acquire special skills. Or, the founder may invest time and money in increasing his/her own capabilities in order to manage the project for the long term.

6. *Create the schedule.* An abbreviated version of the strategic planning spreadsheet described earlier can be used to lay out all of the details associated with the project. The timeline should be reasonable and

tuned to the specific needs of the project's design, implementation, and assessment phases.

7. *Implement the plan.* Put the plan into action by following the steps found in the strategic planning spreadsheet's timeline and in accordance with the goals and resources that have been identified.

8. *Evaluate results and refine/adjust future efforts.* Has the project been completed and is it producing the intended results? Effectiveness and impact should be measured according to the original ambitions of the project. If the photographer and project team launch the new website and attract many new clients as a direct result, then the project should be declared a success. However, there will be an ongoing need to refresh the site with new content and continue evaluating its effectiveness using measurements of web traffic, social media engagement, and revenue generation.

Choose a specific project that is an essential part of your organization, such as marketing, fundraising or product development and distribution. Create a new document and name it Project Strategic Plan. Follow steps 1–8 described above to create an initial draft of your planning document, then work with your team of advisors and co-workers to edit and revise the text until a final version is produced. Place the Project Strategic Plan in your Planning and Assessment folder.

Business Plans

Note: This section can be revisited after reading this book's other chapters and creating materials from the associated exercises, which can be incorporated into the Business Plan for the new venture.

While strategic plans are primarily for the benefit of an organization's internal staff and leadership, a business plan provides valuable insights and information for people both inside and outside of the venture. Business plans are typically constructed as a formal written presentation of the new company's founding concepts and operational approaches to areas such as:

Product development

Organizational structure

Marketing

Fundraising

Legal issues

Financial management

Like the strategic planning process, a business plan's research, development and final execution stages help the founder clarify the intentions of the venture and organize the company's proposed methods of accomplishing its objectives using commonly understood terminology, measurements, and business methods. In this way, the business plan serves its dual purposes:

- Provides insights and guidance for the organization's leadership and staff as they developed the business idea and turn it into a reality.
- Communicates the business concept – and descriptions of its key functional areas – to external supporters such as investors, bank loan officers, donors, partners, advisers, board members, media contacts, and service providers.

A business plan can be a very useful tool for any kind of organization, whether for-profit or nonprofit, small or large, online or brick-and-mortar, domestic or international. Business plans do not need to be overly complicated or time-consuming to produce. The scope should be in line with the overall ambitions of the proposed organization. A neighborhood-focused, one-person company could produce a brief five- to ten-page business plan that covers all the key areas. The final document could be used for the company's guidance and organizational management, as well as sharing the business concept with important external supporters from the community. A more complex venture, on the other hand, could produce a business plan of 20–30 pages that presents in great detail how the company will be formed, how it will evaluate and approach the market for its products, and how it will handle areas such as intellectual property, corporate formation, generating capital, and managing its finances.

Key Elements of a Business Plan

The following sections introduce the key elements of a well-designed business plan. Remember that its purposes are: (1) to provide the company's internal core team with a shared understanding of what the businesses is about and how it will operate; and (2) to communicate to select individuals outside the organization what the venture hopes to accomplish, how the company understands its responsibilities and what the methods are of addressing them.

1. Title Page

The first page of the business plan should include the name of the organization and a logo or some other graphic representation of the brand, the name(s) of the founder(s), contact information such as the company's email, website, social media and phone number, and the date of the document.

2. Table of Contents

The table of contents is simply a list of each section's name and the page number where it begins.

3. Executive Summary

The executive summary presents the business idea in a brief but compelling format. The purpose of this text is to generate interest and focus the reader's attention on the quality of the overall proposal and the venture's likelihood for success. Normally written as one page or less, the executive summary introduces each of the essential components found in the rest of the business plan. Starting with the name of the business and its location, the first few sentences should convey a clear sense of the venture's products and services and the mission of the company. Additional sentences should highlight the founder's understanding of the market and how it will be approached. The executive summary should also describe how the organization's offerings will be produced and delivered, along with an introductory description of the relevant fund raising and legal issues.

4. Vision/Mission/Goals Statement

This section of the business plan provides the reader with an understanding of the founding principles, assumptions, and intended outcomes of the business. Earlier in this chapter, we explored the process of developing a mission statement for a new company, using these five basic questions:

What do we do?

Why we do it?

How do we do it?

For whom do we do it?

What benefits do we provide?

The answers to these questions will produce text that allows the reader to grasp the underlying purpose of the organization. In writing this section of the business plan, the author should carefully construct a convincing premise for the venture's formation. The key operational issues should also be addressed, especially the processes involved in the creation and delivery of the company's products and services. Finally, a clear picture of the target market – and the benefits it will receive – should also be described here. If there are specific goals for the company in terms of the anticipated financial performance or targets for customer engagement, then they should be briefly presented in this section as well. For arts organizations seeking social impact, a description of those outcomes should be highlighted.

5. Organization Overview and Legal Issues

In this chapter, the company's organizational structure is presented, along with a description of the potential legal issues confronting the venture and how they will be addressed.

An organizational chart (see Chapter 8 on organizational design) can be used to show the relationships between the company's Board of Directors, leadership, and staff – along with any dependencies on outside services, such as accounting, shipping, or web design. The organizational chart should be accompanied by several paragraphs of descriptive text that explain the responsibilities of each position within the organization, as well as the expectations associated with external service providers.

A presentation of the company's legal issues (see Chapter 5 on legal issues) should include considerations of the following topics:

- The corporate form chosen for the new organization, either as a sole proprietor, LLC, B Corporation, or other legal entity, along with an explanation of why that form is best suited to serve the company's needs.
- Discussion of the relevant intellectual property issues, such as copyrights, patents, and trademarks.
- Discussion of any contracts that will be necessary to create and operate the company, including agreements with suppliers of raw materials or parts and formal arrangements with clients or distributors.

6. Market Analysis and Marketing Plan

Communicating a convincing vision for the organization's customers – and the most effective methods of reaching them – is an essential part of the business plan (see Chapter 3 on marketing). The marketing analysis should begin with a description of the competitive environment for the new organization, including similar companies that are located geographically nearby or existing firms that create and deliver similar products in another region or country. If the new arts organization can test its products and services with focus groups or early adopters to gather consumer feedback and refine its approach, then the results of these early explorations should be presented here. A comprehensive description of the target market should include consumer demographics and plans for growing the customer base over time.

The marketing plan helps the reader understand how the new venture intends to make its brand visible to the outside world and how it hopes to attract customers as the company becomes established and grows. Rather than general descriptions of marketing ambitions such as "using social media" or "creating and distributing an e-newsletter," the marketing plan should present a thorough, methodical set of strategies for reaching specific consumer types and measuring the effectiveness of the marketing effort.

7. Operations Plan

This section provides a clearly presented introduction to the organization's processes for designing, producing, and delivering its goods and services. A flow chart (or several diagrams of use case scenarios) can, together with some explanatory text, help communicate the venture's operational concepts to the reader and outline the practical steps involved. A company focused on acquiring raw materials and converting them into commercially available finished products should describe each of the steps required in its design, fabrication, and distribution methods.

For example, the creator of unique, artistically conceived hats, caps, and other headwear could demonstrate – through diagrams and written text – the processes involved in acquiring fabric and other materials, creating prototypes and testing them with potential consumers, moving the selected designs into production, developing marketing and distribution relationships with local galleries and stores, and delivering the finished pieces to distributors, retailers, and end-users. On the other hand, an arts education organization could present a vision of its program development and teaching concepts by describing its processes for designing arts-related courses and workshops, hiring instructors, renting appropriate workspaces and studios, connecting with potential customers via relationships with school programs and art supply stores, and working through the scheduling and delivery issues involved in accomplishing its educational mission.

8. Financial Plan

The financial section of a business plan should present a detailed, persuasive description of the organization's actual and/or potential performance in terms of income, expenses, and budget forecasting (see Chapter 6 on money management and entrepreneurial finance). For an established venture, or for a new business being constructed in conjunction with an existing company, the financial plan should use documented, verifiable data from prior and current tax records and financial reports. For an independent new business, the financial planning section will necessarily contain projected figures for income, expenses and other details.

There are several commonly used financial documents, known as *pro forma* statements, that should be included in the financial chapter of a business plan for an arts-related business:

- A *cash flow projection* shows anticipated activity for the venture's income and expenses. Typically constructed with separate columns for future months or years, a cash flow projection presents estimates in each of the categories under the income and expense headings. For example, a painter could develop a list of income categories such as gallery sales, commissions, licensed images, and other income-producing projects such as work for hire, paid lessons for younger art students, canvas stretching and framing, and art conservation services. Under the expense section, the painter would list materials (paint, canvas, framing, and shipping supplies), studio space rental, utilities and communications charges, transportation, and any other business-related costs. If the business generates income in excess of its expenses, then it has a positive cash flow. Although this financial document is a projection showing *anticipated* financial activities, it should be based on realistic figures that are derived from commonly accepted sources (such as trade association publications or community arts organizations) or based on comparative information from similar businesses.

- A *balance sheet* (similar to *statement of financial position* for non-profits) reports the organization's assets and liabilities in order to demonstrate the company's overall financial health and show its current net worth. The categories under the Assets section include cash on hand, accounts receivable, anticipated grant income, and property and equipment, such as company-owned buildings, machinery, and vehicles. The categories under the Liabilities and Net Assets section include accounts payable and credit lines such as credit card or bank loan balances, along with entries for savings and owner's equity.

- A *profit and loss statement* (similar to *statement of activities* for non-profits) shows the company's financial performance over a specific amount of time (typically one year) using the organization's accumulated income and expense data. For an existing business, the figures presented are based on the company's actual financial activity. For a new venture that will begin operating sometime in the future, a projected profit and loss statement should use realistic calculations based on published data or your own research into comparative businesses.

These and other financial documents should be included in the financial section of the business plan, along with narrative descriptions of how the company will produce income, anticipate and manage expenses, and generate either (1) profit for the for-profit venture's founders, investors, and other stakeholders, or (2) net assets realized for the nonprofit venture.

9. Appendix (optional)

The optional final section of a business plan is the Appendix, where references, reports, and other documents cited within the other chapters can be found. The inclusion of materials found from your research (such as census data or industry publications) can help support your overall proposal by demonstrating, via information from external sources, the validity of the assumptions and projections used in describing your proposed venture.

Evaluation and Assessment

Measuring the Financial, Programmatic, and Operational Effectiveness of Your Organization

In this section we consider the various ways an arts-related organization can benefit from the evaluation and assessment of its specific programs and projects, along with measurements of the company's overall performance.

The reasons for incorporating evaluation and assessment into an organization's ongoing activities include:

- *Looking for ways to increase effectiveness and efficiency.* By studying the real-world data – and valuable customer opinions – associated with a business, the venture's leadership can discover opportunities for improvement and take action to make the entire company more productive and better suited to the needs of its market. The range of measurements available – from financial reports to customer satisfaction surveys – will depend on the type of organization and the scale of its operations. All the members of a venture's team, from the founder to the management, staff and volunteers, can benefit from participation in the evaluation process. In addition to encouraging an inclusive atmosphere, the processes involved in measuring business performance – and discussing the results throughout the organization – can enhance the understanding and commitment experienced by everyone in the company.
- *Communicating the company's current and anticipated conditions to board members, advisors and financial partners.* The individuals who provide guidance and resources to help an organization thrive will expect – and deserve – a thorough, evidence-based analysis of all aspects of the company's operations. Reports on the venture's financial activities, production, and distribution methods, marketing strategies, legal and other issues must contain the results of objectively generated assessments and analyses in order to be convincing and useful. For board members, advisors, and consultants, quarterly and annual reports are essential to keep these stakeholders informed and allow them to make fact-based recommendations or reach key decisions for the venture. For providers of financial and other resources – such as investors, bank loan officers, grant program managers, and individual donors – an understanding of all aspects of the company's operations is needed in order to keep these supporters committed, or increase their levels of engagement.

- *Identifying areas for business growth and the introduction of new products.* Evaluation and assessment involves *paying attention* to both the data produced by quantitative measurements and the opinions and ideas offered by people inside and outside of the organization. A sense of openness to insights and new directions for a company should be encouraged by its leadership in order to create a dynamic, responsive environment for positive change and ongoing success. By listening carefully to the suggestions and attitudes expressed by customers, advisers and coworkers, the arts entrepreneur can lead the organization toward a future shaped by an evolving, validated understanding of how the company's products are being received and how its brand is understood.

The terms *assessment* and *evaluation* are defined depending on their context. In education, for example, assessment can refer to the measurement of student engagement and learning outcomes using quantitative data, such as attendance records and test scores. Evaluations, on the other hand, are qualitative judgments that are derived from written opinions from students about teaching quality and learning expectations. For the entrepreneur focused on creating an arts education business, the academic definitions of assessment and evaluation will be very useful as they analyze and adjust their programs in pursuit of continuous improvement and greater student achievement.

For the arts-related business offering products and services in areas besides education, evaluating and assessing the company's operational efficiency, product design and delivery, and marketing and customer engagement are all essential components in developing and running a successful organization. The techniques for measuring and understanding a venture's effectiveness will differ depending on the type of business and the specific product or service being delivered. An art gallery with a physical space and a commercial website will evaluate its business differently than a company that develops and sells apps for musicians and nightclub owners. A community-based performing arts center will measure its programs differently than a company that manufactures and exports artistically designed textiles.

The following sections consider the different approaches to evaluation and assessment taken by arts organizations from a variety of purposes, orientations, and goals.

> An evaluation may serve funders, stakeholders, and partners, in addition to your own interests. Different audiences may want to learn different things from evaluation and value different kinds of evidence.[3]

In *The Fundamentals of Arts Management*, we are introduced to a number of key concepts for evaluation and assessment that are relevant to the needs of an arts entrepreneur:

Who Is the Evaluation for?

Accountability has become an increasingly important component of business development and operations. Funding sources, such as government agencies and private foundations, are increasingly insistent on evaluation and assessment in order to initiate or continue their support. Managers, supervisors, and board members need objective measurements of business performance in order to fulfill their responsibilities. Staff and volunteers, along with the general public, value and respect transparency in the organizations they interact with. Researchers and designers of a company's products require validated input from customers in order to refine and improve quality and align their product's features and benefits with explicitly communicated consumer needs. When designing an evaluation project for your venture, start with a definition of the audience who will be reading and responding to the results. Evaluation can be extremely valuable to the business founder, but it could also be an important tool for other stakeholders in and around the organization.

What Kind of Evaluation Is Needed?

The different kinds of evaluations include needs assessments, process evaluations, and outcome evaluations. A *needs assessment* will study a specific area of the business, such as marketing, in order to examine and propose actions for that area of the organization. A *process evaluation* will focus on production, distribution, or transactional activities (such as ticket sales or customer service interactions) in order to identify opportunities for improvement or increase efficiency.

An *outcome evaluation* looks at the ways an arts organization's products and services influence behaviors, attitudes, knowledge, or understanding. In the case of a company offering arts education services, the outcomes of increased comprehension and students' capacity to apply learning in their professional lives will be important areas to measure. For a business selling art-related products in a physical space, such as a gallery or community arts center, the outcomes might include increased awareness and appreciation of the art forms represented in the work, a greater understanding of the social and political meanings of the art being purchased, and a deeper sense of the artist's mission as an individual or as a member of a movement or a collective group. As we shall see, outcomes are difficult to measure directly. However, they can be evaluated using indirect methods.

The following definitions help clarify the terminology used in designing and conducting an evaluation:

- An *outcome* is a specific result that can be attributed to a program, product, or service. Distinct from the actual object to experience being delivered, the outcome is the result produced *within the recipient*. For example, a life drawing class could produce an outcome such as increased technical skills, a deeper appreciation of arts-related materials such as paper and ink, and an enhanced sense of aesthetics related to different artists throughout history. The outcome of a performing arts experience, such as attending a contemporary dance program, could include the inspiration to study and practice related dance forms, or a renewed commitment to supporting the creation of new dance works. The outcomes of acquiring an artistic product, such as a collection of recently composed music, might be an expanded appreciation of musical styles and an increased willingness to engage with similar artists through purchases of their products or attendance at their concerts.

- An *objective*, or *goal*, is an intended outcome. When designing an arts-related business, it is essential to identify objectives and goals that include intended outcomes. In addition to enrolling students and collecting fees, an arts education company wants to produce learning and skills that will benefit its customers. The founders of a dance company want to sell tickets to their performances, but they also want to inspire their audiences and influence attitudes toward their art form. Composers and musicians want to sell recorded music and encourage attendance at their events, but they also want to spark the imagination and interest of their listeners

- *Activities* can include events, exhibits or other experiences that seek to produce outcomes. Art classes, dance performances, and the enjoyment of recorded music are all activities that can produce the types of outcomes a business owner might want to encourage. The purchase and use of other types of arts-related products and services – such as photographs, apps, or custom-designed jewelry – can likewise be considered activities that will produce outcomes in their users.

- An *output* is the product of an organization's programs or items available via sales transactions. A drawing class, dance performance or music recording is an output, while the understanding and appreciation experienced by the student, audience or listener are an outcome.

- An *indicator* is a way of measuring evidence. Indicators can provide evidence of outcomes, which, as mentioned earlier, are more difficult to observe directly. A customer satisfaction survey can be designed to gather feedback about a consumer's perception of a transaction's quality, the positive or negative associations related to the brand, and the likelihood of a repeat purchase. Surveys can ask the responder to rate their experiences on a scale of 1–5. Then these indicators can be tabulated and analyzed to understand whether or not the company's outcomes have been realized.

Using Outcome Targets

In order to convince an investor or grant program officer that your arts-related business is producing results that align with their interests, it can be important to communicate the organization's outcomes using numbers as well as written text. Outcome targets represent the venture's goals for producing desirable benefits for their consumers. For example, a photography education business could anticipate both the numbers of students attending their classes and workshops and the increased skills acquired by the participants. Because outcomes (such as increased knowledge) are difficult to observe and measure directly, indicators can be used to produce data that will show whether or not the organization has reached its outcome targets. If the photography education business had an outcome target of 50 students over the course of one year who will develop and use new skills to enhance their professional careers, then a survey could be taken after the fact that asks participants how their increased capabilities allowed them to expand their range of photographic techniques and attract new clients or generate repeat business from existing customers. If the outcome target of 50 students with improved, productive skills is compared to a survey result of 40 actual students reporting increases in their business as a direct result of their recent training, then the photography education business could claim an 80 percent success rate, which is a very persuasive number when communicating with financial partners or other supporters of the education business.

Using Benchmarks

Benchmarks are a very effective way to analyze and demonstrate an organization's results. Benchmark data can come from the company's own history, such as attendance figures for a season of theatrical performances or the number of units sold by a music production and distribution company. Benchmark data can also be derived from industry standards and trend analysis documents, such as published reports on national, regional, or local activities that are directly relevant to your arts venture. Organizations such as the National Endowment for the Arts and Americans for the Arts produce surveys and reports that contain information about public engagement with many different art forms. Some arts-related businesses produce annual reports or other publications that describe in some detail their business performance figures, such as attendance, income vs. expenses and net profit or loss. The creator of a new dance company could present data about attendance at national, regional, and local dance events (found in these kinds of surveys and reports) to make a convincing argument in favor of the launch of their new venture. They could also use the externally produced benchmark data to compare their own business performance over time and demonstrate the long-term viability of their organization's concept.

Here are some questions to consider when deciding whether an evaluation might be useful for your arts venture.

When Should an Organization Undertake an Evaluation?

The processes of designing an evaluation, investigating the various aspects of the business and understanding and implementing the results can be time-consuming and demanding of the company's human and other resources. Evaluations should not be constantly pursued, but there are circumstances that could trigger the need for such an effort. A major change in the direction of the overall company, or the introduction of a new program or product within the existing structure would be a good opportunity for a thorough evaluation. As an organization grows and changes, evaluations can help the leadership make informed decisions about the future of the business and establish benchmark data for use in subsequent studies. Also, a new or re-energized fundraising initiative that aims to target appropriate foundations or attract individual donors would benefit from a comprehensive evaluation of the business to produce persuasive material in support of this campaign.

The underlying issues for any evaluation of an arts-related business should be the feasibility of such an undertaking and the specific area(s) of the organization being evaluated. An online gallery could choose to evaluate its sales and customer satisfaction performance on an annual or semiannual basis using a combination of web analytics, financial reports, consumer feedback, and industry benchmark data from relevant external sources.

Who Is the Evaluation for and How Will They Use the Information It Contains?

In the example of a fundraising initiative, an arts organization would design the evaluation with the intent of making a convincing presentation about the venture's overall standing and its needs for additional resources. A company designing, launching, and responding to an evaluation for its own uses will want a broadly focused effort that reveals both successful instances of their business performance and operational areas that need improvement.

Who Will Conduct the Evaluation?

Choose the individuals responsible for an evaluation from within the organization, depending on their skills and responsibilities. Or, hire an outside consultant.

Many arts organizations rely on their internal staff leadership to form a committee charged with the responsibility of designing, implementing, and interpreting evaluations. Other companies will work with an outside consultant with skills in evaluation processes – the arts venture can benefit from the consultant's objective perceptions of the business while deriving value from the efficient application of their capabilities and experience. Another approach would be to combine these two techniques by developing an internal document (or self-study) and sharing it with an outside consultant or team of specialists to incorporate that work into the collective evaluation of the venture. Although using the company's leadership and board members might be less demanding financially on the organization, the cost in terms of time will be considerable. The expenses of hiring an outside specialist or consulting group for the evaluation need to be compared with the time demands on the company's founder and the management team. In either case, it is important to dedicate resources such as time, space, and funds to the evaluation project in order to produce comprehensive, useful results.

Here are the six steps for *planning* for an evaluation:

1. *State the goals* of the evaluation in clear, unambiguous terms. Are you looking to examine and measure all aspects of the organization? Or, is a specific area – such as marketing or production – in need of a focused study? Determine how the evaluation will be used. Will a fund-raising evaluation help the organization improve its ability to attract funding from individuals and regional grant-making programs? Will an evaluation of the company's financial activity and management processes reveal some strengths and weaknesses that are in need of attention? An evaluation's goals should be broadly or narrowly focused, depending on the needs of the organization and the resources available to design, implement and apply the initiative.

2. *Write the outcomes.* Remember that outcomes are the results experienced by your consumers during and after their engagement with your products or services. For an arts education venture, the outcomes will include increased knowledge, understanding, and skills among students enrolled in the courses and workshops. For a company selling original artwork such as photographs or paintings, the outcomes could be customer appreciation for the art form, satisfaction with their purchase, their intentions for possible future transactions, and their willingness to recommend the business to other potential customers.

3. *Write the indicators.* Measurable activity for choosing an evaluation's indicators can include:
   (a) financial details for individual purchases and cumulative totals, calculated over time and sorted by category
   (b) the number of units sold and customers served
   (c) data from a web analytics services
   (d) reviews from print and online media
   (e) results from the customer surveys, questionnaires, focus groups and interviews.

4. *Assemble the evaluation plan.* Once the goals, outcomes, and indicators are identified, the next step is to put together a complete evaluation plan that lays out the steps to follow in order to produce the final written result. The plan can include details about the preparation phase (when gathering background data such as reports on financial history or other benchmark data from external and internal sources), the investigation phase (when the evaluating team gathers new information from targeted sources), and the conclusions phase (where the results of the evaluation are analyzed and interpreted to produce actionable recommendations).

5. *Define the evaluation questions.* Like any good research project, an evaluation needs to start with some relevant, probing questions – about the state of the business, customer engagement and product acceptance, brand awareness, market penetration, and other issues that may need attention. In addition to defining the questions that the overall evaluation project is seeking to answer, specific questions need to be developed for interviewers, focus groups, and surveys that will elicit useful data for the evaluation team's analysis and recommendations. For the arts education business described earlier, the general evaluation questions might focus on instructional quality, financial performance, and marketing effectiveness. The specific evaluation questions for the focus groups and surveys could include customer satisfaction ratings, descriptions of newly acquired skills and their application in the students' professional lives, and the likelihood of recommending the company's classes and workshops to other potential customers.

6. *Assign the evaluation tasks.* With an evaluation plan in place and the general and specific questions identified, the members of the evaluation team need to receive their assignments in order to work through the evaluation process and begin producing useful data. Each individual associated with the evaluation project – whether an employee or executive from within the company, a volunteer, advisor or board member, or a hired outside consultant – needs to understand their responsibilities and be able to accomplish their assigned tasks within the context of the overall effort. Choosing a group of people who can collaborate well for this type of project is especially important, given the fact that they will be working with sensitive, proprietary information about the company and will need to collectively focus their energies on producing quality research results and delivering useful conclusions and recommendations.

The three steps to *implementing* an evaluation are as follows.

1. *Collect the evaluation data.* For an existing business, gather together all of the company's historical records that the evaluation will need to study. A performing arts venture will have information on audience attendance totals for individual events and an entire season or year of

programming, financial data about sales of tickets, merchandise and concessions, and print/online media reviews or customer comments on the organization's website and social media platforms. Creative services such as graphic design, photography, and arts education can also use historical data on new/repeat customers, income, expenses, community engagement, and marketing effectiveness. Arts entrepreneurs who produce and distribute original work can incorporate information about their production and sales processes, profit and loss details, and responses from gallery owners, representatives/agents, and collectors.

For a new business that has yet to produce any information on prior sales, production processes, or customer engagement, there will need to be a collection of benchmark data from sources such as:

- similar businesses in the region, or located elsewhere but highly comparable to the new venture;
- industry reports, publicly available tax filings and published studies;
- relevant documents produced by national arts advocacy organizations such as Americans for the Arts and the National Endowment for the Arts, or similar reports published by regional, state, county and city arts agencies.

In addition to gathering historical information related to the evaluation topic and/or benchmark data from external sources, the evaluation needs to produce new material. This can be generated from:

- assessments of the organization's programmatic activities or product/service creation and delivery;
- observations of consumer behavior, especially for performing arts venues, galleries and other locations where the public interacts directly with the company and its products;
- interviews with influencers and repeat customers;
- focus group sessions designed to explore and reveal customer attitudes toward the company and its products;
- input from media reviewers and key members of the community;
- survey results from a wide range of targeted actual or potential customers;
- demographic studies and economic forecasts that identify trends that could have a positive or negative effect on the business.

2. *Analyze the evaluation data.* As you may have noticed, evaluation data include both *quantitative* information (expressed as numerical data, such as financial reports, production and distribution figures, and survey responses with multiple-choice or yes/no questions) and *qualitative* information (expressed as narrative text, such as transcriptions from customer interviews and focus groups, benchmark interpretations, trend analyses from external organizations, and survey questions requiring short answer or long essay responses).

Because quantitative data is expressed in numbers, it is easier to compare and interpret across internal or external benchmarks. For example, a photographer evaluating the effectiveness of a recent marketing campaign could compare financial activity and customer satisfaction ratings from before and after the campaign's implementation. The numbers will clearly demonstrate whether or not the marketing campaign was effective in increasing business activity – it may also serve to inform the photographer (and interested financial stakeholders such as investors or bank loan officers) as they make decisions about allocating resources to the company's future marketing efforts.

Qualitative data is also valuable when seeking insights into the business operations and the perceptions generated in the minds of its customers and supporters. It can be gathered, studied, and interpreted in its original narrative form. It can also be converted into numerical data and evaluated like the quantitative data described above. The process for this conversion includes identifying specific concepts or keywords and assigning a code to each, then using that code to tag each instance of the concept's or keyword's use. The totals for each code are tabulated and can be compared to the company's previous measurements for those concepts and keywords, or compared to similar studies done by other organizations.

3. *Report the evaluation's results.* Once the evaluation data have been collected and analyzed, the final step is to write an interpretation of the results, along with recommendations for future actions based on what has been learned in the process. An evaluation's recommendations can include:

- proposed improvements to business operations, such as production, marketing, financial control, or organizational structure;
- the introduction of new programs and products to keep the venture and its offerings fresh in the minds of its consumers and remain viable for the long term;
- the reduction or elimination of some products and programs that are not performing at a satisfactory level, as determined by the company's owners and managers;
- proposals for new investment in areas where the organization can expand successfully via new product development, enhanced marketing effectiveness or increased efficiency in production and distribution methods.

A well-designed and executed evaluation can produce many benefits for an existing company or for a new startup with valid external benchmark data that can be used as a reference. General evaluations that look into every aspect of the venture will take more time and effort to create, but will paint a more comprehensive picture of the organization's real strengths and weaknesses – an important tool when negotiating with investors or donors. Evaluations of specific operational areas, such as marketing, production, or fundraising, can help refine and improve those aspects of the business and keep the company on track for continued success.

Chapter Summary

Planning, evaluation, and assessment are important aspects of designing and running a successful business in the arts. The process of developing and using a plan – especially a strategic plan or business plan – can help the founder identify and eliminate potential problems or build on the known strengths and unique qualities of the organization. Business planning builds on the company's vision and mission statements. An analysis of the venture's strengths, weaknesses, opportunities, and threats (SWOT) allows the leadership to examine the organization from multiple perspectives and discover internal and external conditions that will influence the design of the business concept and the operation of the company. Strategic planning starts with the beliefs upon which the organization will be built, including the values, principles, and assumptions associated with the business and its owners. Results are the goals being pursued by the business, such as financial performance, product acceptance, and impact on the community. The methods used to achieve the intended results are the strategies, actions, and assessment techniques used by the organization to address all of its operational needs. To produce a valuable strategic plan, schedule one or more days in a comfortable, business-friendly space and invite a select group of participants to contribute their ideas and perspectives to the effort. Distribute advance materials such as financial statements or marketing or fundraising reports before the planning sessions. During the strategic planning meetings, allow the participants to study the vision and mission statements and evaluate the business from a number of angles. After the plan has been completed, it should be implemented using a strategic planning spreadsheet that identifies strategies, tasks, and individual responsibilities with a timeline for deliverables. After a strategic plan has been designed and implemented, it should be evaluated annually to determine how well the company has accomplished its mission and to make adjustments for its future endeavors. Other types of plans include project plans and business plans. The business plan is an essential tool for shaping the business concept and communicating it to stakeholders within the organization and to external supporters such as advisers, investors or volunteers. The sections of a business plan include the title page, table of contents, executive summary, vision/mission/goals statement, organization overview and legal issues, market analysis and marketing plan, operations plan, financial plan, and an optional appendix for reference materials and data cited within the preceding chapters.

Evaluation and assessment can help measure the company's overall performance and can reveal specific issues in operational areas such as product design, marketing, and financial management. Evaluations can also communicate the company's current and anticipated conditions to board members, advisors, and financial partners. Before designing and conducting an evaluation, the company's founders and advisers should consider whom the evaluation is for and what kind of evaluation is needed. Benchmarks are useful for comparative analysis of a venture's past, present, or anticipated future activities. The six steps for planning and evaluation are: stating the goals, writing the outcomes, writing the indicators, assembling the evaluation plan, defining the evaluation questions, and assigning the evaluation tasks. The three steps involved in implementing an evaluation are: collecting the evaluation data, analyzing that data, and reporting on the evaluations results.

Discussion Questions

1. Why is business planning important and what kinds of results can it produce?
2. What are the key questions that need to be asked when developing an organization's vision and mission statements?
3. How does an arts venture conduct an analysis of its strengths, weaknesses, opportunities, and threats?
4. Describe the differences between beliefs, results, and methods in the context of strategic planning.
5. Who would be good candidates for a strategic planning effort designed to support your business idea?
6. Describe the processes for implementing a strategic plan and evaluating its results.
7. What are the eight steps for a strategic planning effort that is focused on a specific project?
8. What are the dual purposes of a business plan?
9. When designing and conducting an evaluation, what are the differences between an outcome, a goal, an activity, an output, and an indicator?
10. Describe one of the several reasons for choosing to produce an evaluation for business.
11. What are the six steps for planning and evaluation?
12. What are the three steps for implementing an evaluation?

Notes

[1]   Korza, Pam, Maren Brown, and Craig Dreeszen. *Fundamentals of arts management* (Amherst, MA: Arts Extension Service, University of Massachusetts, Amherst, 2007), p. 67.

[2]   Byrnes, William J. *Management and the arts* (Burlington, MA: Focal Press, 2015), p. 151.

[3]   Korza, et al. *Fundamentals of arts management*, pp. 399–400.

3 Marketing

How will your arts venture find customers, sponsors, or supporters to launch and sustain the business? What do you need to learn from your competitors about running an arts organization in your local market? Are there ways to adapt your programs, products, and services to meet the needs of your audience and distinguish yourself from similar organizations? In this chapter we examine marketing tools and techniques – including market research, competitive analysis, and marketing/communications plans – that will help your organization communicate and connect with your audience.

Marketing is a wide-ranging topic, especially in the arts. There are many areas where the arts entrepreneur will need to customize their approach to audience engagement and fine-tune their marketing strategy to suit their unique product or service. Learning the basic principles of traditional marketing will help the owner of an arts organization build a foundation for future marketing efforts, either as the founder of a new business or as an employee of existing arts organization looking to gain experience and develop a network of support.

The arts venture has some special features when it comes to marketing, such as access to compelling audio/visual materials for advertising and promotional campaigns. In addition, arts-related products, services, and experiences can have a deep, meaningful impact on both producers and consumers – a condition not always found in other types of businesses. To further develop an understanding of the many issues involved in marketing for the arts, consult the Further Reading section at the end of this chapter.

Marketing is communication. Whether you represent a cultural group or local arts agency, marketing is central to the fulfillment of your goals. Marketing is a means of telling the public who you are, what you do, and how they can be involved.[1]

Some people equate marketing with advertising, public relations, and the cultivation of a "brand" for their specific product, service, or overall company. While these elements are important factors in the marketing effort, there is much more to marketing than *selling* something to your customers. Marketing is about communication, engagement, and involvement: developing relationships with customers is essential, but so is connecting with sponsors, supporters, internal stakeholders, and the media. Even your programmatic focus or product design can be influenced by what you learn through market research, since connecting with the needs and wants of the *audience* is the key to attracting interest, generating positive word-of-mouth attention, and driving sales. Adopting a customer-centric approach may seem odd to the fiercely independent studio artist, but creative individuals also need to package their "product" and image to successfully navigate the world of commissions, residencies, and gallery representation. The aim is to strike a balance between the extremes: ignoring customer needs can lead to isolation, while adhering too closely to market norms can dilute the unique, compelling features of your distinctive product or service.

In this chapter we explore a range of important marketing concepts and practices for the arts venture, including:

- the role of marketing in shaping your image, educating your audience, and inviting participation
- the exchange model of interaction between producers and consumers
- market research and competitive analysis: understanding customers and the marketing landscape
- strategic marketing plans: designing, implementing, and evaluating marketing programs and campaigns
- internal databases, software, tools, and techniques for planning, execution, and evaluation of marketing
- integrated digital marketing using websites, social media, smart phones, and text for publicity and media relations
- connecting your products and services with the needs and wants of the people in your market.

The Role of Marketing in Shaping Your Image: Educating Your Audience and Inviting Participation

Building an Image

Marketing is a mode of communication focused on certain intended outcomes. The first – and perhaps most important – outcome is creating an awareness among your target audience of the very *existence* of your product or service. Customers can't be expected to engage with your venture if they don't know what you do and where you conduct business. To generate awareness of an organization and its products, many business owners (and their marketing teams) invest time and energy to carefully craft the image/identity/brand they want to convey. This includes elements such as names, logos, and graphic design systems for the company's offerings (as well as for the company itself), written material, such as text developed for web content and social media postings, and audio/video pieces that tell the story behind a specific product, service or unique artist's vision. By introducing these elements to potential customers in a structured, strategic way, the venture's image can be established and disseminated to a series of markets, such as local residents, an online community, or a special interest group, whose concentration area connects with the organization's brand. For example, a new product for digital/analog audio mixing would have its name, logo, features, and technical specifications designed and delivered via multiple marketing channels (media reviews, trade shows, online videos, advertising, promotional materials for specialty retailers) to reach consumers of related products and attract interest. Marketing helps shape the image of both the company and its offerings by launching a brand that inspires and motivates consumers.

Educating Audiences

Generating awareness of your business and products is critical for getting your foot in the door when it comes to generating sales. The next step is to cultivate the interest of the customer via information, examples, recommendations, and testimonials. Some potential consumers of your product or service may already be thoroughly knowledgeable about your offerings. For example, an arts education program featuring advanced digital photography might target customers with beginner-to-intermediate comprehension levels of the processes involved. However, even in this case of marketing to an experienced customer base, it is important to convey the *value* of your unique service: for example, offering training in advanced photographic techniques specifically for sporting events or fashion editorials. Each art venture will have its own special categories of products and services to market to customers who have varying levels of sophistication and understanding – it is the job of the marketing campaign and its associated materials to educate the consumer so that he or she can make an informed buying decision. This is even more important when promoting a new product/service concept to the market: customers have to be informed about *what* it is, *why* it exists and *how* its value relates to them. This explanatory process can be seen sometimes in new app development and marketing, where the product's purpose must be explained and demonstrated before consumers become interested. Customer education can also be encouraged through reviews (both online and in traditional media such as newspapers, magazines, trade publications, radio, and television), endorsements by recognized experts (or celebrities), and recommendations from online communities and special interest groups.

Inviting Participation

Once consumers are aware of your company and its products, have an understanding of the value associated with your offerings (more on this later), and have studied recommendations and reviews from trusted independent sources, they are ready to engage with your organization via a purchase, contribution, or volunteer assignment. The concept of participation covers the full spectrum of relationships between providers and customers: for a performing arts organization, this can include patrons purchasing tickets to an event, donors offering financial and in-kind support during a capital campaign, and volunteers (including advisors and board members) investing time to help the venture succeed. Participation involves the immediate, short-term interactions between provider and consumer (such as a purchase), as well as the longer-term relationships established between a community and its valued cultural institutions. For example, a well-established neighborhood cinema can develop participation via ticket sales to an annual fundraising gala while encouraging ongoing support from local catering and bookkeeping services. Marketing helps inspire and sustain participation because it is part of the overall relationship between customer and provider: it encourages a sense of *connection* between the arts organization and its supporters by communicating value and reaching the target audience.

The Exchange Model of Interaction Between Producers and Consumers

> Marketing: The activity, set of institutions, and processes for creating, communicating, delivering and exchanging offerings that have value for customers, clients, partners, and society at large.[2]

As the definition above indicates, marketing is based on an exchange (usually between seller and buyer) that delivers value for each participant. A live music venue sells a ticket to a patron: the customer receives the experience of seeing and hearing a performance, while the musicians, event staff, and venue owner receive income, recognition, and other rewards. The concept of exchange is central to marketing efforts of all types and for all kinds of offerings, including online experiences, tangible goods, and unique services. Although exchange is commonly understood as a customer's money traded for a provider's product or service, the concept also applies to interactions involving other kinds of value. For example, a web designer might offer services at a reduced price to a new arts venture in exchange for access to the company's customer database for future work. The value for the venture is low-cost web design, while the value for the web designer is the opportunity to attract new clients.

Keep the exchange model in mind when you are determining price points, designing marketing materials, and defining the needs and wants of potential customers. Some keys questions to ask are:

- How does the customer perceive the value of your organization's offerings?
- How can the exchange be structured in a way that satisfies both producer and consumer, with the goal of creating a transactional experience that both parties will want to repeat?
- How can new customers be attracted to your business based on *their* needs and wants?

This last question naturally leads to considerations of who your customers are – or might be, once your business is established – and what motivates them to enter into the exchange process that is specific to your product or service.

Market Research and Competitive Analysis: Understanding Customers and the Marketing Landscape

The overall goal of market research is to learn about your customers: what are their interests, how they make choices about engaging with the arts, where they live, how they learn about new products or events, what *they* consider incentives or barriers to consuming culture. Understanding markets is an essential part of shaping messages and delivery mechanisms for an arts organization's marketing campaigns, but it is also a key factor is designing products and services that people actually *want*. The quality of an idea for an arts venture is measured not only by its innovation and unique characteristics, but also by how well it finds an audience and establishes enduring relationships with individuals within its target markets – this is what can turn a creative concept into a viable, arts-related business.

In this section we will look at market research during the three phases of the business cycle for the arts venture:

- before the launch;
- during the introduction of the concept: promoting and growing a new business;
- once the organization is established.

Market research is not a one-time effort. Learning from – and adapting to – your customers constitute an ongoing continuous practice that keeps your business focused, relevant, and connected.

Before the Launch

There are a number of techniques for learning about your customers once you have an established business, but what about conducting market research before your venture has been introduced to the public? Analyzing the interests, buying habits, and demographics of *potential* customers is different than studying those you already have.

One way to get familiar with future customers is to look at other similar businesses in your category to see where and how they connect with their audiences. If you want to develop an arts education program, the first question would be: how do similar organizations reach customers in your local market? What kinds of people are exposed to – and interacting with – arts education opportunities within your territory? This kind of research (which shares a number of features with the competitive analysis process) can be conducted via several different methods. The most direct path would be to develop a mutually supportive relationship with an existing business that is similar to yours and arrange some data sharing that would allow you to learn about their customers. As mentioned in other chapters of this book, the idea of arts organizations collaborating – rather than competing – is not uncommon. There may be opportunities to share not only data, but also to develop marketing campaigns for two or more similar businesses. For example, a number of galleries within walking distance of one another might organize a Friday night "Art Walk" to attract customers to all of the venues in the same neighborhood.

If receiving customer data from a similar business is not a viable option for your venture, you can still observe consumer patterns and trends by going to local gallery openings, live performances, or artist receptions to see what kinds of people show up. You can even interview a few patrons to find out what they like, where they are from, and how they learn about cultural events. Obviously this won't work for all arts-related businesses, but in some cases you can glean useful, real-world information by interacting directly with the public.

Conducting online market research can produce some useful information as well. Starting with a basic search for businesses similar to yours in the immediate geographic area, you can start building a database of organizations to study. Examine each business to discover what kinds of marketing techniques they are currently employing (print advertising, websites, social media, etc.), how their offerings are being announced and sold (season tickets, discounted prices for students, promotions tied to seasonal events or with partners), and especially *whom* they are reaching with their marketing messages. The insights gained from objectively evaluating who is consuming the products and services of businesses similar to yours will give you important guidance on how to craft and deliver your own marketing messages.

Promoting and Growing a New Business

Introducing a new arts venture to the marketplace is an exciting – and challenging – experience. After incorporating the insights discovered during the "pre-launch" phase, the marketing team needs to develop a focused, strategic plan that reaches the target audience with messages that motivate consumers to act.

Working with the Media

The opportunity to promote a brand new product or service is unique because media outlets (newspapers, weekly periodicals, magazines, radio, television, and web-based sources) are more likely to report the launch as "news" when it is being first announced. Media coverage is important because not only is it free (except for the paid staff time to create press releases and cultivate relationships with editors and other media contacts), it introduces the arts venture to the largest potential audience in the widest geographic area. Knowing that editors are looking for "newsworthy" items to promote, you should develop a database of local media outlets with current contact information (names, email addresses, social media references, deadlines) in advance of your launch date. You can then deliver intriguing, factual, accurate press releases to your list and invite your press contacts to respond to you for more information and – if appropriate – enjoy direct access to you and your organization via site visits, interviews, and pre-opening events, such as rehearsals, press screenings, or product launch meetings.

Do an online search for "Press releases for arts organizations" to discover examples of press release formats and contents.

Defining and Reaching Market Segments

Beyond the widely distributed messages sent through mass media, a new arts organization will need to invest time and money in a targeted marketing campaign to reach customers and generate interest – and revenue. Defining your audience in terms of age, income, location, ethnicity, and other variables is known as *market segmentation*. This aspect of your overall market analysis and strategy seeks to identify specific types of customers who will be likely to have an interest in your product or service. These are the individuals you want to reach with well-defined marketing messages that engage the recipient and inspire action. In addition to defining who and where your potential customers are, market segmentation identifies the appropriate modes of communication for reaching these consumers, such as direct mail, print advertising, web, email, social media, and text platforms.

> Effective marketing communications appeal to a target customer's core values, lifestyles, and interests ... Arts marketers must develop and implement strategies that develop new audiences while continuing to build loyalty and frequency among current audiences.[3]

Think about the age categories your artistic product or service is most likely to appeal to – there can be more than one. Does your music project seek to develop an audience among teenagers and young adults? Is your arts education program designed for children (while needing their parents' approval and financial support)? Will your theater present works that will attract an older, well-educated audience? Make a list of the following age groups and identify which one (or more) fit your product or service, then describe *why* each group will be interested in your offerings:

- young children and pre-teens
- teenagers
- young adults
- mid-career adults (singles)
- mid-career adults (families)
- late-career adults
- seniors.

Try to avoid making your list of target customers too broad. You may believe that your venture has something that will appeal to "everybody" in the age spectrum, but you need to be realistic about identifying who will be a potential customer and why they will be motivated to engage with your business. A very narrowly focused age range can limit your success over time, but it is better to connect with a well-defined audience first and then grow your business to focus on other age groups. For example, a training center for photography might offer courses to mature adults first, then expand the program to provide lessons for younger students.

Next, think about gender and ethnicity as categories that will be especially drawn to your enterprise. Some businesses try to appeal to people of all types, while others selectively target customers based on gender or ethnicity. Start with the categories that are the most genuinely connected to you and your venture's mission, and remember to identify both *who* will be a potential customer and *why* they will be interested.

Now concentrate on the location of your potential customers. Are they from the immediate neighborhood, or will they be willing to travel to your location from across the region? Are your customers online only? If so, what are their preferences in terms of consuming arts-related products and services? Do they find businesses like yours through search engine results, or through referral websites, blogs, email campaigns or social media recommendations? Make a list of locations (physical and virtual) that are relevant to your target customer base.

Finally, think about income categories for your desired market. Does your venture focus on high-income individuals, or middle-income families, or low-income youth, or some other economically defined group or groups? Make a list of income categories that are appropriate for your venture and indicate why your product or service appeals to that segment.

Other market segmentation categories for you to consider include sexual orientation, mobility, education level, and employment status. For more information on demographics and market segmentation for arts-related businesses, see the research/publications materials offered by arts advocacy organizations, such as Americans for the Arts,[4] Grantmakers in the Arts,[5] and the Wallace Foundation.[6]

Create a folder named Marketing. Start a new document and compile your lists from the above sections on age, gender, ethnicity, location, income, and other features. Create profiles of your target customers based on these categories. Name this file Customer Demographics and place it in the Marketing folder. The Customer Demographics file will be used in later sections of this chapter.

Once the Organization Is Established

Having a database of existing customers gives you access to a wealth of useful information. Not only do you have a prequalified group of patrons to market to in the future, you also have a valuable resource for research to learn about your target customers' needs, wants, preferences, buying habits, and perceptions regarding your business (and your competitors).

As with any research project, it is a good idea to identify a specific problem you are trying to solve at the beginning. Your performing arts venture is experiencing declining ticket sales for its full season subscriptions – why is this occurring and how do you address it? Your website selling fine art is experiencing a shift in browsing activity and sell-through of merchandise – what are the causes and how do you react? Your art education business has plans to introduce a new program for younger learners – what kinds of marketing messages will you use to attract interest and grow participation?

Once you have defined a research problem and have a set of specific research questions you want to pursue, the next step is to develop a strategy for gathering useful data. Consider some or all of the following opportunities to engage with – and learn from – your customers;

- *Direct interaction* with consumers can be accomplished at your next public event, such as an artist reception, live performance, or open house. Observing people's habits as they move throughout your space to purchase tickets, read about upcoming events, and communicate with one other (and your event staff) will tell you a number of things about how well your facilities are organized and their contribution to the overall experience. Set up an information table staffed by marketing personnel (and yourself) to ask targeted questions about the customers' likes and dislikes vis-à-vis your organization – or simply circulate throughout the event and strike up conversations with individuals, couples, and groups about their experiences with your business. Consumers appreciate having their opinions heard and considered, especially if the owner or another high-level person is involved.
- *Surveys* are often used at live events to gather information from as many customers as possible. These can be introduced at any point during the customer's contact with your business: when a ticket or product is being purchased, at the beginning or end of a performance, or after the event/purchase is completed and sent via surface mail, email, social media or text message. The process of designing surveys, implementing them effectively, and analyzing their results is both an art and a science. Your choices include everything from traditional paper or postcard-size handouts/mailers to online platforms, such as surveymonkey.com. Your survey questions should be tied to the research questions identified previously, and the quality of the results depends on the way your questions are framed. Help can be found by searching online for books and articles on "marketing research surveys" and questionnaire design, hiring a professional consultant to create and run your survey, or working with an organization such as the Research and Survey Services team at Americans for the Arts.[7]
- *Focus groups* allow you to explore a number of valuable research questions with a small group of individuals who have been carefully selected and invited to participate – usually they receive a modest payment for their time. Again, the questions and guided interactions with focus group subjects should be handled by a professional, preferably someone who has experience designing, conducting, and analyzing results from a similar investigation involving patrons of the arts in your area.

Create a document named Market Research and Competitive Analysis. Compile all of the information you have gathered about customer attitudes/behaviors and comparable businesses in your area and place the file in your Marketing folder.

Strategic Marketing Plans

Audit

As described in other chapters in this book, the first step toward developing a plan of action is to make an objective audit of your current situation. For marketing, this means creating a thorough, realistic analysis of your organization's operations, image, and reputation, along with its capacity for launching an effective campaign to attract interest, and inspire participation.

Businesses that are already established will be able to look back through their recent history to identify key aspects of their organization and measure the performance of previous marketing efforts such as print advertising and social media activity. For the new arts venture in its planning or startup phase, these same audit categories should be described as future activities, plans, and commitments based on the *intended* outcomes of the overall business. A well-designed marketing plan should be able to paint a convincing picture of what *will* happen once the venture is established.

The marketing audit should look at:

- the organization's mission, values and goals'
- the current range of projects, programs, and specific products or services it offers to the public;
- the current capacity for developing and executing a marketing program, including resources such as funding, personnel, time, and space allocations;
- the current commitments of any of the above resources toward future marketing efforts, such as advertising contracts, partnerships with other organizations or agreements with artists for future exhibitions, performances, or other events;
- analysis of previous marketing efforts for the past year (if they exist).

Create a folder named Marketing Audit. Write a thorough, objective audit of your organization's actual (or intended) internal activities related to marketing. Place it in the Marketing folder.

Marketing SWOT Analysis

As with your efforts to introduce strategic planning concepts into your overall business development, discussed in Chapter 1, a SWOT (Strengths, Weaknesses, Opportunities, Threats) analysis focused on marketing will help clarify your understanding of your venture's current position and prospects for future success. A SWOT analysis will also help organize your thinking around specific issues that will expand awareness of your brand and encourage acceptance of your products and services.

A marketing SWOT analysis follows the same structure as an overall SWOT analysis for the entire arts organization. Consider scheduling a brainstorming session (or series of sessions) with advisors and stakeholders from inside and outside the organization to get the broadest range of perspectives and input on marketing your business:

- A company's *internal strengths* for marketing purposes can include any number of positive attributes associated with your products, services, company history, current profile (founders, leadership, staff), location, and overall brand. Encourage your brainstorming group to come up with as many phrases, words, concepts, and images as possible that identify legitimate strengths of your business across all categories. Examples include very high quality and attention to detail in the design and delivery of your products or services, the integrity and reputation of your personnel, and the favorable opinions of existing customers toward your business.
- *Internal weaknesses* for marketing should be likewise identified and listed in a comprehensive, realistic fashion. Common marketing weaknesses include lack of money and/or expertise to develop and carry out effective marketing campaigns, along with the absence of any internal systems (such as customer databases or project management software tools) to keep marketing programs on track. Factors such as staff morale and internal decision-making processes should also be considered.
- *External opportunities* should include enhancement of existing marketing efforts along with expansion into new, untested areas. For example, translating your current marketing materials into relevant foreign languages can help reach additional local customers, while introducing social media into your publicity mix can attract interest from entirely new categories of consumers. Think of external opportunities for marketing across the full spectrum of possible categories (e.g. paid advertising, media relations, publicity, events, social/mobile/text campaigns, etc.).
- *External threats* for marketing may encompass customer opinions and attitudes, increased competition from other businesses in your category and location, and changes in marketing opportunities, such as the closing of a local newspaper. Other developments such as negative economic trends or changing demographics should also be considered.

A SWOT analysis is a good tool for any business seeking to evaluate its prospects for success and growth, and a marketing SWOT analysis is especially good for focusing attention on ways to connect a company's products and services with consumers. For artists – and owners of art-related businesses – a marketing SWOT analysis is particularly useful because it opens up the possibilities of seeing the venture from different points of view. Artists and business owners can sometimes concentrate all of their energy and ambition on creating the unique object or experience they want to share with the world, which is understandable given the time it takes to develop skills and refine one's particular set of productive techniques. A marketing SWOT analysis (especially one done in collaboration with trusted advisors and stakeholders) allows you to step outside the role of creator and see the larger issues around bringing your special product or service to a *market*. The SWOT exercise naturally leads to the development of specific, actionable tasks that can be accomplished as you establish or expand your creative venture – this is the first step in the formation, implementation, and evaluation of your company's Marketing Plan.

Create a document named Marketing SWOT Analysis. List all of the ideas in each category from your brainstorming sessions, then place the completed file in your Marketing folder.

Goals and Organizational Needs

With the information from your marketing SWOT analysis in place, you can now move on to defining specific organizational goals and needs. Like other forms of planning for your business, this step will be shaped by a number of factors, including the types of products and services you intend to offer, where your venture is located, how much funding is available to support your marketing ambitions, and how established your business is in terms of public awareness. For example, a new company could identify a goal of announcing its brand to a defined market to generate awareness of something new, while a venture that has been around for some time might choose a marketing goal of improving relationships with existing media contacts.

Reaching Audiences

Finding ways to attract customers is something every business pursues, whether they are a brand new venture or a well-established enterprise. Try to describe your vision of this goal with as much detail as possible, using information from the Customer Demographics file you created earlier and the External Opportunities section from your marketing SWOT analysis. You can include specific information about your intended customers, as well as numerical targets for how many people you want to reach and how many of those contacts might become consumers or patrons of your business. Setting realistic goals for new audience development can be challenging for a start-up venture that doesn't yet have a track record of customer engagement or sales, but you can always adjust your numbers as you go along to align your ambitions with reality. The point is to document both your *intended* levels of new audience development and your *actual* results so you can measure how well your marketing program is performing.

Here are some examples of marketing goals.

For a New Business

- Create brand awareness among new customers from a defined demographic profile, including age, gender, ethnicity, location, and income.
- Identify new customer needs and wants in relation to your general product/service category.
- Set target numbers for reaching new consumers, based on the analysis of available data from similar businesses in the same market.
- Convert general brand awareness among new customers to measurable sales.
- Generate traffic to a new company website or social media channel.
- Populate email and text databases with new contacts.

For an Established Business

- The goals listed above for a new business are also important for an established venture: existing organizations need to continually look for ways to attract new customers.
- Improve, change or re-direct your existing customers' perceptions of your brand and its products/services. Like other marketing goals for an existing venture, this will require input from your customers via interviews, focus groups, and surveys.
- Refine or alter your company's understanding of how its products/ services address the needs and wants of customers.
- Analyze the success of previous marketing campaigns and set new targets for future marketing efforts.
- Expand existing audiences by growing customer engagement within previously identified demographics.
- Increase diversity within your range of audiences by reaching out to new *types* of customers.
- Increase traffic to established website(s) and/or social media channels.
- Increase the number of contacts in email and text databases.
- Reduce or otherwise adjust marketing expenses to increase efficiency of marketing budget.

The last point above on budget reduction hints at another category of goals for your art-related business: internal policies, procedures, and tools to help develop and manage your marketing program.

Create a document named Marketing Goals and Needs. List all of the ideas in each category, then place the completed file in your Marketing folder.

Marketing policies are the general guidelines you'll want to have followed in your marketing efforts, along with the reasons for making certain strategic and tactical choices. The point of creating internal marketing policies is that it allows your marketing staff – either working in-house or hired outside as a consultant or agency – to understand clearly what your company's priorities and expectations are when it comes to designing, implementing, and evaluating marketing activities. The process of developing a clearly stated set of marketing policies also gives the owner an opportunity to think through the various options for marketing and express certain preferences/emphases in an objective manner – this benefit alone helps the overall marketing plan take shape. Marketing policies can cover a wide range of topics, from how budgets are determined and tracked, to how marketing effectiveness is measured, and how the company's image and brand are crafted. Large corporations have time and staff dedicated to developing and implementing marketing policy documents, but a smaller business should concentrate on creating a succinct, focused set of guidelines to get started.

Suggested marketing policy and procedural topics include:

- definition of terms (product, brand, advertising, promotion, web content, etc.);
- guidelines for creating marketing content for products, services and the overall company:
  - graphic design style guide
  - writing style guide.
- guidelines for interacting with media representatives (editors, reviewers, podcast and blog hosts);
- guidelines for interacting with outside services (photographers, illustrators, writers, web developers);
- guidelines for hosting public/private events to support the marketing program;
- internal mechanisms for developing marketing budget;
- policies for developing collaborations and partnerships with external organizations, including contracts and intellectual property agreements;

- methods of evaluating marketing effectiveness (annual, semi-annual or quarterly review of marketing activities and results).

Create a document named Marketing Policies and Procedures. List all of the ideas in each category, then place the completed file in your Marketing folder.

Internal Databases, Software, Tools, and Techniques for the Planning, Execution, and Evaluation of Marketing

How your company manages information and accomplishes marketing tasks is an important part of running your marketing programs and overall business. There are a number of options for keeping up-to-date records and using software programs to manage marketing efforts.

Marketing Management Systems

An online search for "marketing database management software" produces a wide range of choices for tools designed to help manage marketing programs. Some have highly sophisticated (and expensive) features that integrate email lists, analytics for web page visits and social media activity, return on investment (ROI) evaluation, and other reporting functions. Many of these software tools and apps are available as subscription services, with monthly charges of $100 to $1000 per month and more. Whether you choose to invest in this type of service will depend on how your arts venture is structured and whether your funding model supports this level of ongoing expense. Keep in mind that your budget will need to cover not only the software tools that help you manage your marketing program, but also the payroll associated with people doing the work of entering and analyzing marketing data – along with the costs of the marketing program itself, such as graphic design, copywriting, advertising, website development, and search engine optimization (SEO) fees.

Individual Software Programs

For the arts entrepreneur with a limited budget and less expansive marketing ambitions, there are other solutions to capture data, deliver messages to a target market, and analyze results. A common spreadsheet program like Microsoft Excel, for example, can be used to record basic information about your customers, such as name, mailing address, email address, phone number, social media presence, and even purchasing habits such as transaction history and specific likes/dislikes relative to your product. Organizing your customer list alphabetically in Excel (or a similar program) allows you to quickly generate labels for a direct mail campaign, for example, or sort customers by location for targeting guests to invite to a special event. Spreadsheets can also be used to record contact and other information about advertisers, media representatives, suppliers and services (photography, printing, web hosting), and other participants who help you execute your marketing program. FileMaker Pro is another choice for database management software, with many customizable features that can be tailored to your particular type of business.

Create a document named Marketing Databases. Describe your approach to record-keeping with software or other techniques, then place the completed file in your Marketing folder.

Websites

After the physical location of your arts venture, your website is the most important place for marketing to – and interacting with – your customers. Of course, if your organization is a web-based business, then your website is both an important marketing vehicle for – *and* the place of – your organization. In either case, developing and maintaining an effective web presence are a crucial component in marketing and running a successful arts-related business.

Many arts entrepreneurs work with experienced web developers (individuals or companies) to work through the conceptual and structural issues involved in designing and running a website. Other business owners are comfortable taking on the responsibilities for developing and maintaining their own web presence. Whichever path you choose, note there will be costs in terms of time and money: designing and maintaining your own website will be less expensive than hiring a professional firm, but your time will be impacted by the ongoing tasks associated with managing your site. Add to this the complexities of integrating social media, email, and mobile/text to your marketing mix and you will see how quickly the responsibilities accumulate. Just like bookkeeping and legal obligations, a business owner should carefully evaluate the efficiencies of using an outside service vs. handling everything themselves. In the end, an objective cost-benefit analysis should help determine the best approach for your venture.

Cost Benefit Analysis

A cost benefit analysis (CBA) is a decision-making tool that typically compares the financial consequences of different scenarios. A simple CBA would study a specific project by using consistent units of measure (usually dollars or other currency) for all of the expenses (costs) and income (benefits) associated with having the project proceed or not proceed. For example, an arts organization could conduct a CBA for a marketing project involving the expense of $10,000 to buy advertising in a local newspaper. The analysis would measure the anticipated benefits of proceeding with the ad purchase by projecting the number of additional tickets sold to a series of performances. If the anticipated revenue exceeds the cost of the advertising, then the decision to proceed could be chosen. On the other hand, if the scenario for not proceeding with the ad purchase saves the organization the expense and some alternative low or no-cost marketing options are selected instead, then that scenario could be chosen. Much of the accuracy of predictions concerning potential future expenses or income is based on actual data from similar projects in the arts organization's past, or from the experiences of other organizations in the same field. Try some scenarios in a CBA for your website creation project to see how the anticipated expense/income figures compare, using expensive/moderate/low cost models for web development and maintenance.

The following steps will help you create your strategy for designing, launching, and maintaining an effective web presence.

Identify Goals

Think about the purpose of your website and how you will accomplish your marketing mission. Are you primarily looking to sell products or services directly online, or are you seeking to direct customers to a venue, such as a gallery or performance space? Do you want people to sign up on your site to receive announcements and return often to check on news and to post comments? Do you want multiple layers of content within your site for your visitors to explore (such as artist bios or audio/video examples), or do you want a straightforward navigational experience that drives web traffic to a "buy now" opportunity? Make a list of realistic goals for your web presence and use categories such as Sales, Multimedia, Announcements, and Interactive Content to keep your ambitions organized. Visit a number of well-designed websites in your general focus area and research how other organizations develop their content.

Define Your Audience

Your current and potential customers are, of course, a key part of the audience for your website. There are other visitors to consider as well, such as investors, vendors, media reviewers, grant-makers, partners, and suppliers. Using the Customer Demographics information you created earlier, make a list of all the customer attributes that are relevant to your organization. Make additional lists of other audiences for your website, including their relationships to your business and the ways they might interact with your web presence.

Create Brand and Image

This is where the web page layouts are developed, using components such as photography, illustrations, different text styles (fonts) and sizes, product and company logos, video, audio, and other elements. Searching online for "website design ideas" will give you an overall sense of what is possible and currently popular in the world of web design "look and feel" concepts. Explore the websites of organizations similar to yours to inspire you with some ideas about how to present your own mix of web content. There are also a number of print/online magazines for professional web designers (*Communication Arts*,[8] *How*,[9] *Net*[10]) that feature innovative site layouts and publish "best web design" issues that showcase industry trends. If you hire a professional web designer, you will likely receive some examples of their work as a starting point.

The degree of unique layout details and overall customization for your site will depend on the skills you (or your web designer) employ using web content management platforms, such as Drupal or WordPress. Some businesses simplify the process by selecting pre-made templates within these platforms, or by using website builders such as Squarespace or Wix. Once again, the choices on unique vs. boilerplate design options should be evaluated by conducting a CBA that compares the various web scenarios relevant to your venture. For example, a small theater company may self-manage a simple website built in Squarespace to announce upcoming performances and generate ticket sales, while an online gallery for painting and sculpture may work with an experienced web design firm to launch an elaborate, content-rich web experience that is influential, deeply informative, and transactional.

Keep in mind that your website choices regarding logos, colors, typography, and even writing style should be consistent with your other marketing methods, such as print advertising, direct mail, social media, and email/text messages, not to mention packaging, signage, interior design, and other branded points-of-contact involving your customers. A skilled graphic designer can help your venture develop an integrated "identity system" that works effectively across many platforms and builds brand awareness with an integrated approach to concepts, images, and messages.

Make Design Decisions Based on Goals and Audience

This is where everything comes together: your business identity, your product/service mix, your customers' demographic profiles and their specific needs and wants, your goals in reaching people to develop brand awareness and inspire action, etc. All of these – and other – key considerations should be taken into account when choosing what to include (and exclude) in your web design direction.

To get some sense of the many technical aspects involved in making web design decisions, do a web search for "web design terminology" and review some of the information under topics such as Navigation (the ways users move from page to page), Wireframe (the underlying layout of the site's content, such as images, text, and other elements), Call-to-Action and other terms. This research will help you understand the common language and concepts used in the field, should you end up hiring a professional web designer. If you choose to build and maintain your own site, study the design choices (and examples) offered by website builders such as Squarespace or Wix. Or, you could invest some time and money in your own web development training using resources such as local workshops, vocational training programs at community colleges, or online learning services.

Testing Your Website and Measuring Results

There are many important aesthetic and functional elements to test before and after your new website launches. Does the site look good using different browsers (Chrome, Firefox, Safari) and on different devices (desktop computers, laptops, tablets, smart phones) using different operating systems and from different eras? Is it easy to add new content or edit existing content? Do the customer interaction functions work properly, including online point-of-sale transactions and email list sign-up requests? Does your site's relationship to your email messages and various social media channels (Facebook, Instagram, Twitter, etc.) perform as intended, driving traffic to and from each instance of your company's online presence? Working through these and other issues will be part of your website's design, development, launch, and maintenance phases.

To measure a website's performance, many organizations start with Google Analytics, a free service that tracks and reports on website traffic. Configuring your Google Analytics account might require some expert support, depending on your experience level and which features you want to use. Web analytics is an evolving field and there are other free or paid options for measuring online activity for websites, social media, and email campaigns – try an online search for "web analytics for arts organizations" and explore some options that fit your venture's goals and budget.

Refresh, Refine, Improve

Once your website has been planned, developed, and launched, the next question is how and when to add new content. Visitors to your site will include first-time viewers who are forming their initial impressions of your venture and its products and services, as well as people returning (hopefully often) to discover what's new about your business. Here are some tips on keeping your website engaging.

Make Your Homepage Interesting and Exciting

Decisions about exploring a website by first-time viewers can take place in 10 seconds or less, so design your homepage in a way that inspires curiosity and engagement. For some businesses, this means filling the space with colorful photography and bold text, for others, it means an elegant, refined layout with minimal content. Some sites incorporate audio and animation into their homepage, while others present a spare, simple opportunity to enter into the organization's world. However you choose to proceed, your homepage should tell the story of your business and invite further interaction.

Add New Content on a Regular Basis

Remember that marketing is all about communication. Your web content is not only sending messages to your visitors, it is also providing opportunities for interactions, such as purchasing a ticket for a performance, ordering a custom print, or simply signing up to receive announcements via email or text. Some arts organizations post new web content on a daily basis, while others update weekly. Create a web marketing calendar for up to one year and populate it with regular content update deadlines that coincide with your offerings. Web updates can be timed with monthly or seasonal events, such as holidays, or can be scheduled around your specific plans for introducing new products or services to your customers. Prepare your text, images, audio, and other content in advance, publish new content using your web update schedule, and measure effectiveness using Google Analytics and/or other tools.

Use Graphics, Photography, Video, and Audio

Along with well-written text, using audiovisual content that is interesting, relevant and well executed can grab the attention of website visitors in a way that is immediate and engaging. Artists and arts organizations are in an exceptionally good position to capture and publish compelling imagery related to their products and services, so set aside some time (and budget) to produce an ongoing series of high-quality audiovisual content. Because of the costs and technical issues involved in hosting large video or audio files on their local web server, some businesses place their audiovisual content on sites such as YouTube, Vimeo, or SoundCloud.

Inspire Visitors to Act

Marketing programs often include a "call to action" for the recipient. The idea is that your potential customer is invited to do something specific, such as make a purchase, submit a donation, leave a comment, or opt in to receive announcements via email. In the case of your website, this means placing opportunities for your visitors to act in places that encourage engagement. For example, a calendar of upcoming concerts would have a "Buy Tickets Now" button next to each event.

There are several important concepts to keep in mind when integrating calls to action into your web marketing materials:

- Think of how each opportunity connects with its perceived value by the customer. Remember from this chapter's previous discussions on consumer research and demographics that effective marketing communications appeal to a target customer's core values, lifestyles, and interests. Each call to action on your website should be designed with your customers' interests and values in mind.
- Make the action easy to understand and accomplish. This means Buy Now buttons for purchases or Sign Me Up web forms for email lists should be designed so the call to action is a straightforward, clearly described, and easily completed process.
- Have a small total number of calls to action on your website. This will make each opportunity stand out and generate interest.
- Place calls to action in strategically relevant places on your site. Invite visitors to make a purchase, receive announcements, add a comment or download some content where it is contextually appropriate and leads to other interactions.

In summary, there are a number of key functions that a website can provide to the arts entrepreneur:

- *Communication* that informs visitors about the organization, its purpose, people, and offerings.
- *Marketing* that connects products or services with customer needs and wants, then offers a call to action to inspire engagement and build relationships.

- *Fundraising* via Support Now links and other development opportunities.
- *Social media* interaction that connects a company's website to Facebook, Instagram, Twitter, YouTube, and other channels.
- *Email* contact to keep customers up to date about upcoming events, special offers, or time-limited opportunities.
- *Comments/blog* to encourage a sense of participation and dialogue between the arts venture and its customers. Some careful attention to managing comments on your site may be warranted if visitors need to have their postings moderated due to inappropriate content.
- *Multi-platform engagement* that delivers a high quality experience on a variety of browsers, devices, and operating systems
- *Analytics* that provide insights into your website's performance, including visits by new or returning viewers, purchases or other transactions (conversions), length of time visitors spend on the site, etc.

Search Engine Optimization (SEO)

How do you increase and measure the ability of web surfers to discover your site and its associated pages? Search engine optimization (SEO) refers to the techniques used to make your web content appear higher up on the list of search engine results in Google, Yahoo, Bing, and others. Keywords are an important part of the strategy for improving "discoverability" online, but so are images, well-organized content, page titles, and meta-descriptions. Try a search for "Search engine optimization (SEO) for arts organizations" and explore some options for improving your web content's ranking in search results.

Although SEO refers to no-cost options for improving your rank in search results (except for SEO management software licenses or fee-based SEO services), there are also paid techniques for increasing your web content's visibility such as Google Ad Words.

Create a document named Website Development. List your goals, target audience, design strategy (in-house or outsourced), site maintenance, assessment plans and content update schedule, then place the completed file in your Marketing folder.

Integrated Digital Marketing

Social Media

The growth and influence of services such as Facebook, Twitter, and Instagram have reached the point where every arts entrepreneur must consider engaging in some type of social media presence, especially for their marketing program. The ability to join networks and communities of like-minded individuals, deliver messages across demographic categories, and reach new customers makes social media a natural choice for both individual artists and established or developing arts organizations.

Many readers of this book will already have considerable experience with one or more of the many forms of social media, while others will be new to the concept and preparing to use these services for the first time. An additional complexity lies in the fact that many of the features and techniques employed by social media users change frequently, as social media companies themselves change the way their products are used by offering new features and changing or terminating others. In this section we will review underlying concepts for social media users of all experience levels, introduce basic techniques for new users and highlight some areas of interest for intermediate and advanced users.

Underlying Concepts

Like the approach taken for developing your overall marketing program (as well as other areas, such as fundraising, financial management, product/ service design, organizational growth, etc.), breaking your social media efforts down into basic *planning*, *execution*, and *evaluation* components will help keep your business focused on those specific, measurable activities that will help your venture achieve success.

Facebook

Launched in 2004, Facebook has grown into an enormously popular service that allows users to connect with each other via smart phones, tablets, and computers. Many people use Facebook to keep in touch with family and friends, follow celebrities, or keep up with the news. The range of relationships possible on Facebook is as varied as the users themselves, which include individuals, families, interest groups, public institutions, and private companies.

How does the arts entrepreneur approach Facebook as a marketing tool? One key factor lies in the creation of an online *social media identity*. This refers to the type of person (or organization) you want to project out into the social network – and what purpose that identity serves. Some people establish their Facebook presence at a young age and post a variety of messages, images, videos, and links that may seem appropriate at the time, but can end up working against the goal of reaching an engaged market of interested consumers for your arts organization. The distinction between a *private* social media identity and a *public* or *professional* one should be considered at the outset – you may not want your posts from high school or earlier connected with your initial attempts to attract customers to your new arts-related business. One way to solve this is to create a new, independent Facebook account that is conceived and curated with your business goals in mind. This is part of the planning process for social media: deciding who you are trying to reach, what messages and other media they will be receiving, and how they will be inspired to take action that relates to your business. If you have already developed a large following on Facebook, you can always direct your community to your new, independent account and invite them to discover what you have prepared for your network of prospective customers, supporters, and partners. All of your social networks can be contacted when announcing a new venture, introducing a product or service, or launching a crowdfunding campaign. As your business-oriented Facebook presence becomes established, tools such as Facebook Insights can help you measure the number of people who have clicked, Liked, commented on, or shared a post on your Page. You can discover a range of other software tools to help you measure and evaluate the effectiveness of your social media presence, For example, if you announce a reception for a new gallery exhibit on Facebook, you can use social media analytics to measure online activity before, during, and after the event – this can help you refine your messaging and timing for the next instance.

The planning, execution, and evaluation steps for social media can be thought of as a cycle of activities that continually turns to refine and improve your identity, reach, and impact. For Facebook, do the following:

- *Plan* a social media account that reflects the kind of identity you want your customers to experience. This should include sufficient text, images, and contact information so that the visitor becomes interested in your product or service and is compelled to take action, such as making a purchase, leaving a comment, Liking, or sharing your page.
- *Execute* your plan by creating and following a schedule of social media postings for a month, quarter, or year. Keep your postings informative and engaging. Likewise, reach out and follow, comment on, or share other Facebook users and their postings, to both increase your visibility and become an active, recognized member of your online community.
- *Evaluate* your Facebook activity using Facebook Insights and other tools for social media analytics. The information gleaned from these tools will help you plan your next month/quarter/year of Facebook activity and continue refining your approach.

Twitter

Twitter allows artists and arts organization to connect with their network in a quick, informative (and hopefully, inspiring) fashion. Like other forms of social media, attracting a substantial number of followers to your Twitter presence will take some time. Starting with only a few followers at the beginning may be discouraging, but by tweeting regularly, keeping your messages lively and interesting, and reaching out to connect with others, you will be able to increase your numbers over time and develop a solid network of people interested in you and your work.

To make Twitter useful as an arts marketing tool, do the following:

- *Plan* a series of Tweets around a focused event or series of actions. This can include updates on works in progress, a public or private event such as a gallery opening, premiere performance, or new product launch, or a new development in your professional or personal status, such as moving to a new location.
- *Execute* your thematic Twitter campaign over a brief time period to keep followers engaged and motivated. Provide links to your Facebook page, website, or other online presence so followers can learn more about you. Follow other Twitter users and participate in exchanges focused on *their* interests. Tweet about a variety of topics of interest to you personally, not just your arts marketing ambitions.
- *Evaluate* your activity using Twitter Analytics and other tools to identify areas that are working well or need some attention to become more successful. Use the information you gather to plan and execute your next Twitter marketing campaign.

Instagram

Artists of all types have discovered that Instagram is a very effective environment for displaying their work, connecting with followers, and generating sales. Because Instagram is primarily visual (rather than heavily text-based), it is well suited for arts consumers who want to see a variety of work from different sources without the interpretive written content that traditionally accompanies artwork in the marketplace. Instagram also allows your followers to develop a connection with your entire career – including your creative working methods and non-arts interests – and become engaged with your life as an artist and/or business owner and not just your finished work.

All of these Instagram practices relate to arts organizations as well as individual artists. To make Instagram useful as an arts marketing tool, do the following:

- *Plan* on posting at least once or twice a day, but probably not more than six or eight times a day. Use high-quality photography with good lighting to represent your work at its best. Present a variety of images and video content (some arts-related and some not) to paint an overall impression of yourself as a working artist. Use interesting, well-chosen hashtags for your postings, and resist the temptation to pile on too many in order to attract attention. Follow other artists on Instagram, and Like/comment on their work.

- *Execute* a strategy. As your following grows and interest in your work inspires sales inquiries, execute a strategy for managing financial transactions by setting up an Instagram shop or linking to your website or other online selling platform. Remove sold items promptly from your image feed and follow through with shipping, receipts, and thank you messages just like any other regular sale.
- *Evaluate* your activity with free or paid Instagram analytics tools, which can be found via online research.

More Social Media Tips

There are many other social media platforms to explore, including (as of this writing) Pinterest, Behance, LinkedIn, Snapchat, Tumblr, YouTube, and others. The future will certainly see even more opportunities for arts entrepreneurs to leverage the power of social media to reach a wide audience. The best way to keep up to date on the best (or newest) social media for artists is to keep up with arts-related websites and blogs that focus on trends and emerging arts-related products and services: Americans for the Arts (americansforthearts.org) and the New York Foundation for the Arts (nyfa.org) are just two examples. Or, a simple Google search on "best social media for artists" should reveal some recent online articles and postings.

Once you identify and set up your selected social media channels, it can be helpful to use a management platform such as Hootsuite (hootsuite.com) to manage your activity by scheduling messages and tracking activity. Paid services such as this can be an efficient way to organize and deliver a variety of content across multiple social media channels.

Email

Developing and regularly using a mailing list for email newsletters and customized messages is one of the most efficient ways to reach fans and customers of your arts venture. The availability of email marketing services such as Mailchimp and Constant Contact has greatly simplified the process for managing lists, creating email messages, and tracking results.

On his internet marketing website "The Abundant Artist," consultant Cory Huff provides some tips for artists who want to use email marketing:[11]

1. *Collect names, email and physical addresses*: Whenever you present your work to the public, make sure to invite people to subscribe to

your e-newsletter by filling out a form or writing their information in your email "guest book." Offering an incentive such as a free print, digital file, or other gift can increase your success rate in attracting subscribers. Make signing up for email prominent and easy to use on your website, social media, and text/SMS messages.

2. *Use an email management service*: As mentioned above, services such as Mailchimp (mailchimp.com) and Constant Contact (constantcontact.com) help users manage their email lists, design and distribute attractive, consistent messages, and track results of email campaigns. Huff also recommends ConvertKit (convertkit.com) for email marketing.

3. *Start digital, go physical*: Printing and distributing an attractive, well-designed brochure or catalog is a great way to stay in touch with your patrons. Physical objects occupy a different place than digital messages, especially when your customers keep your printed material in their home or office as a reminder of upcoming events, or to show to their friends and relatives.

4. *Frequency*: Arts organizations that have frequent events should communicate often with their audience – at least weekly, if appropriate. Other ventures with a more infrequent schedule should contact their database with a monthly newsletter, then distribute additional emails during busy periods.

What to Talk About?

Developing interesting content for your readers is of utmost importance in designing and implementing email campaigns. Some ideas for what to write about include:

- *Curation*: Regularly review performances, gallery shows, or other recent cultural events that you like (or dislike) to give readers a sense of your aesthetic judgment and personal preferences.
- *Tell small daily stories*: Describe some interesting episode in your arts or non-arts life that readers can relate to or be surprised by.
- *Show off work in progress*: Write about (and show images of) what you are working on in preparation for a future public event. This is the same type of content you would develop during a crowdfunding campaign to give supporters a sense of connection to you and your work.
- *Events and shows*: Give readers advance warning of your upcoming events, with reasons to consider attending and maybe discounts for early ticket purchase.

Keep It Simple

The graphic design aspects of your email messages and e-newsletters don't need to be complex or overly stylized. Keep layouts simple and easy to read. Also, think about maintaining a recognizable "look and feel" across your email, website, social media, and printed materials to reinforce your brand and encourage recognition of your enterprise: use consistent (or at least complementary) fonts, colors, and layouts across all of your marketing materials.

Text/SMS

Texting and SMS (Short Message Service) are essentially the same thing: users send and receive brief written messages of up to 160 characters on their smart phones, often including emoticons, photographs, video, and/or audio files. The immediacy of sending and receiving texts make the experience easy, compelling, and conversational. Texting is extremely popular among younger users, although people of all ages use the service for all kinds of communications. Companies such as banks, airlines, and pharmacies use text alerts to notify their customers of financial transactions, flight updates, and prescription refills.

How does the arts entrepreneur integrate text messaging into their marketing program? Like adding people to your email notification list, start by inviting patrons to provide their cell phone number to be notified about upcoming promotions, discounts, and invitation-only events. Keep the information gathering process simple by asking customers for everything at once: name, physical address, email, and mobile number. In addition, you should create opportunities for your fans to "opt in" to text notifications on your web pages, email messages, and social media postings.

Once you have a database for text messaging, plan a series of messages that are tied to a specific opportunity or call to action. For example, if a new event has been added to your calendar that is likely to sell out, send a text to your list and invite people to purchase tickets soon. It is important to note that recipients of your text notifications may not respond well to frequent messages about opportunities they can learn about easily via social media, email, or traditional advertising. The aim is not to overwhelm customers with too many messages, but to use texting for urgent, special announcements that will provoke interest and require timely action. Using texts to simply reinforce messages found in other formats will alienate your users and encourage them to opt out – save texting for special promotions or occasional announcements.

In addition to marketing, many nonprofits use texting as a way to inspire donations via text-to-give campaigns. Arts organizations can follow this method, especially at the end of year "donation season" in December when patrons are making plans for charitable giving to maximize tax deductions.

CRM Software

With all of these digital options at your disposal (websites, social media, email, text messaging), how does one keep track of multiple channels of marketing activity and measure effectiveness? CRM (Constituent Relationship Management, aka Customer Relationship Management) systems provide a convenient way to organize materials, schedule output, and track results. Although these paid services require training and upkeep, they are very useful for the *planning*, *execution*, and *evaluation* of all your marketing efforts – this includes traditional methods, such as phone calls and direct mail. Ticket sales and other transactions can be entered into CRM systems to provide a complete picture of customer involvement with your products and services. To explore the latest CRM technology available for arts-related planning, sell-through, and customer tracking, try a web search using "CRM for the arts" and investigate some of the many options.

Create a document named Digital Marketing. List all of your ideas for websites, social media, email, and text marketing, then place the completed file in your Marketing folder.

Print Advertising

Although the opportunities (and reasons) to advertise in newspapers, magazines and other print media have changed dramatically in recent years, there is still a case to be made for including print advertising in your overall marketing mix if your business warrants it. Many arts patrons – especially those in an older demographic with disposable income and a background in arts appreciation and support – still turn to their local newspapers, magazines, and free weekly periodicals for information about cultural events in their market. Many cities and regions have free "alternative" weekly publications that cover the local arts scene in depth, providing listings for upcoming events such as gallery exhibits, film screenings, or live performances along with editorial coverage highlighting specific artists or emerging cultural trends of interest to their readers. The free weeklies also feature local businesses selling products or services such as workshops or other educational programs. Many daily newspapers, free weeklies, and regional magazines also have online editions, so ad buys can reach customers via both print and web-based channels.

Developing a relationship with your local print media takes time and money, but it can pay off if your consumers fit the demographics served by the publication. This is especially true if your customer base is concentrated geographically in an area served by the publication's circulation. Newspapers and magazines can provide detailed information about their readership (location, age, income, discretionary spending habits) along with the publication's rates for printing ads of different sizes and run once or over a series of installments. The cost for print ads goes down dramatically per instance if you commit to a series of ads over time – having a regular advertising presence in a publication also reinforces your organization's image in the minds of the readers and (like your website) can help to inspire responses to a call to action.

Print ad design should be approached with the same careful consideration of your brand that you use for other marketing materials such as your website, business cards, or social media graphics. The idea is to reinforce a consistent image and messaging in the minds of your customers so they become familiar with – and increasingly attracted to – your company and its products or services. Fortunately, most artists and art organizations have access to engaging visual material simply because of the nature of their business. Make your ads visually arresting, with key information such as dates, location, web address, and other logistical details clearly presented. The challenge is to selectively build a brand identity over time via print advertising that produces measurable results. Most publications with print/online editions can help their ad customers develop assessment techniques to measure ad response activity, especially when web-based advertising is linked to a transaction opportunity on *your* site – that can then be tracked by Google Analytics or other tools.

For information on connecting your arts venture to a publication's editorial division, see this chapter's discussion of *Working with the Media*. A publication's advertising and editorial departments are separate entities and require different approaches to cultivate successful relationships and produce beneficial results.

Radio

Like print advertising, choices about investing in radio advertising have changed dramatically over the years. Radio was once considered an essential ingredient in a venture's marketing mix, especially for new businesses trying to establish themselves by reaching listeners throughout a wide geographic region. Like buying newspaper or magazine advertising, radio ads can make sense for an arts venture if the demographics of the station's listeners align with the organization's target audience. For example, a local classical music radio station might be an excellent choice for a performing arts venue that wants to advertise a concert by a famous singer – the demographics of the station's listeners would likely be a very good match for such an event. If your company's products or services are designed to appeal to younger consumers, don't overlook college radio stations or local/regional community stations – just like the commercial stations, these outlets often support online listening and can reach people all over the world.

Television

Advertising on television is an expensive but potentially powerful option for an arts organization, especially one that already has strong market presence, brand identity, and dedicated customers. The upsides of buying local or regional television ads include the ability to reach very large numbers of potential consumers and the creation of immediate interest around an upcoming event or other time-limited opportunity. Having a presence on television can also distinguish your business from others in the same market, while reinforcing other advertising channels such as print, web, and social media postings. Like other forms of mass media such as print advertising and radio, TV provides opportunities to deliver your marketing messages to a large audience that includes people familiar with your organization as well as new customers who may be discovering your products and services for the first time.

Direct Mail

Despite predictions about the digital age creating a paperless world where nearly all information and transactions would be transmitted online, we still live in a time when many paper-based marketing pieces arrive in our home or office mailboxes every week. Although sometimes derided as "junk mail," direct mail can actually be a very effective method of reaching customers, generating interest, and producing measurable sales results. The key to designing and running a successful direct mail campaign starts with the quality of the mailing list used in the project. For the established arts business, there should be a well-maintained mailing list of home addresses for past customers who will be very interested in receiving an attractive, inspiring postcard, flyer, brochure, or sales catalog from you. For the new venture, there are opportunities to rent or purchase a targeted mailing list that allows you to reach potential consumers who fit your demographic criteria. Along with the quality of your mailing list, there is the importance of creating a well-designed print piece that draws the reader's attention with enticing graphics and compelling messages, especially offers of time-limited discounts or other transactional incentives. Direct mail campaigns often employ special codes or other response measurements to help quantify how many respondents took action after receiving a postcard, flyer or other print piece – this allows the business to evaluate the effectiveness of the mailing project and make decisions about refining or expanding future efforts. The best way for your venture to experiment with direct mail is to work with a graphic designer or advertising firm with extensive experience in developing, distributing, and measuring direct mail campaigns.

Events

An art gallery advertises a reception for the opening of a new exhibition ... a performing arts venue invites the public to a free daytime event ... an arts education program holds an open house to promote upcoming workshops and classes for children and adults ... an individual artist joins a weekend open studio tour that attracts experienced and novice art patrons from around the region ... a manufacturing and distribution company schedules a product launch event at their headquarters or a local hotel for the press and invited VIPs ...

There are many ways for arts organizations to produce events that raise awareness of their products and services while promoting direct interactions with their known (and potential) customers. The variety and frequency of marketing events for your business may be limited by your capacity to accommodate the public in a space you already occupy, such as a warehouse, storefront, or business reception area. Many restaurants, bars, nightclubs, and hotels have rooms for business functions that can be used for public or private events, the advantages being built-in access to parking and catered food and beverage services for your guests. Marketing events for an arts venture should be primarily social and subtly informational – you don't want to impose an aggressive sales pitch on guests at a cultural reception. At the very least, consider hosting a launch party for your new organization when it opens for business (and when you reach an important milestone in its development) – people will naturally want to help you celebrate the accomplishment of turning your dream into a reality. Remember from this chapter's discussion about Working with the Media that public events can be considered newsworthy by daily newspapers, free weeklies, magazines, and other print/online media outlets – you can send press releases announcing your event to your list of editorial contacts in the hopes of getting valuable (and free) media coverage about you and your organization.

Create a document named Advertising. List all of your ideas for print, radio, TV, direct mail, and events, then place the completed file in your Marketing folder.

Now that you have identified your potential customers using market research, evaluated other businesses in your market using competitive analysis, and developed a list of marketing channels to reach your audience, such as free publicity/press relations, organizational websites, social media, email, text/SMS, and the various paid advertising opportunities, it's time to create a marketing plan that communicates the value of your products and services to your target market.

Connecting Your Products and Services with the Needs and Wants of the People in Your Market

To develop your approach to marketing your company's offerings to customers and make productive connections with *their* interests, work through the followings steps:

1. *Define your product/service general category*: Take a step back and imagine your arts venture as part of a *general* category of similar businesses. This category can be as broad as "music" or "photography" and serves to locate your business concept within your customers' general perceptions about what kind of organization you are operating.

2. *Define your product/service specific attributes and value for customers*: Bring the focus in to illuminate the details of your venture's offerings. For example, "hypnotic electronic dance music with a Brazilian flavor," or "provocative black and white photography that inspires engagement with pressing social issues." Describe the specific attributes of your products and services in terms of the *value* provided to customers, such as "a unique, exciting live performance" or "beautiful, inspiring fine art photography." Develop as many descriptive terms as possible, both from your own viewpoint and from your customers' perspective.

3. *Define your customers in general categories*: Take another step back and consider your actual (or potential) customers in general terms, such as "adults living in major U.S. cities" or "experienced collectors of fine art."

4. *Define your customers in specific details (location, age, gender, interests)*: This is where you apply the insights developed in this chapter's previous focus on defining and reaching market segments. Identify all of the demographic information and other details for your specific customers. Try to be both realistic about what kinds of consumers your business can attract now and ambitious about the possibilities for connecting with a robust mix of future customers for the long term.

5. *Define your specific customers needs/wants in relation to your product/service category*: Now that you have described your customers in some detail, what are their needs and wants with respect to your general product/service category, such as "music," "photography" or some other term? This step requires some research into what your actual (or potential) customers think about and want from businesses in your general category. Again, review this chapter's section on defining and reaching market segments for ideas on how to identify your customers' needs and wants.

6. *Connect your product/service attributes and value with your specific customers' needs/wants*: This is where the business owner and his or her marketing team brainstorm all of the ways to connect their product/service details (from Step 2) with what their customers are

seeking (from Step 5). For your organization, try to approach this step with an open mind and as much creative input as you can gather. Bring in trusted advisors, friends, potential consumers, or even an experienced marketing consultant for this (and the other) steps to capture as many perspectives and ideas as you can.

After completing this series of marketing analysis and idea-generation steps, you should have a good supply of material ready use to build your Marketing Plan.

Create Your Marketing Plan

Like other planning efforts, putting together a comprehensive marketing plan serves several important functions:

- It causes you to organize your thinking around a series of clearly defined actions that produce specific, measurable outcomes.
- It communicates to others in your organization what is happening and why, so they can rally around the cause and apply their best efforts toward a shared goal.
- After the completion of a marketing campaign, it provides the structure to analyze each action to evaluate its effectiveness and consider improvements, modifications, or entirely new approaches.

The sections of your marketing plan should be as detailed and strategically focused as necessary to both guide the actions of the marketing team and assess the effort's results (and help generate future plans). The documents you created earlier in this chapter will provide background material for a formally written marketing plan. Let's work through the sections in your marketing plan, using the documents you have prepared earlier.

Introduction, Goals, and Resources

In this section you describe the overall condition of your business, what kinds of marketing goals are being established (increased attendance at a series of events, financial targets for sales of a specific item) and what you have to work with in terms of people, time, space, and funding to execute a successful marketing program. Use information from your previously created *Marketing Audit* to write an objective presentation of your organization's marketing resources that can be put to use in the campaign. Refer to your *Marketing SWOT Analysis* for additional material on your venture's marketing strengths, weaknesses, opportunities, and threats. Your *Marketing Goals and Needs* document will help you write a focused description of exactly what your marketing ambitions are designed to accomplish. Use the information from your *Marketing Policies and Procedures* file and *Marketing Databases* data to write about these topics and how they support your marketing efforts.

Identify Marketing Opportunities

Use material from your *Customer Demographics* file to describe your target audience. Your *Market Research and Competitive Analysis* document should help you write a comprehensive presentation of your market and your competition – make sure you include examples of how you will distinguish your product or service in the minds of your intended customers.

Develop Materials

This section is where you spell out exactly what you will create, distribute and maintain in the service of your marketing efforts. Focus on each of the areas covered in these documents:

- free publicity/press relations
- website development
- digital marketing (social media, email, text)
- advertising (print, radio, TV, direct mail, events).

Train Your People

Who will perform the many tasks associated with your organization's marketing program, including the research, development, distribution, and assessment of your marketing materials? Use this section to describe who does what, and how they will be trained to accomplish their duties. If your company chooses to hire professional help for its marketing, write about how that service will be researched, selected, and managed.

Create Schedules

Most marketing plans describe at least one full calendar year of activity (and sometimes more) to identify actions before, during, and after a campaign runs. At the very least, write out a monthly to-do list of marketing activities that is coordinated with the seasonal ebb and flow of your venture's business volume during the year. The more detailed and specific your marketing schedule is, the easier it will be to keep on track once things get busy.

Evaluate Results and Refine/Adjust Future Marketing Efforts

This section describes how you will measure the effectiveness of your marketing efforts and how you will respond to the insights provided by these measurements. Include not only quantitative sales data in terms of units and dollars, but also the numbers of new/repeat customers, qualitative data from focus groups and interviews, ad response rates from print ads and direct mail, and online data from Google Analytics and other sources.

Chapter Summary

Marketing is about understanding and communicating with your customers. The arts entrepreneur uses marketing techniques to build an image, educate customers and inspire action such as sales, website comments, or some other forms of participation. The exchange model of interaction shows us how to approach current or potential consumers with *their* needs and interests in mind. By conducting market research and competitive analysis, the arts business creates a valuable collection of information about the market for its products and services, including the presence of similar businesses and how to create a unique identity. Market segments are identified via demographic research, while qualitative data from customers can be generated from surveys, interviews, and focus groups. An audit (with SWOT analysis) of your organization's current conditions and resources for conducting a marketing campaign is an important step in building your overall marketing plan. Define your company's marketing goals, policies, and infrastructure to help clarify your marketing campaign's direction and organizational capacity. The development and maintenance of an effective website are important, potentially complex undertakings with many positive marketing aspects. Likewise, incorporating social media, email, and text channels into the marketing mix can help the arts venture efficiently reach current and potential customers. Traditional paid marketing options such as print advertising, radio, television, direct mail, and events can still have a productive role in your marketing mix, especially if the demographics served by the medium align with your target customer base. A comprehensive, well-organized marketing plan will allow an arts organization to develop, execute, and measure success across all aspects of the effort.

Discussion Questions

1. How does a marketing campaign communicate an arts organization's value to current and potential customers?

2. Describe how the "exchange model of interaction between producer and consumer" applies to your business concept and its target audience.

3. What are the ways to conduct market research on similar (perhaps competing) businesses in your area?

4. Describe the demographic categories relevant to your customer base.

5. What are "media relations" and how does an arts venture develop and nurture these connections?

6. For an established business, what are the techniques for gathering useful marketing information from existing customers?

7. How does a marketing audit with SWOT analysis help a company create an effective marketing plan?

8. Name three essential marketing goals for your organization.

9. What are the options for website design and maintenance, from the simplest to the most complex choices?

10. Describe which social media channels your business will use and why.

11. What are the potential advantages of using "traditional" marketing methods, such as print advertising, radio, television, direct mail and events?

12. List the ways your product/service attributes and values address the needs and wants of your target customers.

Notes

[1] Korza, Pam, Maren Brown, and Craig Dreeszen. *Fundamentals of arts management* (Amherst, MA: Arts Extension Service, University of Massachusetts, Amherst, 2007), p. 297.

[2] Kotler, Philip, and Kevin Lane Keller. *Marketing management* (Harlow: Pearson Education, 2016).

[3] Bernstein, Joanne Scheff. *Arts marketing insights: the dynamics of building and retaining performing arts audiences* (San Francisco: Jossey-Bass, 2007), p. 25.

[4] See www.americansforthearts.org/

[5] See www.giarts.org/

[6] See www.wallacefoundation.org

[7] See www.americansforthearts.org/by-program/services-and-training/services-for-your-organization/research-and-survey-services

[8] See www.commarts.com/

[9] See www.howdesign.com/

[10] See www.creativeblog.com/net-magazine

[11] See http://theabundantartist.com/newsletters-so-easy-an-artist-could-do-it/

Further Reading

Bernstein, Joanne Scheff. 2007. *Arts marketing insights: the dynamics of building and retaining performing arts audiences*. San Francisco: Jossey-Bass.

Bhandari, Heather Darcy, and Jonathan Melber. 2017. *Art/Work: everything you need to know (and do) as you pursue your art career*. New York: Free Press.

Korza, Pam, Maren Brown, and Craig Dreeszen. 2007. *Fundamentals of arts management*. Amherst, MA: Arts Extension Service, University of Massachusetts, Amherst.

Kotler, Philip, and Kevin Lane Keller. 2016. *Marketing management*. Harlow: Pearson Education.

Kweskin, Amy, Nancy Hytone Leb, Yesenia Sanchez, Greg Victoroff, Nancy Walch, and Richard Walch. 2012. *Business of art: an artist's guide to profitable self-employment*. Los Angeles, CA: Center for Cultural Innovation.

Michels, Caroll. 2018. *How to survive and prosper as an artist: selling yourself without selling your soul*. New York: Skyhorse Publishing Company, Inc.

New York Foundation for the Arts, Peter Cobb, Felicity Hogan, and Michael Royce. 2018. *The profitable artist: a handbook for all artists in the performing, literary, and visual arts* (2nd edn). La Vergne, TN: Allworth Press.

4 Fundraising

How will you raise money to establish and sustain your nonprofit arts organization? After your venture's mission and purpose, this is probably the most important question you will face as an arts entrepreneur.

Raising money requires significant investments of time, planning and effort, but the support provided in terms of cash, in-kind contributions and professional relationships can be crucial to the success of your business. In this chapter we will examine:

- the importance of contributed income to your overall financial picture;
- ways to connect your organization's mission and needs with funding sources;
- techniques for finding and approaching different types of donors;
- developing and implementing plans for your short-term and long-term fundraising goals;
- collecting and storing data on people and funding organizations;
- evaluating the effectiveness of your fundraising program to help your venture thrive.

Why Is Fundraising So Important for a Nonprofit Arts Organization?

The non-profit arts venture seeks revenue from two distinct categories: (1) earned income; and (2) contributed income.

Earned income is proceeds from the sales of:

- tickets (to performances, exhibitions, lectures or other events);
- merchandise (t-shirts, CDs, posters, gift shop or café revenue);
- space rental (renting out your concert hall, gallery or other venue to another user);

- any other exchange of money for goods or services provided by your organization.

Contributed income refers to donations in the form of:

- cash or cash equivalents, such as stocks and bonds, real estate, and investment income;
- in-kind contributions of equipment, such as lighting, sound gear, tools, machinery, and construction materials;
- supplies, such as food and beverages, flowers, paint, and cleaning materials;
- services, such as printing, web hosting, hotel and airline expenses, legal advice, and accounting support.

Fundraising refers to contributed income only, not the income generated by sales of products, services or "experiences," such as live performances or internet-based exchanges.

Arts organizations in the US typically find less than half of their total budget needs met by earned income. The National Endowment of the Arts 2012 publication, *How the United States Funds the Arts*,[1] describes the ratios between earned income, contributed income, and interest for non-profit performing arts groups and museums as follows:

40.7 percent	earned income
44.9 percent	contributed income
14.4 percent	interest and endowment income.

If the typical non-profit arts organization relies on roughly 45 percent of its total income from donations, then your venture will need to carefully develop and implement a comprehensive fundraising plan to cover expenses.

In the US, institutional grants, gifts and other tax-deductible contributions normally require the recipient to have 501(c)(3) "charitable organization" status from the Internal Revenue Service (IRS). Most new arts organizations don't have that status when they start out, so they work with a *fiscal sponsor* to attract tax-deductible donations. See Chapter 5, Legal Issues, for more information.

Every Business Has Different Needs

You may have a special concert presentation in mind for next season that requires sponsorship to support additional costs. Your online arts community might need a complete website overhaul to keep up with an increasing user base and an expanding range of interactive content via mobile apps. Your training center for young actors may need more space for rehearsals and set construction. In addition to these exceptional circumstances, you may find that your regular operating expenses, such as payroll, rent, utilities, and insurance are not being covered by your earned income from regular sales.

Your fundraising efforts can help pay for your regular and exceptional expenses while supporting your organization's overall ambitions. By creating and following a Fundraising Plan, you will be able to articulate your venture's purpose, mission, and goals in a way that inspires donations from individuals, foundations, corporate programs, and government agencies.

Your Organization's Purpose, Mission, and Goals

Your organization's mission, structure, and marketing components have all been developed from your initial inspiration to bring art and business together around an artistic theme or practice that you value. Likewise, your fund-raising plan should be an outgrowth of your organization's purpose and goals. An arts venture that consistently builds its infrastructure upon a solid conceptual foundation will be recognized – and hopefully well supported – by virtue of its integrated approach to practical necessities, including fundraising.

Developing Fundraising Materials

The following elements can be used to develop a fundraising plan and communicate with funding sources to inspire support.

Mission Statement

A mission statement gives the reader – in this case, a potential funder – a brief, clear description of what the organization does, whom it serves and where it is located (see Chapter 2, Planning and Assessment). Here are some examples:

> The Springfield String Quartet brings powerful, unique expressions of classical music to listeners of all ages in and around Springfield.

> The purpose of PaintersForum.com is to bring together professional, amateur and student artists from all around the world to discuss their work and provide ideas, guidance, and encouragement to help one another succeed.

> The Uptown Theatre Company's New Visions program gives young actors and playwrights in Upville County opportunities to learn from experienced professionals and create new plays based on their own life experiences.

Starting with a brief version of your mission statement from Chapter 2, write an expanded version that gives the reader more information about how your venture was formed (organizational structure), the needed products or services you provide (value for consumers), who your customers or "clients" are (target market), what you are trying to accomplish (goals) and how you intend to achieve your objectives (strategies).

This expanded mission statement serves several purposes:

- It requires you to think through the important aspects of your venture's "reasons for existence" and write clear, compelling text for readers who have little or no direct experience with you or your organization.
- It gives you experience writing from a brief, focused starting point and expanding your communication outwards to provide a fuller, more detailed picture of your venture.
- It organizes your company's overall image into specific categories that help people inside and outside the organization understand and – most importantly – want to support your ambitions.

This process of starting from a small, focused mission statement and expanding outwards to a more detailed, fully articulated view is a good approach for all kinds of writing related to your venture. For the purposes of advancing your fundraising program, continue writing on each of the themes you developed in your expanded mission statement:

- Organizational structure
- Value for consumers
- Target market
- Goals
- Strategy

Organizational Structure

The next step is to describe the people who are part of your organization, their roles in operating the business and the management relationships between individuals and departments. Non-profits have a Board of Directors overseeing the entire business, with an Executive Director (you) reporting to the Board. A Business Manager, Marketing Manager, and Sales Manager could report to you, and an Assistant could report to each of these Managers. Don't forget to include volunteers or interns if your operation has opportunities for these important roles. Or, you may have a group of partners working together with equal levels of authority and responsibility for the organization's decisions and actions. An *organizational chart* helps the reader understand the people and relationships within your specific business (see Chapter 8, Organizational Design).

Value for Consumers

Describe the benefits derived from people who interact with your organization from the outside, primarily your customers. What products or services does your business provide that are perceived as valuable by the recipient? Value can be measured in different ways, from monetary worth (a customer buys your artwork and it increases in market value over time), to meaningful experiences in the performing arts, to educating aspiring artists, to raising awareness of social issues via artistic engagement.

Target Market

Describe who your customers are: where they are located (in geographic terms if your organization has a physical location, or in behavioral terms if your business is exclusively online), their age range, economic category, and purchasing preferences as consumers. See Chapter 3, Marketing, for more information on demographics and customer identification.

Goals

List your venture's specific goals for the near term and the long term, including:

- financial income and expense targets;
- market reach – the number of customers you will attract, where from, and how you will connect with them;
- organizational structure, especially if you plan on expanding in the future;
- impact of your product or service on society – this can include all kinds of positive changes in people's perceptions, attitudes, and actions in relation to your organization's focus.

Strategy

Describe how you will achieve the objectives listed in the Goals section above. You can address each goal individually, or you can use an integrated approach that demonstrates the synergy found in pursuing several Goals together. For example:

> Organization X has a business growth strategy that relies on expanding its market reach through frequent exposure via social media and mobile apps. As our transaction count and net income (after expenses) increase over time, we will add more staff, especially in the Content Development department. Our central mission of inspiring young artists through online learning will remain intact as we touch more lives and have a greater impact on artistic practice in underserved communities that lack accessible training programs in the arts.

Write at least one page on each of these themes (Organizational structure, Value for consumers. Target market, Goals, Strategy) and place the documents in a folder named Fundraising Materials. You are now ready to move on to painting a picture of your venture's needs.

Organizational Needs

There are several categories of need that your organization may have, including:

- programmatic
- operational
- infrastructure
- capital projects.

As we examine each of the areas, keep in mind that your donors will be interested in some – but not necessarily all – of your categories of need: your goal is to match a specific need with an appropriate funding source. For example, a foundation might provide grants for program-related costs (artists' fees for performances), but not operational expenses, such as administrative overhead and office supplies. An individual donor might be a good match for funding a capital project (the construction of a new teaching space for digital artists) but not a good choice for supporting ongoing infrastructure expenses, such as web hosting and utilities.

Programmatic Needs

Does your organization offer classes, support artist residencies, produce concerts or other events, provide online content, develop community-based art projects, or engage in other similar activities? These are just a few examples of program-related work: the actual services or products your venture provides to consumers. Since every non-profit arts organization has – by definition as a charitable organization – some positive social benefit associated with its mission and purpose, program activities are the key "deliverables" that the business provides to its market. Programmatic needs, therefore, are the expenses associated with program-related activity: salaries and benefits for teachers and artists, transportation costs for bringing live events to underserved communities, or advertising charges for making your customers aware of a new product or service. This category of expenses is different than operational, infrastructure or capital projects in that it includes only costs exclusively related to a specific program's development and implementation, not the ongoing, general expenses associated with your organization.

The good news is that many foundations, public agencies, corporate philanthropy programs, and individual donors are very interested in seeing arts programs succeed and will, if you are selected for a grant or other support, provide financial and other assistance to help make your "deliverables" available to your target audience. The challenge is that a smaller percentage of potential funders are willing to provide financial support for general administrative expenses, such as office space and non-program personnel (see the section on Operational Needs).

Make a list of expense categories that are exclusively program-related. Then, add expense figures for each category. Finally, write a one-page description of your programmatic needs (categories, expenses, and intended results) that ties the successful delivery of your organization's product or service to its mission. Try to express your programmatic outcomes (see Chapter 2, Planning and Assessment) as *solutions* to a problem (or multiple problems) you have identified. This is your statement of Programmatic Needs – it will be an important component for your overall fundraising strategy as you seek support from a variety of sources.

Operational Needs

Making a distinction between programmatic and operational needs can be a bit tricky: is the company vehicle programmatic because it brings art teachers to public schools, or is it operational because it is also used to move office supplies from a vendor's warehouse to your organization's central workspace? The aim is to identify expenses that are associated with your non-programmatic activities and raise funds from donors that support operational or administrative costs. In the case of the company vehicle above, you could have two separate uses for the same resource and could identify both programmatic *and* operational costs related to each functional category.

Other operational (non-programmatic) costs include:

- salaries, benefits and payroll taxes for non-programmatic personnel (managers, administrative staff, paid interns);
- rent, utilities and insurance for leased office/workspace;
- general supplies needed to run your organization;
- outside services, such as legal, accounting, facilities maintenance, website hosting, phone/internet providers, and email support;
- fundraising costs, including expenses for events, mailers, personnel, and travel.

Make a list of expense categories that are exclusively operational. Then, add expense figures for each category. Finally, write a one-page description of your operational needs (categories, expenses and intended results) that ties the operation of your overall organization to successfully realizing its mission. This is your statement of Operational Needs – it will be a key element in raising funds from donors that do provide support for administrative and other non-programmatic expenses.

Infrastructure

This refers to systems, structures and facilities that your organization relies on to conduct its business. Examples included Ethernet network cables, switches and routers, electrical and plumbing systems, and buildings, workshops or other physical structures. Like your operational needs above, your infrastructure expenses will qualify for some – but not all – support opportunities from funding sources, such as foundations. Make a list of infrastructure expense categories and amounts for each – this will be added to your Operational Needs when seeking donations from selected funders.

Capital Projects

If your organization needs to construct a new building for its operations and programs, or wants to develop a large endowment fund that will provide reliable interest income into the future, then a capital project is the appropriate way to convey your needs to donors. Capital projects involve raising significant amounts of money (often totaling millions of dollars) for needs that have a long lifespan: construction of new buildings, extensive renovations to existing spaces, or establishing an endowment fund that is large enough to provide operational or programmatic resources for many years. For your organization to attract enough funding to support a capital project, you will need to have been in existence for a number of years, have a solid reputation in the community for providing needed products and services, be widely recognized as a successful and well-managed operation and have an extensive network of potential donors with the capacity to give large amounts of money. If this sounds like something your organization is ready to undertake, then you will need to fully describe the costs of your capital project throughout its lifespan (planning, implementation, results, long-term sustainability) and the anticipated impact it will have on your programmatic and operational capacity.

Create a folder named Needs Statement and place your Programmatic, Operational, Infrastructure, and/or Capital Campaign documents inside it.

Evaluating Funding Methods

Now that you have developed an expanded mission statement and needs statement, it's time to move on to selecting the types of donations you will be targeting. Remember that your overall goal is to match your organization's needs with support types and funding sources that are a good fit – you don't want to expend time and effort pursuing donors that don't have a reasonably high likelihood of connecting with you, your organization, and your explicitly described goals.

Gifts

Gifts are donations of cash or cash equivalents, such as stocks and bonds, real estate, and investment income. Individual people provide most gifts, while some come from corporations with unrestricted giving programs. Since a gift is not usually tied directly to a measurable outcome, there is freedom to apply the funds in any way that suits the organization's needs. This is especially important when seeking funds to cover operational expenses. The overall message with a gift is that the donor supports the overall mission, strategy, management, and outcomes of the arts venture. The gift expresses the donor's wish to provide resources to help the organization continue its work in general.

An exception would be a gift that it made as part of a capital campaign: in this case, the gift is tied to an expectation that the campaign's objectives will be met using gift funds from multiple donors. Sometimes donor recognition is an important component of capital campaign gifts – for example, when your donors' names (as individuals, couples, or corporations) are listed in a publication, plaque, or engraved wall and sorted by giving level.

Grants

Grants are usually focused on a particular project or program run by the organization, or a desired outcome as defined by the donor. Foundations have grant programs that are organized by location, program focus, organization size, and other parameters. Corporate and government grant programs are also usually structured according to areas of interest that they have identified as warranting support. Examples include:

- The James Irvine Foundation: The Exploring Engagement Fund provides risk capital for arts non-profits with innovative ideas about how to engage new and diverse participants.[2]
- Through Our Town, subject to the availability of funding, the National Endowment for the Arts will provide a limited number of grants for creative placemaking projects that contribute toward the livability of

communities and help transform them into lively, beautiful, and resilient places with the arts at their core.[3]

- Bank of America: Arts & Culture/Partnerships: We provide vital support to cultural institutions and arts organizations throughout the world via our extensive program of sponsorships and grants.[4]

Methods for finding, applying for and receiving corporate, foundation and government grants are covered later in this chapter.

In-kind Support

In-kind support means anything donated that is not cash or cash equivalent. When a catering company or winery donates their products and services to your fundraising event at no charge (or at a reduced amount) – often with an acknowledgment on your website and other marketing materials – this is considered an in-kind donation. There are many types of in-kind donations, from reduced rent on your workspace to contributions of office supplies, graphic design services, or legal counsel. Although donors providing materials are not giving cash, they can still deduct the value of their contribution from their taxes. Donors who provide services can deduct some costs related to their service (such as travel expenses) as a charitable gift. This makes the possibilities for in-kind donations very attractive to supporters in your community who wish to see your arts venture succeed but don't have disposable income for cash gifts or grants.

Planned Giving

Your range of potential donors may include individuals from different age groups and socio-economic levels. Many arts organizations offer planned giving opportunities if the age and wealth of their donor base warrant solicitation of larger gifts in the form of real estate, securities, life insurance policies, or cash held in a trust or annuity. Planned giving provides benefits to both the donor and the recipient: donors can receive tax deductions,[5] future income for themselves and their beneficiaries, and exemptions from probate; while recipients can attract significant current and future funding for endowments or operating expenses. The underlying principle with planned giving is the same as for other contributions: the donor has a strong interest in the arts organization's mission and wants to see it thrive both now and in the future.

The forms of donation developed through planned giving are unique. Here are some examples:

- *Bequests*: a donor can amend his or her will (using a specific document called a codicil) to leave a gift for an arts organization in the form of cash, property, or other assets. This type of gift gives the donor an immediate tax deduction and reduces estate and inheritance taxes in the future.

- *Trusts*: By placing a gift in a trust, a donor can contribute to an arts organization's future needs while receiving annual payments and tax reductions. An *annuity trust* provides income for the donor at a fixed rate, while a *unit trust* makes payments to the donor based on the annually adjusted value of assets.
- *Annuities*: Donors who place cash or securities in an annuity can receive tax deductions for their charitable gift while generating income for themselves. Annuities can generate income either at the time of the donation or later as in the case of a *deferred gift annuity*.
- *Real estate*: There are several ways to donate property to an arts organization, including arrangements where the donor and his or her survivors continue to occupy a residence until a mutually agreed upon transition in the future. This type of gift also provides immediate tax benefits to the donor.
- *Life insurance*: A donor can include an arts organization as a beneficiary of a life insurance policy – or donate a fully paid policy to the organization – and receive tax deductions immediately.

It is important to note that planned giving requires expert advice and counsel for both the donor and recipient, usually provided by attorneys, accountants, financial planners, and other trained professionals. Because of the many functional and legal details associated with planned giving strategies, it is essential that donors and arts organizations seek and follow the advice of consultants who have relevant experience in preparing and executing these types of agreements.

Annual Campaign

The annual fund drive – or annual campaign – is an important component of the overall fundraising strategy:

- It reaches out to large number of current or prospective donors and attracts them to your organization's cause.
- It provides much-needed financial support for general operating expenses, such as staff, workspace, and infrastructure expenses.
- It can be organized to integrate with – and reinforce – your capital campaign and special project fundraising efforts.

Annual campaigns have traditionally used direct mail: letters, brochures, catalogs or a combination of all three, usually with some form of response, such as a postcard. Contemporary annual campaigns also employ email, social media, and text or SMS communications to connect with donors who prefer digital media. In either case, the annual fund drive is usually timed near the end of the calendar year (mid to late December) to remind donors of the opportunity for last-minute tax deductions for their charitable gifts. Another logical time to launch an annual campaign would be around the anniversary date of an organization's founding, or just before the beginning of a new cycle of activities such as an educational program, a live performance season, or a special exhibition of a compelling artist or genre.

Since annual campaigns are designed to attract a broad range of donors, the gift or pledge amounts often start at a fairly low level (as little as $20 or $50 for the year) and scale up to higher levels, with associated higher benefits. Sometimes a membership in the arts organization is offered as part of the appeal, but often the gift is solicited purely as an expression of support for the venture's mission and purpose. Rewards for higher gift levels can include VIP access to pre- or post-event receptions, special mention in the organization's annual report and on their website, or opportunities to meet visiting artists in person.

Major Gifts

> Major gift fund raising – with its emphasis on face-to-face contact and solicitation – is effective for sponsorships, funds for special projects, pace-setting operations contributions, and capital and endowment campaigns.[6]

The definition of a "major gift" will depend on the scale of your organization's overall funding picture: a small operation may consider $1000 as a major gift, while a large institution might define a major gift as one million dollars or more. Regardless of a major gift's size, the important point is that it is based on an established relationship between the donor and the organization. Major gift donors are very engaged with an organization's mission and purpose – they may have started as individual donors at a lower level and gradually enhanced their giving based on their desire to provide high-level support for programs and projects. Or, they may have an increasingly vested interest in the institution's impact in the local community. Major donors may also have strong social/professional links with members of the board of directors, along with other key players in the organization's support network. Identifying potential donors for major gifts is a very important aspect of your overall development strategy. The process for researching and approaching major gift prospects is examined later in this chapter.

As the quote above indicates, there are several categories of support that are a good match for major donors:

- *Sponsorships*: Special events provide an attractive opportunity for major donor support. These can include a VIP dinner, auction, special event, or other gathering. A major donor can underwrite the costs of an event, allowing the organization to earn contributed income from the participants. In addition to providing a lively social atmosphere, special events are also an efficient way to reach groups of potential supporters for the future.

- *Special projects*: Like foundation support for a specific project, major donors can provide funding for a programmatic need. For example, you might notice an acknowledgment in a concert program: "Tonight's performance made possible thanks to generous support provided by J. Smith." This means that a major donor underwrote some or all of the costs related to a single artistic presentation. Sometimes major donors will support an entire series – or season – of performances that align with their interests. The same is true for gallery exhibitions, educational programs, and other initiatives. The key is to connect your organization's projects and programs with the interests of a major donor.

- *Operations*: For ongoing expenses, such as space rental, administrative salaries, outside services, and general supplies, major donors can provide support in the form of annual, quarterly, or monthly donations. These "unrestricted" contributions help underwrite the overall activities and goals of your organization – they can also be renewed annually and provide an important component in sustaining your organization over time.

- *Capital and endowment campaigns*: Raising large sums of money takes time, patience and perseverance. Relationships with major donors must be "cultivated" to produce significant contributions for your organization's growth and continued success. The rewards for the donor are also significant: they are involved in building and sustaining an arts organization they care about. Ultimately, the donor participates in the institution's mission via contributed support and receives public recognition for helping the organization attain its goals.

> Write up to one page each on the funding methods your organization will use to raise money: gifts, grants, in-kind donations, planned giving, annual campaign, and major gifts. Create a folder named Funding Methods and place your documents inside it.

Crowdfunding

The term crowdfunding refers to a fundraising strategy for attracting a large number of donors who contribute mostly small amounts of money to a specific project or other outcome – the collective resources generated by the "crowd" allow the project's creators to accomplish their ambitions. The online versions of this relatively recent phenomenon have become extremely popular, with platforms such as Kickstarter and Indiegogo helping individuals and organizations – especially those in the arts – raise money for a wide range of interesting projects. The crowdfunding industry continues to grow rapidly, with new platforms emerging every year. There are some key differences that distinguish each crowdfunding platform, for example, Kickstarter requires a campaign to reach or exceed its stated monetary goal before the creators receive any money, while Indiegogo allows creators to keep what they have earned even if they don't reach their goal. Despite these and other differences, there are some basic concepts and techniques that apply to all forms of crowdfunding.

The History of Crowdfunding

Many sources acknowledge a music tour as the first instance of online crowdfunding.[7] In 1997, the British rock band Marillion found itself without enough financial resources to undertake a planned US tour, so a fundraising campaign was launched on the internet to help them achieve their goal. An even earlier instance of non-internet crowdfunding was the 1885 campaign to raise money to finish the pedestal for the Statue of Liberty in New York – this newspaper-based effort attracted over 160,000 donations, mostly of very small amounts.[8] Although these early examples occurred under very different conditions than the ones we experience today, the underlying reasons for their success are consistent with those found in contemporary crowdfunding campaigns: they had the ability to attract large numbers of small donations through a network of supporters to reach a well-defined goal.

What Are the Elements of a Successful Crowdfunding Campaign?

There are a number of key ingredients that will help your organization raise money using a crowdfunding platform:

- a clear, compelling story, told with engaging content, including text, photos, videos, audio, and other materials;
- a network of friends, family, and other potential supporters who know you and your work and are likely to make a contribution;
- a well-crafted communications plan that keeps actual and potential donors informed, inspired, and entertained by your story as your campaign develops ... and beyond;
- an effective mobile/social media infrastructure that employs email, texts, instant messages, and a variety of updates and regular new content on platforms, such as Facebook, Instagram, Twitter, and YouTube.

Content

The best way to start learning how to develop a successful crowdfunding campaign is to study websites such as Kickstarter or Indiegogo, where online fundraising projects are hosted. There you will discover the importance of telling a compelling story via words, images, and sound. A well-crafted presentation will convey your project's goals to prospective donors and entice them with rewards to provide support.

The materials you developed earlier in this chapter (expanded mission statement and value for customers) provide a good starting place for your crowdfunding campaign. This information provides the background for your project, which should be a specific, achievable, and reasonably priced goal that is central to your organization's mission. Examples include an event such as a concert tour or recording project for musicians, a gallery exhibit or published catalog for visual artists, or a set of instructional materials and new website for an arts education program. There are many examples of successful projects in the arts that have used crowdfunding to attract support – take some time to explore both the campaign guidelines and sample projects found on the websites of several crowdfunding platforms before you design your own project.

Developing clear, compelling written content is an essential part of your organization's overall public presence. This includes your marketing materials, planning documents, and – especially – fundraising statements. In the context of a crowdfunding campaign, your written materials should be less formal than other situations: a more casual, friendly, and informal tone works better when communicating with online donors, since many of your supporters may be your own family and friends. Read through all of the text used by several successful crowdfunding campaigns to get a sense of what kind of writing style might be appropriate – and successful – for your campaign.

Audiovisual content is also very important for your project. The introductory video you create for your campaign should be lively, informative, entertaining, and brief. Good quality video and audio content are essential, although many people produce excellent results using only a smart phone and basic video production software. The video that explains your project should tell an engaging story in a way that represents your personality and that of your organization – your donors will feel a connection to your project's organizers (you and your company) and will want to participate in helping you reach your fundraising goals. Keep your video simple and entertaining: be yourself, have a sense of humor, and get your message across in direct, unambiguous terms.

Most crowdfunding campaigns offer rewards to donors, with high-level contributions providing higher-level rewards. For example, a $10 donation might offer an acknowledgment of the donor's name on your website, while a $250 donation might include a private lunch where the donor gets to meet your organization's key staff. Look over some sample campaigns in your venture's general category to get a sense of how to structure your reward levels.

There are many ways to design a crowdfunding campaign, from a simple project with modest goals (raising $500 to produce and distribute original art prints) to ambitious, large-scale initiatives (raising $50,000 to develop an arts residency center). The key to making your campaign stand out from the competition is to keep your project focused on your unique personality and vision: create videos, still images, and text that tell an interesting story in an entertaining way and people will notice you and want to get involved. The same can be said of your other outreach efforts using email, text/IM, social media, and websites.

Network

Who will you contact to solicit donations for your project? Some artists or arts organizations launch their first crowdfunding campaign with an extensive network of family, friends, and professional contacts already in place. If you have hundreds – or even thousands – of contacts via email, text, or social media, such as Facebook, Twitter, Instagram, LinkedIn, etc., then you are well on your way to attracting a significant number of donors to your cause. If, on the other hand, you have a fairly modest number of people in your email database or social network, you can still launch a low-level campaign to test the potential for funding your project. For example, a photographer could create a $500 campaign to raise money for a photo essay – donors could receive a signed digital print of an image from the series. If the crowdfunding effort is successful, the next project could be more ambitious as more people become aware of the artist's work. Keep in mind that crowdfunding platforms not only provide opportunities for raising money from people you already know, they also promote your project to people you haven't met yet, who are browsing through Kickstarter, Indiegogo, etc. and looking to become involved in interesting creative projects.

If crowdfunding is high on your list of fundraising strategies, you should proactively develop as many connections as you can via email and social media. Over time you will have more people to communicate with about your projects and a greater likelihood of running successful campaigns. Growing and curating your contact list for crowdfunding campaigns is no different than expanding your marketing network. In fact, crowdfunding is an excellent way to "advertise" your work to an audience of potential patrons/consumers who may want to continue supporting you and your organization into the future.

The Campaign Cycle

Some arts organizations and individual artists use crowdfunding repeatedly to build a community of support and sustain their ambitions through a series of compelling projects. The level of donor involvement in your artistic practice is key in attracting and retaining supporters for your projects. Publish regular updates on your campaign's progress and your project's success to keep people connected to you and your mission. Follow through by quickly distributing rewards and sending post-campaign messages to help build credibility and continuity for your organization.

These steps will help you launch your first crowdfunding effort, successfully raise money for a project, grow your network of supporters, build a sustainable organization, and achieve your goals through a series of campaigns:

- Spend some time on Kickstarter, Indiegogo, and other online fundraising platforms to learn about the rules, strategies, and techniques involved in using their services.
- Examine active and completed projects to learn about campaign structure (project descriptions and financial goals, reward levels) and content development, such as videos, messages, and web links. Note how each creator tells a "story" about themselves and their project.
- Outline one or several ideas for projects of your own that would be well suited to crowdfunding. Design projects that reflect your interests, ambitions, and unique talents. Based on your study of similar campaigns, choose rewards that are appealing to prospective donors but not too expensive or difficult to deliver (especially at the higher giving levels).
- Make a comprehensive list of all of your contacts who might be potential candidates for donating to your campaign.
- Scale your campaign deliverables and financial goal according to the size of your network of contacts. Make your first campaign easy to fund, the project easy to complete, and rewards easy to distribute.
- Organize your campaign content and contact list, then launch your online project, making sure to notify and stay in touch with as many potential or actual supporters as you can through email, websites, social media, and text/IM channels.
- After your campaign finishes, make sure to thank your supporters and distribute rewards quickly to earn credibility and generate interest for future projects.

Once you have successfully completed your first campaign:

- Document your project by organizing and archiving the content (video, photos, text, and other materials) and store everything in a location that is easy to find for future reference.
- Keep detailed records of who supported your campaign, what their interests are and how to reach them.
- Design your next campaign – or series of campaigns – around ideas and themes you developed during your initial research and have refined or augmented as a result of your first experience with crowdfunding.
- Continue acknowledging and expanding your network of supporters to develop an ever-growing donor base.

Fundraising Via Email, Websites, Social Media, and Text/IM Channels

> Those nonprofits that focus on creating content and use as many communication channels and fundraising tools as their budget allows are the most successful in achieving their fundraising goals.[9]

The traditional methods for communicating with donors – such as postcards, letters, brochures, and phone calls – are still very effective at reaching people and cultivating relationships that provide support. With the widespread use of new media, we now have an additional set of opportunities for contacting individuals, raising awareness, and attracting contributed income. Designing and implementing a fundraising strategy that incorporates communication channels such as websites, email, social media, and text/IM requires a good deal of effort to effectively plan, organize, and execute. The results, however, can be significant, and may end up providing financial and other support at levels that exceed traditional methods.

Websites

Most arts organizations and individual artists create a website that serves a number of purposes:

- to present their mission, structure, products, and services using text and visual and audio content;
- to announce events and attract an audience;
- to sell tickets, subscriptions, and merchandise;
- to express opinions, give information, and tell anecdotes via articles and blogs;
- to invite visitors to interact via comments and other postings.

Like other aspects of your arts business, such as marketing and organizational development, introducing an effective fundraising component into your website takes some careful planning, quality execution, and regular evaluation to produce results. Many of the people you hope to attract as potential donors will want to visit your website to learn more about you and your organization. This is especially true if traffic to your site is being driven from sources such as search engine results, online ads, referrals from other sites, links embedded in email and text messages, or postings on social media.

There are some important web design concepts for fundraising that focus on ease of discovery and ease of use. Discovery means both how people find their way to your site and how they navigate to a donation opportunity once they are there. Use refers to the donor's online experience: finding the donation page, selecting a contribution amount, entering name/

address/credit card information, completing the transaction, and receiving an acknowledgment. Your web presence should be designed to *look* and *function* as well as possible, given your resources for hiring a web designer or capacity for programming your own site. Study the donation pages of existing non-profits (they don't necessarily have to be arts-related) to learn about visual designs and functional methods for accepting contributions.[10]

Web design tools and techniques are constantly evolving, so plan on having your web designer (or yourself) regularly investigate the latest programming techniques for improving your site's look and functionality with respect to fundraising. Placing a large "Donate Now" button on your home page may not be the best, or only, solution to attracting contributions on your site. Making your web presence easy to navigate from different devices is also becoming increasingly important: many arts organizations construct dynamic websites that perform equally well on multiple platforms, such as desktop or laptop web browsers, smart phones, and tablets.

Email

Although email has in some ways been surpassed by social media and text/IM as the communication channel of choice for younger users, there is still a great deal of value in building and regularly using a database of email contacts for your arts organization. Email allows the sender to develop messages that have more written and visual content than a typical text or social media posting. This gives you more space to develop your fundraising appeal and connect with a donor – by distributing an e-newsletter, for example.

Many fundraisers use email communications software such as MailChimp or Constant Contact to maintain email lists, send announcements, and track the effectiveness of their email campaigns. Your email can include attachments such as an e-newsletter or other document, links to your website or donation page, or other interactive content, such as buttons that initiate donations, event RSVPs, or other actions. As with your website, designing your email to be mobile-compatible is the best way to reach the largest number of prospective donors, since many people use smart phones to read and respond to email. Like your website and printed materials, your email messages should be easy to interact with and visually appealing. All of your electronic communications should convey the personality of your organization in a compelling, accessible fashion.

Social Media

The opportunities to reach prospective donors through Facebook, Twitter, Instagram, YouTube, and other platforms are something every arts organization should evaluate. If you already have extensive connections via social networks, then it makes sense to incorporate these existing contacts into your overall fundraising strategy. If you want to attract donors to a new venture by using a selected group of integrated web, mobile, and social media channels, you should be able to initiate and grow a community of supporters with relatively low financial costs, especially compared to traditional print advertising or direct mail. The challenges are in your ability to plan, execute, and evaluate productive fundraising campaigns using social media. It takes time and skills to create effective, regular donation appeals in any medium ... will you be able to dedicate enough hours to this aspect of your business while developing and running your programs, managing bookkeeping, marketing products, and supervising staff and volunteers? The payoffs of using social media for fundraising and marketing can be significant, but it is important to remember that there is a cost in terms of *time* to make this strategy work. To explore ways to incorporate social media into your overall fundraising strategy, visit some social media pages of arts organizations in your general category and look for focused donation appeals, time-limited giving campaigns, or ongoing opportunities to provide support. As with crowdfunding, there is a lot to learn from existing examples of social media fundraising – adapting and applying strategies developed by other arts organizations is a good way to get started.

Text/Instant Messaging (IM)

The importance of mobile compatibility for your website and email has been discussed above because so many people now use mobile devices for most, if not all, of their communications needs. Mobile alerts and text-to-give campaigns are efficient methods for reaching potential donors directly on their smart phones or tablets. Text-to-give campaigns are focused on urgent, time-sensitive situations where raising money quickly is a necessity – the mobile giving response to the Haiti earthquake in 2010 raised over $35 million in a few weeks. In the case of an arts organization, text-to-give should be employed sparingly – for example, if there is a budget shortfall for an upcoming performance or at the end of the year to encourage tax-deductible donations.

Mobile alerts are notices sent via text or instant messaging (IM) – including photo or video sharing – that provide information and invite involvement in some activity. Contacting your donor base via mobile alerts is an effective way to draw people's attention to an upcoming event, promote media exposure such as a favorable press review, or encourage participation in a special giving opportunity. Each message can contain a link to a specific page on your website or social media channel, allowing the reader to explore the content of your announcement and reserve a seat for a concert, learn about your crowdfunding campaign, or volunteer some time to help organize a social event.

Even though recipients of your mobile alerts and text-to-give messages have offered their contact information because they support you and your organization's mission, the people on your contact lists shouldn't feel pressured or overburdened with too many messages and requests. Don't overuse the opportunities to reach donors via text/IM and they will reward you with support when you do contact them.

Special Events

> Special events have the potential, if undertaken properly, to generate substantial funds and to cultivate prospects. Special events increase an organization's visibility, producing greater public awareness of its programs.[11]

Bringing people together in the same physical location is an excellent way to introduce your organization to supporters and customers, especially if your arts business has its own space. Even if you have to rent or borrow a ballroom, theater, nightclub, or other venue, organizing a special event has many benefits:

- You and your staff can interact one-on-one with a variety of participants.
- Visitors can ask questions and get to know about your organization's people and programs on a personal level.
- You can develop the essential word-of-mouth recommendations that come from people interacting in a social setting.

Raising money from a special event takes careful planning and preparation. It is all to easy to overspend on catering, music, decorations, advertising, and other services, so scale your event to a level appropriate to your donor base. Special event income can be generated by sales of tickets (for example, $500 per person), which are attractive to donors because the expenses can be tax-deductible. (Note: The Tax Cuts and Jobs Act of 2018 increased the standard deduction for taxpayers, which might cause some donors to revise their charitable giving strategies. See the reports on this topic published by the National Council of Nonprofits.[12]) The first step is to develop an invitation list from the personal contacts: your own, those of your board of directors, your staff and your high-level volunteers, to see if an income-producing event is likely to be successful, given the number and giving capacity of the guests/donors you identify.

One way to keep costs down and make your event financially successful is to seek in-kind donations from local business owners who can provide food and beverage services, invitation printing, space, and other support. Your in-kind donors can receive valuable exposure to your carefully chosen guests for their future business, which is especially attractive to new companies looking to become established and develop their customer base.

Write up to one page each on fundraising concepts for your arts organization using crowdfunding, email, websites, social media, text/IM channels, and special events. Place them in your Funding Methods folder.

Once you have articulated your organizational needs and identified funding sources and techniques that are appropriate to the ambitions and scale of your operation, it is time to turn your attention to the donors themselves.

Understanding Why and How People Give

Understanding the reasons why people give to individuals or organizations will help shape your fundraising tactics and provide a basis for your overall development strategy. The commonly heard phrase "People give money to people" is true enough in terms of focusing on the importance of personal relationships at the core of most donations. However, there are some valuable insights to be gained by examining the range of motivations that compel people to give to a cause they support.

> Myriad reasons exist for people giving of themselves and their wealth through volunteerism and philanthropy ... Most scholars find that philanthropic gifts and prosocial behaviors are motivated by a blend of altruism and self-interested motives ... Some gifts are given out of a motivation to receive recognition, whether it is for access to networking opportunities, to receive tax deductions, or to see their name etched into a building or on an endowed professorship.[13]

Altruism refers to the capacity to give selflessly for the benefit of others. As the quote above indicates, most people are motivated to donate money, time, and other resources to a cause they support through a blend of altruism and self-interest. An individual might provide a substantial contribution to a fundraising campaign because the money will be put to good use *and* because the donation provides recognition, social status, and other rewards to the donor. In this regard, the arts and culture are similar to other social causes, such as health, education, and environmental issues. There are some unique features to artistic practice and engagement that will attract some donors but not others – it very much depends on the interests and motivations of the individual.

Below are some ways to think about what motivates donors to give:

- *Public good* is a highly selfless form of giving that is purely for the benefit of others. This kind of contribution is driven primarily by the needs of the recipient, rather than by the interests of the donor.

- *Private good* refers to the connections donors feel with the person or organization being supported. The donor feels a sense of identification with the recipient, so the support is partly a reflection of the donor's promotion of his or her own values and aspirations.
- *Relationship marketing* and *social exchange* are concepts that emphasize the value found in long-term connections (relationships) between donors and recipients, or transactions (exchanges) between funders and charitable organizations that are built on mutual interest and reciprocity. Alumni campaigns are an example of relationship marketing, where strong sentiments and associations with the brand (for example, the donor's former school) are cultivated to inspire giving. Naming a project, program, or building after a donor is an example of social exchange, where the supporter receives public recognition and other benefits in return for their gift. Other types of returns to donors include reaching specific targets for program development, expanding audience engagement, or achieving new levels of financial stability for the organization.
- The term *venture philanthropy* describes donor-recipient relationships where venture capital practices in business management (such as risk management, growth, and return-on-investment) are applied to charitable organizations.

The range of donor motivations can be envisioned as a spectrum, with purely altruistic, selfless giving on one end and highly managed and measured venture philanthropy on the other. Most donors would be located somewhere between these two extremes.

Understanding donor motivation is essential when designing cultivation strategies for approaching individuals, but it is also useful when researching foundations, corporations, and government programs. Arts organizations offer donors opportunities to support a cause they feel connected to on both an emotional and intellectual level – a major donor to your arts education program might have strong feelings about the role of arts in society and be motivated by the opportunity to make a positive impact on the lives of young artists and the broader community. Developing an awareness of the donor's hopes and aspirations is the first step toward building a productive relationship that serves the interests of both the giver and the beneficiary.

Researching Funding Sources

Individuals

Most arts organizations have a board of directors or advisory panel to provide guidance and support as the business grows and evolves. Even small arts-related ventures need a group of experienced specialists to help plan and execute the mission. This could include advisors with experience in legal, accounting, or marketing issues. Outside of this core team will be the owner's close personal relationships, such as family, friends, and professional contacts. Beyond this group will be informal contacts, social media followers, and "friends of friends," who may have heard about the organization but haven't (yet) interacted with its products and services. The community of stakeholders expands outward in concentric circles, with the strongest allies in the center and potential supporters toward the outer edges. This map is the basis for understanding and approaching your individual giving prospects.

Some arts organizations require substantial financial contributions from their board members, while others rely on their leadership for access to members of the community who have the interest and capacity to give to the venture. Fundraising from the inside out is an effective way to send a compelling message to prospective donors: "The core team has already given to the cause; join us and be part of making this extraordinary venture a success."

Starting with yourself, your staff, and your closest advisors or board members, create a confidential database of current and prospective individual donors that includes the following information:

- name and contact information: mailing address, phone numbers, email addresses, web and social media links
- current employment
- professional career, educational background, awards or other recognition
- affiliations
- personal information: date and location of birth, family members' names
- interests, especially those related to your arts organization's mission
- financial data: income, net worth, property and other assets
- giving history (if relevant).

This data should be safely stored in an environment that is only accessible by the company's owner or a designated fundraising professional. Confidential information about prospective donors should never be shared with others because it undermines trust and risks damaging the credibility of the entire operation.

Building on this base of internal stakeholders, ask each member of your core group to provide as many names of potential donors as possible. The aim is to create a list of contacts who have both an interest in helping your organization succeed and the capacity to give at some level – you are seeking donors who are capable of giving small amounts as well as major donors who can provide large contributions. Reaching out through the existing personal networks of your colleagues and advisors allows you to attract interest to your organization through established channels. These informal communication pathways allow you to reach out to new donors while keeping your internal stakeholders engaged and productive. Personal relationships are essential in establishing trust and attracting support, especially if your venture is new and just beginning to create a track record of results.

To add referrals to your database of potential individual donors, you need to conduct some research via local media sources, online prospect research sites, and conversations with people who can supply information about the donor's background, interests and giving capacity. The Foundation Center website has an excellent list of online resources for conducting prospect research for individual donors.[14]

The outermost "circle" of prospective individual donors includes social media contacts, email list subscribers, and other people whose relationship with the arts organization is established yet somewhat more distant. Collect all of these contacts into a list for distributing news about your venture and sending out event announcements and invitations to giving opportunities, especially for crowdfunding campaigns. You never know when an initially distant contact might become a close supporter of your business, so it is important to convey information to everyone in your network of potential donors in an engaging, professional manner.

Keeping a database of current and potential donors is essential for helping arts organizations achieve their fundraising goals. Along with a growing database of prospective individual donors, an active development effort should include databases for foundations, corporate giving opportunities, and government programs.

Foundations

Grants and other support from foundations are key ingredients in the fundraising strategies of most arts organizations. Just like the research and data collection efforts focused on individual donors, building a foundation database and cultivating productive relationships via your network of contacts can produce vital contributed income to help your venture succeed.

The motivations for giving associated with foundations are different than those for individual donors: foundations are legally obligated to distribute at least 5 percent of their assets each year. Like individuals, foundations have a variety of interests and desired outcomes associated with their giving. Foundations also have different expectations in terms of engagement and oversight: some will provide a grant and ask for little or no feedback or reporting from the recipient, while others will require detailed interim and final reports on a funded project, along with expecting other information and interactions.

The giving policy of a particular foundation will often reflect the interests of the foundation's original donor, the donor's family, or the foundation's board of trustees. Many foundations determine the focus of their philanthropy by identifying problems in a particular discipline. The needs of the local community or issues of national or international concern may also affect a foundation's giving policies. Awards are granted to institutions that have projects designed to solve those problems.[15]

There are several different types of foundations:

- *Family foundations* are usually created by an individual donor. Their asset management responsibilities and grantmaking programs are often handled by other members of the same family.
- *Corporate foundations* are designed to advance the philanthropic interests of companies. Often there are specific local or regional causes linked to corporate giving programs, as well as certain expectations regarding publicity and other acknowledgments of the company's support.
- *Community foundations* pool together resources from individuals in a city, county or region. Their grant programs are focused on local issues and are distributed by a board of community representatives.
- Instead of managing their own programs, *private foundations* provide grants to other organizations for programs they run.
- *Operating foundations* provide funds for their own programs, sometimes distributing small grants to outside organizations.
- *Trusts* are funds or foundations that have seen their operational management pass to friends or professional contacts. Trusts are often managed by bank officials or law firms.

How does an arts entrepreneur identify foundations that are good candidates for supporting their venture? The opportunities for foundation support are many and varied, with a wide range of thematic interests, locations, and support levels to consider. The good news is that established programs exist in the foundation world for many art forms – chances are you will be able to find more than one grant program that fits your programmatic focus. The challenge lies in the competitive nature of grant-seeking in this environment: your application for funding will be evaluated alongside many other worthy proposals, and only some will be selected for support.

The first step is to develop a list of foundation targets that fit your area of interest. The Foundation Center has excellent resources for exploring grant opportunities and developing skills to write successful grant proposals. Created in 1956, the Foundation Center has a wealth of information and training programs for people looking to make connections with grant funding from a variety of sources.[16] In addition to their field offices in New York, Atlanta, Cleveland, San Francisco, and Washington, DC, their website provides access to foundation research tools such as GrantSpace and the comprehensive Foundation Directory Online. Although there is a fee for using some of the Foundation Center's most valuable services, their online resources can be accessed for free via Funding Information Network locations, such as libraries, community foundations. and other non-profit resource centers.

There are also books, articles, and other websites devoted to grant writing that have information to help you find foundations and develop award-winning proposals. You can also research other arts organizations in your thematic area and geographic location to see who has been funding programs similar to yours. Don't overlook the importance of person-to-person communication: talking with your advisors and peers about fundraising for your venture can reveal information about giving opportunities that might not be discovered through online or printed sources.

Once you have chosen your research tools, the next step is to design a strategy for identifying and applying for funding opportunities that are a good fit for your venture's projects and programs. Using keyword searches (music, dance, film, education, etc.) in the Foundation Center's *Foundation Directory Online* will produce results showing grant programs that address those areas. Further refinement of your search can restrict results to local or regional geographic areas – this is a good way to identify foundations that are in your vicinity that might have some awareness of you, your organization or your board of directors and network of advisors. Developing relationships with local foundations is a good way to become established and grow your community of supporters: in some cases, your database of nearby contacts may include members of a target foundation's grant review committee. Just like your search for individual donors, your search for foundation grant programs should start with your closest potential geographic and thematic sources and expand outward to more distant (but still relevant) funding opportunities.

Corporations

In addition to the corporate foundations investigated during the research described above, there are giving programs located within corporate departments such as community relations, corporate responsibility, and public affairs. Some companies encourage their employees to donate to causes they support by providing matching funds or other incentives. Researching non-foundation corporate giving programs can be accomplished using the same tools and techniques used for foundations: the Foundation Center's GrantSpace site has a wealth of information about corporate philanthropy, including articles, web links and webinars.[17] Use their *Foundation Directory Online* to find local, thematically appropriate candidates for your database of prospective corporate donors. In addition, search online and in local libraries for books, articles, websites, etc. that provide information about fundraising from businesses.

Another approach to corporate giving is to work through your network of contacts to identify local business owners, CEOs, and public relations directors – especially people you and your core team know personally – who might be attracted to the idea of supporting your arts venture. The direct, personal approach can be successful if the proposed support serves the interests of both the donor and the recipient. Remember that in-kind donations (catering, advertising space, printing, or other services) can be just as valuable as cash when seeking support from business owners. Your venture should offer some kind of recognition in return for this type of corporate support, usually in the form of acknowledgments on your website, social media and e-newsletters, as well as in printed materials that are distributed or displayed at public events.

Government

Although the opportunities in the US for arts funding from government sources are less pervasive than those found in other countries, there are still a number of public grant programs worth investigating for possible support, including:

- *Federal programs*, such as the National Endowment for the Arts (NEA), the National Endowment for the Humanities, the Institute of Museum and Library Services, the Corporation for Public Broadcasting, and the Department of Education. There are also art-related funding programs in the United States Geological Survey, the Department of Defense, the General Service Administration and other federal agencies.
- *State/regional arts agencies* are supported in part by appropriations from the NEA, along with funding from state budgets, donations and other income.
- *Local arts agencies* include cities and counties, as well as neighborhood organizations.

Your research into opportunities for government funding should follow the same approach used for foundations and corporations: start with the Foundation Center's GrantSpace site and *Foundation Directory Online* to conduct keyword searches by theme and geographic region, search online and in libraries for additional information on federal/regional/state/

local public grants, explore what other arts organizations in your area have accomplished in government grant-seeking by looking at their websites (usually under "Support") and annual reports, and talk with your advisors and peers about ways to attract support from government sources.

Create a database of prospective donors, with separate sections for individuals, foundations, corporations and government programs. Populate each section with as many appropriate candidates as you can, keeping in mind that your time to engage with each of these opportunities should be in line with the overall scale of your arts organization. In other words, don't start with a database of hundreds of grant programs if you only have the capacity to apply to a dozen or so each year. Try to identify the best fit between external funding sources and your internal programmatic and operational needs.

The Fundraising Strategy

Research –> Cultivation –> Solicitation –> Stewardship

After identifying donor prospects through research and analysis, the next step is to design and execute an overall fundraising plan to help your arts organization reach its financial goals via contributed income. There is considerable competition among non-profit organizations of all kinds – arts, education, health, environment, etc. – for resources from donors, but there are also many opportunities to connect your specific venture with donated funds. In its report on philanthropy during 2017, *Giving USA* noted a recent trend towards increased donation levels:

> In total, *Giving USA* estimates that $410 billion was donated to charity in the United States in 2017 by individuals, corporations, and foundations.[18] This is the eighth consecutive year of growth in giving, following what was an unprecedented two-year drop in giving during 2008 and 2009.[19]

In the area of interest for arts entrepreneurs (Arts/Culture/Humanities), *Giving USA* estimates $19.51 billion were given in total donations during 2017, an increase of 8.7 percent over the previous year (6.5 percent adjusted for inflation).[20] How will you design an effective strategy to compete for grants, gifts, and in-kind support?

Although each arts business has a development approach tailored to its particular needs and circumstances, a good way to start shaping your fundraising strategy is to look at how other arts organizations raise money. For example, data from the National Endowment of the Arts 2012 publication. *How the United States Funds the Arts* shows the proportions

Table 4-1 Different funding sources for not-for-profit performing arts groups and museums, 2012.

Source of funding	(%)
Individuals	45
Foundations	21
Corporations	19
Local government	7
State government	5
Federal government	3

of different funding sources for not-for-profit performing arts groups and museums (Table 4-1).[21]

Individuals are clearly the largest category of donors in this example, which is also the case for many arts organizations in other disciplines. This breakdown of donation sources would be a good starting place for deciding where to focus your attention when seeking contributions. Over time you can adjust your "donor mix" according to what works for your business.

Your fundraising strategy will contain four basic elements: research, cultivation, solicitation and stewardship. Each of these activities will require careful preparation and follow-through to deliver results. Fundraising needs to be managed year-round to keep your efforts engaged and productive.

For conducting research on fundraising opportunities, this chapter's previous section on researching funding sources lays out the concepts and techniques for building databases of prospective donors, including individuals, foundations, corporations, and government agencies. For a new arts venture, it is probably more important to focus on the *quality* of your initial donor candidates rather than the *quantity* – you want to establish a successful track record of attracting grants and gifts to your business early on, then grow your contributed income across all categories by building on (and frequently referring to) your prior successes.

Cultivation refers to relationship building that inspires interest and forms connections with prospective donors. This is important when working with individuals, especially those in a position to make a major gift to your organization. In-person contact is essential when cultivating individual giving prospects – this is why special events such as VIP tours, invitation-only performances, or other social/professional gatherings are considered the norm when engaging with people who can provide support for your venture. Remember that working from an internal core of advisors, staff, and volunteers outwards toward your network of qualified fundraising prospects is the best way to communicate your organization's mission and attract giving.

Cultivation can also be a factor in developing productive connections with foundations, corporations, and government programs: there are people at the center of each of these programs who will evaluate and sometimes select your grant proposals for funding. Reaching out to people in grant-making positions via email, phone, or in person is part of the process of developing mutually beneficial relationships – this becomes increasingly important as your arts organization becomes established and is able to attract recurring support from reliable sources.

Solicitation refers to the actual "ask" for a contribution, especially in the case of approaching individual donors who may be providing major gifts. Many books, articles and websites have some version of this old adage: "Successful fundraising is the right people asking the right prospects, in the right way, for the right amount, at the right time, for the right reason."

Asking a prospective donor for support requires tact, sensitivity, and a professional demeanor – it also requires that research and cultivation efforts have been productive in identifying the donor's interests, giving capacity, network of relationships, and other connections to the arts organization that is requesting support. With all of this preparation accomplished and communications established between the prospective donor and your organization or its intermediaries, the next step is to schedule an in-person meeting to formally make the request and get feedback.

Here are the six steps to a "model" solicitation from Stanley Weinstein's *The Complete Guide to Fund-Raising Management*:[22]

1. Build rapport.
2. State the case for support.
3. Encourage involvement.
4. Summarize benefits and close.
5. Be quiet.
6. Respond appropriately.

Since asking for support from a donor is part of the ongoing dialogue between the prospect and the arts venture, the solicitation should be both natural and specific. Donors understand their participation is an important part of any arts organization's contributed income. Make a compelling case in the right context to a sympathetic person for a reasonable gift and you will likely find success in attracting contributions from individuals. If a prospect declines the opportunity to give, thank them for their time and evaluate whether to follow-up at some future date – some donors require multiple solicitations to eventually provide support for a cause.

For grants from foundations, corporations, or government agencies, solicitation takes the form of a formal proposal that follows published guidelines. Although some grant programs from smaller foundations only ask for a request letter, most opportunities in this category require a carefully crafted grant proposal that addresses all of the qualifications, project details, and institutional themes laid out by the funding source.

Stewardship and donor relations are about responsibly receiving and managing contributions, privately acknowledging the person or organization making the gift, publicly recognizing the donor's support (when appropriate), and reporting back to the donor on how their donation produced tangible results. The overall goal is to grow and maintain positive relationships with donors via different forms of interaction and engagement.

Keeping these four elements of your fundraising strategy in mind, attention can now be focused on developing and carrying out a comprehensive fundraising plan.

Creating and Implementing Your Fundraising Plan

In this section, you put all of this chapter's previously developed background information, written materials, databases, and strategies into direct practical use to raise money and other support. The fundraising plan is both a map to follow as you launch and sustain your pursuit of contributed income *and* a set of tools for measuring results and refining your future endeavors.

> Create a new folder named Fundraising Plan. Write one page or more for each of the following sections and place the documents in this folder.

1. Fundraising Audit

In this first section you write an objective, detailed account of the resources currently available to pursue grants, gifts, and in-kind donations. This includes:

- *People*: Yourself and other staff, volunteers, or consultants who will be dedicated to fundraising activities.
- *Funds*: From your start-up budget, or specially allocated money from another source.
- *Workspace*: Office or other environment with computers, printers, phone, web access, mailing supplies, etc. Also potential venues for fundraising events such as performances or VIP receptions.
- *Time*: A work schedule that allows for fundraising meetings, planning sessions, research, donor interactions, special events, campaigns (including online and in-person projects), and all other activities related to your development program.

You can adjust the categories within your fundraising audit as you fill out the remaining sections of your plan. The aim of this section is to develop an honest picture of your fundraising *capacity* at this point in time. Like other components of your fundraising plan, this section will change as your arts organization matures: after a year of operating your business and realizing success in attracting contributed income, you will be able to write a new audit based on your evolving capacities.

2. Goals and Organizational Needs

Using materials written earlier in this chapter, develop a clear list of what you will be raising money for: programmatic needs such as staff and space for a new arts education program, infrastructure needs such as computers, web design, and hosting for an online project, etc. Make your list comprehensive but also time-constricted: your goals should be accomplishable within a reasonable time period (six months, one year, two years) that aligns with the expectations of your prospective donors.

Note that this part of your fundraising plan is intended for internal planning and analysis purposes only. When it comes time to develop materials for cultivating donors, writing grant proposals and presenting giving opportunities, you will want to focus on *external* problem solving and public benefits, not your *internal* issues and concerns. Donors, including individuals and foundations, will be persuaded less by your venture's needs and more by the positive outcomes, impacts, and results your programs will deliver to a defined community. The "Goals and organizational needs" section of your fundraising plan serves to identify areas where donations will improve your organization's programmatic and operational functions – when writing productive fundraising materials for prospective donors, your focus should be on your venture's unique and effective capabilities for solving problems and delivering benefits to society.

3. Identify Funding Sources

In this chapter's earlier section on researching funding sources, the concepts and techniques were laid out for identifying prospective donors, including individuals, foundations, corporations, and government programs. Since the databases associated with your donor research will be changing constantly – with new, updated information being incorporated regularly and prospects being added or deleted over time – this part of your fundraising plan should be a snapshot of your best targets for funding in each category at a given moment. Based on your research and input from close advisors and consultants, list the major donors, foundations, corporate programs, and government agencies that you believe have the highest likelihood of providing support based on your funding proposals.

4. Develop Materials

As you can tell from the assortment of writing tasks throughout this chapter, there is a wide range of materials that need to be produced when conducting a successful fundraising program:

- an expanded mission statement with descriptions of your organizational structure, value for consumers, target market, fundraising goals, and strategy;
- descriptions of your programmatic, operational and infrastructure needs, and capital project ambitions;
- materials to support an annual campaign and major gift initiative;
- content for your crowdfunding campaign, including compelling background information on yourself and your project, scripts for introductory videos, and copy for email, texts, and social media postings;
- invitations and collateral material for special events;
- externally focused solicitation letters, grant proposals, and support materials that persuasively communicate your organization's ability to solve problems and deliver benefits to society;
- internal documentation on your research, cultivation, solicitation, and stewardship strategies, and productive implementation.

Each of these categories requires a significant amount of time and concentration to produce effective, carefully crafted documents. Take grant writing, for example:

> Grant writing is like a cross between preparing a holiday dinner and running a marathon. The process takes stamina, perseverance, focus, and a lot of effort before the big day. In fact, it takes more preparation than you can ever imagine, especially if you've never done it before.[23]

There is no one-size-fits-all approach to developing effective fundraising materials because there are so many options to choose from in terms of funding sources; add to this the complexity of designing just the right development approach for each specific arts venture and it becomes clear that some professional support or targeted training are required to produce consistent results. For the arts entrepreneur who is just starting out there are two choices:

1. Hire a professional fundraiser to help develop materials tailored to your unique venture, or
2. Train yourself to produce effective content via workshops, books, webinars and other learning resources.

As mentioned earlier, the Foundation Center website (foundationcenter. org) has some excellent online training to help you develop writing skills for fundraising, such as their Proposal Writing Boot Camp. More resources are listed in suggested Further Reading at the end of this chapter.

5. Train People

Along with educating yourself on effective techniques for developing and implementing your fundraising plan, it will be necessary to invest time and other resources in training your staff, volunteers, and other representatives, such as board members. Development staff play a key role in attracting contributed income to most arts organizations, so paying for staff participation in fundraising workshops and courses helps them learn how to deliver results that support the interests of the entire venture. Creating clear lines of communication between managers and staff – and using those channels to reinforce the organization's mission, focus, and fundraising strategies – will inspire greater effort and keep the donation levels on target. Coaching board members and volunteers is especially important in donor cultivation and solicitation: take extra time to rehearse the language your representatives use when meeting with prospective donors to explain the importance of your organization's work and the positive benefits made possible with their contributions.

6. Create a Schedule

Like any other project management situation, fundraising needs a detailed, reasonable schedule that can be constructed, understood, and followed by all stakeholders in the development effort. The schedule organizes fundraising activity into monthly, quarterly, and yearly deadlines, with sufficient time to develop, execute, and evaluate each task. For example, a yearly fundraising schedule might include monthly (or quarterly) grant proposal deadlines, an end-of-year annual campaign, two or more crowdfunding campaigns and monthly goals for soliciting major gift prospects. Some managers use spreadsheets, online calendars, or custom-created documents to generate and follow schedules, while others use commercially available software that is specially designed for project management and scheduling. Like your databases of prospective donors, your fundraising schedule can be stored online and made accessible to (and editable by) your development staff and volunteers.

7. Implement the Plan

Once the elements above are in place (fundraising audit, goals, sources, materials, training, and schedule), it's time to put the fundraising plan into action and produce results. Weekly meetings are a good way to organize and implement your development strategy: usually each member of the fundraising team will report on progress, ask for clarifications or assistance on specific issues, and collectively focus on upcoming deadlines, where the goals and schedule are of particular importance.

The insights gained from your fundraising audit will help guide the scope of your development ambitions so that the sum of all efforts is achievable with the resources (people, budget, space, and time) that are available. As your fundraising efforts produce results and your contributed income grows, more staff and other resources can be added to help build on the momentum.

8. Evaluate Results and Refine/Adjust Future Fundraising Efforts

Assessment is a key concept used by funding sources such as foundations, corporate programs, and government agencies to understand how effectively their donations are being used and measure engagement (people who benefit) and impact (how significant the funded project's results are to external and internal stakeholders). An arts organization should have evaluation systems in place to objectively monitor its fundraising effectiveness and compare results to intended outcomes. Evaluation can be as simple as quarterly reports on contributed income to complex, detailed analyses of donor cultivation/solicitation activities and focus group data on the organization's development efforts.

Like foundations and other funding agencies, the successful arts venture uses insights from unbiased assessment information to make decisions about future goals, strategies, and productivity. For example, an arts education program should regularly measure the grants won, students served, learning produced, and budgets balanced to evaluate past fundraising activity and make plans for the future.

Data Management

Documenting Donor Information, Use of Funds, Reporting for Funders

Keeping accurate records is an essential part of building a sustainable development program. Creating and maintaining databases of prospective donors is one part of the data management effort – documenting how donated funds are actually used is another important element.

Create separate folders for each funded project and store individual documents, such as:

- proposal development materials and correspondence
- income/expenditure data
- narrative reports on programmatic and operational activity and assessment
- other relevant information such as press reviews, photos, videos and quotes from project participants.

Most grants have specific reporting requirements both during and after a project's timeline, so it is imperative to anticipate documentation needs early and gather all of the information needed to produce accurate, compelling reports and other feedback for your supporters. The same is true for individuals, such as major donors, who often receive a customized package of information on the positive results made possible by their contributions. The storehouse of data on donors, proposals, and funded projects should be securely maintained: it is a valuable resource for your current fundraising initiatives and a wellspring of inspiration and content for your future development projects.

Chapter Summary

Fundraising for the non-profit arts venture is an essential part of establishing and sustaining a business. Your investments of time, planning, and effort can produce much-needed support, but it pays to be organized and detail-oriented.

To develop materials for a fundraising program, start with an expanded mission statement and descriptions of your organizational structure, value for customers and target market for consumers. Development plans have specific goals and address institutional needs, such as operations, programs, infrastructure, and capital projects. You can connect your venture's needs with different funding methods, including grants, gifts, and in-kind donations. There are many types of fundraising approaches and sources of support to consider: annual campaigns that attract donations from the regional community, major gifts from individuals with significant resources, crowdfunding from large numbers of donors giving small amounts, other online campaigns using email, websites, social media, and text/IM channels, and special events that bring people together in the same space to interact with the organization's representatives and learn about its programs. People give for different reasons – some are motivated by a selfless, altruistic drive to improve conditions and solve problems in society, while others are motivated by self-interest and the desire for recognition.

Researching prospective donors will help you identify individuals, foundations, corporations, and government programs that can support your arts venture. Your fundraising strategy (research –> cultivation –> solicitation –> stewardship) will be shaped by the intersection of your organization's specific needs with donors whose interests best align with your program's social benefits. To create and implement a successful development plan, conduct an audit to determine your fundraising capacity, describe your goals and needs, identify funding sources, develop materials, train people, create a schedule, implement your plan, and evaluate the results. Keeping detailed records of all your giving prospects, proposals and funded projects will provide the information needed for writing donor reports and developing future fundraising plans.

Discussion Questions

1. Why is fundraising important for a non-profit arts venture?

2. What are the written materials needed to begin developing a successful fundraising plan?

3. How would you describe your arts organization's programmatic, operational, infrastructure, and capital campaign needs? What are the top priorities for attracting support? What funding methods will be best suited to your needs?

4. Imagine you are advising an arts venture as they prepare for a crowd-funding campaign: What are the materials needed to tell a compelling story and attract donations at low, medium, and high levels?

5. Why is it important to safeguard data acquired from your donor research?

6. What are the different motivations for giving?

7. Identify a medium-to-large arts organization in your general thematic area and research all of the funding sources listed on their website and other published materials. What types of funding does this organization attract? How will your venture resemble or differ from this organization's approach?

8. After conducting your fundraising audit, how would you describe your organization's capacity to launch and sustain a complex, multi-dimensional development program? What are the areas where you need the most additional support: personnel, budget for fundraising activities, space to conduct development work, or time to plan, execute, and evaluate fundraising effectiveness?

Notes

[1] National Endowment for the Arts. *How the United States funds the arts*. 3rd Edition (Washington, DC: National Endowment for the Arts, 2012).

[2] See www.irvine.org/arts

[3] See http://arts.gov/grants-organizations/our-town/introduction

[4] See https://about.bankofamerica.com/en-us/what-guides-us/arts-and-culture.html#fbid=KK0-YWNL1PB/hashlink=partnerships

[5] See Chapter 5, Legal Issues, for more information.

[6] Weinstein, Stanley. *The complete guide to fundraising management* (New York: John Wiley & Sons, Inc., 2002).

[7] See www.ukcfa.org.uk/what-is-crowdfunding

[8] See www.bbc.com/news/magazine-21932675

[9] Mansfield, Heather. *Mobile for good: a how-to fundraising guide for nonprofits* (New York: McGraw-Hill Education, 2014).

[10] See http://wiredimpact.com/blog/great-nonprofit-donation-pages/

[11] Hopkins, Karen Brooks, and Carolyn Stolper Friedman. *Successful fundraising for arts and cultural organizations* (Phoenix, AZ: Oryx Press, 1997).

[12] See www.councilofnonprofits.org/how-tax-cuts-jobs-act-impacts-nonprofits

[13] Drezner, Noah D., and Frances Huehls. *Fundraising and institutional advancement theory, practice, and new paradigms* (Hoboken, NJ: Taylor and Francis, 2014).

[14] See http://grantspace.org/tools/knowledge-base/Funding-Resources/Individual-Donors/cultivating-individual-donors#websites.

[15] Hopkins and Stolper Friedman. *Successful fundraising*, p. 67.

[16] See http://foundationcenter.org/

[17] See http://grantspace.org/

[18] See https://givingusa.org/giving-usa-2018-americans-gave-410-02-billion-to-charity-in-2017-crossing-the-400-billion-mark-for-the-first-time/

[19] See http://givingusa.org/encouraging-news-in-the-latest-giving-usa-report/

[20] See https://givingusa.org/tag/giving-usa-2018/

[21] National Endowment for the Arts. *How the United States funds the arts.*

[22] Weinstein. *The complete guide*, pp. 124–125.

[23] Payne, Mary Ann. *Grant writing demystified* (Dubuque, IA: McGraw-Hill. 2011).

Further Reading

Margolin, Judith B. 2008. *The grantseeker's guide to winning proposals.* New York: Foundation Center.

Payne, Mary Ann. 2011. *Grant writing demystified.* Dubuque, IA: McGraw-Hill.

5   Legal Issues

What are the choices for establishing the legal structure for your business? How can arts entrepreneurs protect their creative work via copyright and other mechanisms? How are taxes and liability issues managed? How will your venture be organized in terms of supervision and decision-making?

This chapter introduces important concepts and practices in legal issues and organizational structure for the arts venture, including:

- the benefits of nonprofit status, and how to attain it;
- working with fiscal sponsors;
- for-profit corporate forms and their different attributes;
- recent developments in business models: B Corporations, L3C (see Chapter 2);
- artist's rights under the law: copyrights, patents and trademarks;
- understanding and executing contracts;
- managing taxes, insurance and business risks;
- creating and operating within an organizational structure that suits the needs of your venture;
- documentation requirements for businesses: licenses, permits, accounts.

Disclaimer

This chapter presents a general overview of legal issues for artists and arts organizations. The information is not an exhaustive examination of current, local laws, or optimal legal strategies for each individual situation. Nor is it to be considered legal advice, which should be sought from a qualified, experienced attorney.

Choosing a Corporate Form

Establishing a new business requires a number of key decisions, such as the organization's location, management, and product/service offerings. Identifying an appropriate legal structure is another foundational element in creating and sustaining your arts venture. For example, choosing between for-profit or not-for-profit status will have many implications for tax issues, preparing and filing required documentation, and seeking opportunities for your business to raise money.

Many new businesses – especially those with only one owner – start as a sole proprietorship because it is a simple, direct way of launching the venture using the founder's existing social security number. Others choose a limited liability corporation (LLC) or other corporate form to manage liability and attract investment. New arts organizations looking for charitable contributions from individuals, foundations or other donors will need to connect with a fiscal sponsor as they work towards acquiring their own 501(c)(3) tax exemption from the Internal Revenue Service (IRS).

The following sections describe different options for your arts organization's legal status. Evaluate each one in terms of how well it fits with your business plan and your intended relationship to your organization as the owner or Executive Director. It is possible to start out as a sole proprietor and eventually adopt another corporate form later on, such as an LLC, S Corporation, or 501(c)(3) nonprofit.

Legal Structures for Arts Organizations: Not-for-Profit

Some people misinterpret the phrase "not-for-profit corporation" as a business that doesn't make any money, or that doesn't pay its owners or employees, or that has less intrinsic value than a for-profit business. In fact, quite the opposite is true: nonprofits can be very successful financially, can pay their ownership and staff well, and do create value for both stakeholders and society at large.

The key concept that distinguishes non-profits from other corporate forms is based on the notion of benefits to society. According to the IRS requirements for attaining federal tax-exempt status:

> To be tax-exempt under section 501(c)(3) of the Internal Revenue Code, an organization must be organized and operated exclusively for exempt purposes set forth in section 501(c)(3), and none of its earnings may inure to any private shareholder or individual.[1]

The exempt purposes included charitable, religious, educational, scientific, literary, and other objectives. Arts organizations typically claim educational purposes when seeking tax-exempt status from the IRS because creating and presenting art is considered a valid educational activity. Along with an organization's exempt purpose, earnings must be applied to something other than the personal gain of an owner or shareholder. For example, a nonprofit might apply excess revenue (income after expenses) to reducing debt, expanding staff, repairing or improving facilities, increasing marketing efforts, or launching new programs.

The benefits associated with 501(c)(3) non-profit status are considerable, but there are some complex record-keeping, disclosure, and reporting requirements that accompany them. The upsides are:

- exemptions from sales, property and income tax;
- donors who give to 501(c)(3) non-profits can claim tax deductions for their charitable contributions;
- most importantly, 501(c)(3) nonprofits can apply for grants from foundations, corporate programs, and government agencies.

If attracting donations from individuals and grant programs is an essential part of your business concept, then acquiring 501(c)(3) nonprofit status will be a priority as you develop and launch your venture. (See the latest information on the IRS website[2] for up-to-date details on the application process to become a nonprofit, federal tax-exempt organization.) The timing and processing of your application are important details to understand, along with the reporting requirements once nonprofit status is granted. For example, the IRS states that: 'organizations required to apply for recognition of exemption must notify the Service within 27 months from the date of their formation to be treated as described in section 501(c)(3) from the date formed."[3]

and ...

A charitable organization must make available for public inspection its approved application for recognition of exemption with all supporting documents and its last three annual information returns. The organization must provide copies of these documents upon request without charge (other than a reasonable fee for reproduction and copying costs).[4]

There are numerous responsibilities associated with applying for, acquiring and maintaining 501(c)(3) nonprofit status. For some arts entrepreneurs, this will be a worthwhile investment of time and effort because of the unique tax exemption and contributed income possibilities available to nonprofits. Other business founders might choose to retain their for-profit status while providing "benefits to society" as part of their core mission. Fortunately, there is a method of attracting contributed income as a for-profit organization, and it entails working with a fiscal sponsor.

Fiscal Sponsors

Fiscal sponsors are intermediary organizations that already have their 501(c)(3) nonprofit designation. They work in partnership with arts ventures (such as sole proprietors, LLCs, etc.) and apply for grant funding on their behalf. By *sponsoring* the work of a for-profit arts organization, a fiscal sponsor helps the business get access to grant funding they would not otherwise be qualified for. Examples of fiscal sponsors that specialize in the arts include Fractured Atlas[5] and Intersection for the Arts.[6] You can search for a fiscal sponsor in your area using the Fiscal Sponsor Directory (www.fiscalsponsordirectory.org/).

In order for a for-profit arts venture to work with a fiscal sponsor to seek grants and other contributed income, the organization must have a project or program that benefits society and qualifies as an exempt purpose under the IRS rules. Note that your fiscal sponsor will retain a percentage of the income they help generate (typically around 5–10 percent, sometimes more) to offset the administrative and other costs associated with submitting, managing, and reporting on grants that provide resources for your business. Because fiscal sponsors have varying degrees of responsibility and liability associated with grants they manage on your behalf, they may exercise some oversight and financial control over your funded projects. Weighing the pros and cons of working with fiscal sponsors will take some research and evaluation on your part, but if you intend to raise money from donations, this method can be very successful in providing essential contributed income for your venture.

Legal Structures for Arts Organizations: For-Profit

Not every arts organization is a good candidate for 501(c)(3) nonprofit designation from the IRS, and even those that are will need to decide if they want to follow the many rules and regulations associated with acquiring and maintaining their status as a charitable organization. The following descriptions of for-profit business forms provide an overview of the different options you can consider when planning and establishing your arts venture:

Sole Proprietorship

You do not have to take any formal action to form a sole proprietorship. As long as you are the only owner, this status automatically comes from your business activities. In fact, you may already own one without knowing it. If you are a freelance writer, for example, you are a sole proprietor.[7]

The sole proprietorship is the simplest, most direct choice for creating a business that is owned by one person. The organization's tax identification is the same as the owner's social security number, and business income and expenses are filed as part of the individual's tax return. Although there can be other requirements for running a business (for example, a business license, insurance, an Employer Identification Number, and a fictitious business name registration), the sole proprietorship provides the easiest, least expensive pathway to creating a business. Since the owner and the company are essentially the same "person," there are fewer issues with management and control of the operation when compared with partnerships or corporations that have governance rules and multiple shareholders.

The downsides of operating your arts venture as a sole proprietorship include liability, continuity, and access to capital. Since the organization is tied directly to the owner, any debts or claims against the business are the owner's responsibility. Insurance can help mitigate a sole proprietor's exposure to business losses, but both business and *personal* assets can be at risk under this form of ownership. Continuity refers to the essential link between the owner's availability and the organization's ability to operate: if the owner is sick, injured, or otherwise not actively engaged in daily operations, then the business ceases to function, although having competent staff can reduce this dependency. When raising money to create or sustain a business, sole proprietorships can be less attractive to banks and investors, although some business lending programs such as the Small Business Administration (SBA) can provide support.

Partnership

What if your business concept involves more than one owner? Partnerships are an excellent way to combine talents and resources around a shared vision to help launch and operate an arts organization. Setting up a partnership usually involves two or more people reaching consensus on all of the venture's conceptual and operational details – it is highly recommended that this informal agreement be turned into a partnership contract (with the advice of a qualified attorney) that spells out the roles of each partner, along with other aspects of running the business. Sharing a new organization's responsibilities and costs among multiple partners can be an attractive option for some entrepreneurs, even if the profits and decision-making must also be shared. Like a sole proprietorship, the income and expenses from a partnership are reported on each partner's individual tax return according to the percentages spelled out in the partnership agreement. A partnership offers the same flexibility and freedom as a sole proprietorship in terms of managing the arts venture – there is also a legal structure known as a *limited partnership* that provides some advantages in attracting investors.

Limited Partnership

Corporations that issue stock can secure investment by selling shares in the company. The investors' ownership is represented by the amount and type of stock that is held. Stockholders can easily enter into – or exit from – a vested interest in a corporation by buying or selling shares.

A *limited partnership* provides some of the advantages of this mechanism by selling *limited partnership shares*. For example, a for-profit arts organization could raise money through the sales of 10 limited partnership shares at $10,000 each, totaling $100,000 of investment capital to develop, launch, and sustain the venture. Profits are split among the limited partners according to their percentage of ownership. A limited partner can leave the partnership by selling his or her share to another investor, including another limited partner in the same organization. Unlike the partnerships described previously, limited partners are not involved in the direct management of the company's operations – running the business is the responsibility of the *general partners*. Tax liability is the same as partnerships and sole proprietorships: a limited partner's profits are taxed as personal income. Limited partners are less exposed to potential business losses because their personal assets are not at risk, while general partners are more exposed because debtors can target their personal assets.

Corporation

Forming a corporation allows an entrepreneur to establish an independent entity for his or her business that is legally distinct from the individual who owns and operates it. Corporations are like virtual people: they can enter into contracts, buy and sell property, create and distribute products and services, generate and retain profits, and pursue legal actions against other entities. Different states have different laws governing the creation and ongoing operations of corporations, so researching the rules in the state where you will be conducting business would be a good first step in exploring this option.

Because incorporation establishes a separation between the owner and the arts venture, some entrepreneurs choose this form of ownership in order to reduce the liability of their personal assets in case of any unforeseen business losses or debt recovery. Corporations do provide some protection for investors and owners, but there have been instances where courts will ignore this separation and hold corporate officers and shareholders personally liable for business debts – this is called "piercing the corporate veil."

If forming a corporation for your arts venture sounds like a good fit for your overall business strategy, there are several different options to consider:

A *Standard or C Corporation* provides limited liability for investors and stockholders. It can attract investment through the sales of stock, distribute or retain profits, compete for highly skilled employees by offering stock options, and maintain continuity over time by keeping the company intact while transferring ownership via stock sales. However, a C Corporation is complicated and costly to set up and maintain. Depending on whether the corporation is private or public, there will be many local, state, and federal regulations to comply with. Double taxation is another factor: the corporation pays its own taxes as an independent entity, while the recipients of the company's profits (owners, shareholders) pay an additional tax on their personal income.

An *"S" Corporation* has some of the advantages described above for partnerships. It provides some liability protection because it exists as a separate legal entity from the owners and managers. Since an "S" Corporation's profits are not retained (they flow directly to the stockholders), double taxation is avoided because there is no corporate tax, only personal income tax. The limitations of an "S" Corporation include a maximum of 100 shareholders, the requirement to distribute all profits to individuals (causing those individuals to pay tax on that income and reducing the corporation's ability to retain earnings) and other restrictions on stock classes, tax year definitions, and passive income sources.[8]

LLC (Limited Liability Company)

A Limited Liability Company (LLC) is similar to a limited partnership in that it offers limited liability for the ownership. Although not actually a corporation, an LLC can attract investors and distribute or retain profits. Businesses sometimes choose to form as an LLC in cases where the venture has a pre-determined life span, for example, a movie production company with an operating schedule that has fixed beginning, middle, and end dates.

A Cooperative

A cooperative is owned by its members and is usually focused around a specific service or industry, such as agriculture or collective purchasing of raw materials. Arts ventures formed as collectives give members equal responsibilities for (and rewards from) running the business. Organizations such as the Network of Bay Area Worker Cooperatives[9] provide information and resources on setting up and running a cooperative.

The Benefit or B-Corporation

A recent development in legal forms for businesses, the Benefit or "B" Corporation could be a good choice for an arts organization that doesn't intend to pursue not-for-profit status via 501(c)(3) designation but *does* include benefits to society as a central part of its mission. Becoming a B Corporation allows an arts venture to seek both economic returns and social impact, which is different from other corporate forms (C Corp or S Corp) that could penalize managers for including non-financial interests in their strategies and operations.

> Benefit corporations, also known as "B-Corporations," are designed to allow a for-profit business to be more socially responsible even if it results in lower profits without the risk of liability for managers ... The B-corporation is a great concept for entrepreneurs who want to promote social or environmental objectives.[10]

Although B Corporation status primarily protects managers who wish to pursue both financial gains *and* social benefits, there are other positive aspects to consider as well. B Corporations are certified by an independent agency that evaluates the organization's structure and programs. Once the business is approved as a BCorp, they are able to use a special logo on their printed materials, website, social media, and other communication vehicles. The B Corp designation becomes part of the organization's brand – it tells the world that "this is a company that values benefits to society as well as profits to shareholders." Many consumers are supportive of businesses that actively promote positive social impact on issues such as environmental change, healthcare, and educational opportunities for underserved communities. Having a B Corp certification for your business can signal your organization's core social values while building awareness and engagement among a community of like-minded consumers, investors, and other supporters.

Examples of companies doing business as a B Corp include Ben & Jerry's (ice cream), Patagonia (outdoor clothing and equipment), and Method (home, fabric, and personal care products), although the spectrum of B Corp organizations covers a wide range of many different products and services. At this time the B Corporation designation is not available in all states or all countries, but the trend toward its adoption is growing. Resources for learning more about why and how to become a B Corp can be found at http://benefitcorp.net/ or www.bcorporation.net/.

Some examples of arts organizations that integrate social issues into their mission include:

- a fine arts gallery that features visual works and live events focused on environmental awareness;
- a theater space that encourages local residents to tell stories of triumph over economic or social adversity by developing and performing original plays;
- a multi-disciplinary studio space that supports collaborations involving artists and political activists.

The growing trend around social responsibility for organizations of all kinds is a sign that more business owners – along with their customers and other stakeholders – are committed to engaging with social impact in their professional and personal lives. Arts entrepreneurs who sympathize with this trend should evaluate the B Corp as an appropriate designation for their venture.

L3C Corporation

Another recent addition to the variety of legal forms for businesses is the L3C Corporation, also known as a low-profit, limited liability company (the L3 stands for *low-profit, limited liability*). A variation on the Limited Liability Company (LLC) described previously, an L3C is a for-profit company that can pursue social benefits as part of its mission.

> What sets it apart from regular LLCs and other for-profit entities (i.e. corporations, partnership, etc.) is its ability to pursue charitable, educational or socially beneficial objectives as its primary motive. Although the L3C can also pursue profit-oriented objectives, they are secondary to its social goals. The L3C is a hybrid entity taking on the flexible characteristics of an LLC in combination with a low-profit socially beneficial objective.[11]

An L3C organization actually places its social benefits *before* its profit-seeking ambitions, so in some ways its mission can be even more tied to social impact than a B-Corp. Because of this emphasis on positive benefits to society, an L3C can qualify for funding from a foundation in a specific category known as Program Related Investment (PRI). This makes the L3C a rare case of a for-profit company that can apply for foundation funding without 501(c)(3) nonprofit status *or* a fiscal sponsor. As with the B Corp, the L3C designation is not currently available in all states, and places that do have it are still in the early stages of seeing whether companies will take advantage of the opportunity in significant numbers. More information on L3Cs can be found at http://americansforcommunitydevelopment.org/

Evaluating the Many Choices of Legal Forms for Your Arts Venture

With all of the options available for your business (not-for-profit, for-profit sole proprietor with or without a fiscal sponsor, partnerships, LLCs, cooperatives, C and S Corporations, B Corporations, and L3Cs), it can be challenging to identify the *best* choice for your specific arts venture. One way to work toward a decision is to identify and interview several local art-related businesses in your area to determine why and how they established their legal form – ideally these organizations should be similar to the business idea you are developing. You may discover a local gallery, arts education program, or online business that has experience with one or more of the possible legal forms and can share their experience as you consider your options. Another method is to consult with a lawyer who has specific experience in corporations and other legal forms for artists and arts organizations – some preliminary conversations with an objective, experienced professional can be a very efficient way to evaluate what might work best for you. Also, take a look at the people working in your local law schools: there are professors and staff who know a great deal about legal forms for businesses. You may end up connecting with someone who can help you form your corporation or other entity and advise you as your venture develops and expands.

Create a folder named Legal Structure. Write at least one page describing the choice of legal structure for your arts venture (not-for-profit, for-profit sole proprietor with or without a fiscal sponsor, partnership, LLC, cooperative, C or S Corporation, B Corporation, or L3C). Your description should include *why* the choice of legal form is the best one for your business and *how* you will create that particular form of business.

Artists' Rights under the Law

In this section we focus on legal issues related to the creative product itself. Although laws that concern artists do not address art objects or related actions directly, they do address the *rights* of people who create, distribute, or purchase art, especially in cases where there is some potential for disagreement about ownership and use of original creative work. For example:

- a photographer may find her images included in a private company's advertising campaign without prior consent;
- a musician may discover their composition being copied by another artist and sold under someone else's name, although permission or acknowledgment was never requested;
- an author may learn about a feature film based on his previously published novel.

These scenarios describe instances of *infringement* on the rights of the art object's creators. Legal protections for artists fall under several categories.

Copyright

Probably the most important area of legal protection for artists, copyright law applies to creative works that are "fixed in a tangible medium of expression." This means that the artwork must have been printed on paper, captured on film, or recorded on tape (or as digital data on a disk) before the originator can claim authorship. The categories covered by copyright law are:

literary works

musical works, including any accompanying words

dramatic works, including any accompanying music

pantomimes and choreographic works

pictorial, graphic, and sculptural works

motion pictures and other audiovisual works

sound recordings

architectural works.

Note that copyright protection applies to creative expression only after it has been fixed in some medium, not while it is only an idea or concept. According to the Copyright Law of the United States of America:

> In no case does copyright protection for an original work of author-ship extend to any idea, procedure, process, system, method of oper-ation, concept, principle, or discovery, regardless of the form in which it is described, explained, illustrated, or embodied in such work.[12]

Under copyright law, the rights of authorship are immediately applied the moment the originator's work is fixed in a tangible medium of expression. Although no additional action is required to assert ownership of original creative work, there are additional legal benefits associated with register-ing a copyright with the U.S. Copyright Office. These include the ability to initiate actions for copyright infringement and to seek damages and/or recovery of legal fees, within certain time limitations.

Once authorship has been established, the artist has "exclusive rights to do and to authorize" any of the following:

> To reproduce the copyrighted work in copies or phonorecords;

> To prepare derivative works based upon the copyrighted work;

> To distribute copies or phonorecords of the copyrighted work to the public by sale or other Transfer of ownership, or by rental, lease, or lending;

> In the case of literary, musical, dramatic, and choreographic works, pantomimes, and motion pictures and other audiovisual works, to perform the copyrighted work publicly;

> In the case of literary, musical, dramatic, and choreographic works, pantomimes, and pictorial, graphic, or sculptural works, including the individual images of a motion picture or other audiovisual work, to display the copyrighted work publicly; and

> In the case of sound recordings, to perform the copyrighted work pub-licly by means of a digital audio transmission.[13]

These protections put the creator in control of original work at its incep-tion. Artists can license others to display, perform, reproduce, and distrib-ute their work by assigning exclusive or limited copyright. The terms of these assignments are spelled out in written agreements that are signed by the copyright owner. Arts organizations that want to sell or perform work originated by someone else can negotiate mutually acceptable terms with the copyright holder via contract.

If an artist creates work as part of a salaried position in a company, this is considered *work made for hire* and the copyright belongs to the employer. Work done by independent contractors can also fall into this category, depending on prior written agreements and relevant state laws.

How long does a copyright last once it has been established? If a work was created on or after January 1, 1978, the copyright is in effect for the author's lifetime plus 70 years. After that the work enters the *public domain* and is no longer covered by copyright.

Work that is copyright protected can be used without express written consent in special circumstances known as *fair use*. Copyright law says that fair use of another's original work "for purposes such as criticism, comment, news reporting, teaching (including multiple copies for classroom use), scholarship, or research, is not an infringement of copyright."[14] There are a number of factors that help determine cases of fair use – these should be evaluated with a qualified attorney or other specialist.

The ability to electronically distribute and discover digital artwork such as images or sound files has greatly increased access to copyrighted material. However, this ease of access comes with risks – if you put someone else's photography or music on your website without permission and without proving fair use, you may be liable for copyright infringement.

A nonprofit organization called Creative Commons[15] was established in 2001 and has introduced several new forms of licensing designed to encourage open content and more freedom in the exchange of information. The Creative Commons licenses address varying degrees of attribution, modification, and commercialization for protected work.

Trademarks

> A trademark is a brand name. A trademark or service mark includes any word, name, symbol, device, or any combination, used or intended to be used to identify and distinguish the goods/services of one seller or provider from those of others, and to indicate the source of the goods/services.[16]

Companies use trademarks to establish their brand and make their products or services stand out from the competition. There are many trademarks around us, for example, the Nike "swoosh" graphic, or the name and distinctive typeface used by Coca-Cola. A trademark refers to unique identifiers for an organization's products, while a service mark refers to the same thing for a company's services: for example, the FedEx name and logo.

Artists and arts organizations use trademarks to establish their unique identity in an environment where there are competitors, to promote their business through reinforcement of the mark in advertising and other communications, and to identify themselves as the source of their specific product or service. Like copyright, a trademark exists at the moment it is created and used commercially. However, registering a trademark is a more complex and costly process – it also provides more protections in cases of infringement.

Your trademark application may be approved or denied depending on the existence of other trademarks in the marketplace. The first step in establishing a trademark that can be registered and legally protected is to visit the United States Patent and Trademark Office (USPTO) website and search their database to see if someone else is using similar wording or design. Information on the trademark application process and fees can be found here: www.uspto.gov/

Patents

Patents are less commonly used by arts ventures because they are designed to protect inventions that have a functional application, for example, a new process to develop and deliver a specialized medication. Design patents are sometimes sought to protect creative works, but the process is exceptionally expensive and time-consuming relative to its value. For more information, see the website for the United States Patent and Trademark Office: www.uspto.gov/

Trade Secrets

Artists who develop and employ unique techniques – for creating visual art, music, digital content, etc. – can seek trade secret protection under state law. Some organizations guard their secret information by requiring a signed confidentiality agreement or non-disclosure agreement (NDA) from the people they interact with. Most states provide protection under the Uniform Trade Secrets Act – consult with an experienced attorney or other specialist to explore your local options.

Contracts

Artists of different kinds encounter a wide variety of written, oral and implied contracts ... Contracts for the rendition of personal services are also common, such as contracts for musical, dance or theatrical performances, photography, agent's or artist's representative services, model releases and publishing, distribution and commissioned works agreements.[17]

The variety of contracts encountered by artists and arts organizations underscores the importance of incorporating legal expertise into the group of advisors you will develop around your business. There are many guidebooks, articles, and websites that can help entrepreneurs understand different types of contracts, but actually entering into a contract with someone else requires you *understand* and *consent to* all of the terms and conditions spelled out in the document. Contracts can be straightforward or complicated, but their overall purpose is to state in precise detail an agreement between parties that describes the responsibilities of each participant in unambiguous terms. The aim is to define the actions of – and relationships between – the parties so that each, upon execution (signature) of the document, comprehends and agrees to everything in the contract.

Some examples include:

- a live music venue and a musician enter into a performance contract that spells out the date, time, payment, and other details of an upcoming concert;
- a freelance writer signs a contract with an agency for employment on a content development project for a new website;
- an arts educator agrees to a contract with a school to create and teach a new course on fabric design techniques.

According to Peter Cobb and colleagues: "A contract tells the story of the way the relationship is going to look and work: the who, what, when, where, why and how of the relationship."[18]

Settling on a mutually agreeable contract can take some time and negotiation. An initial version of a contract will spell out an *offer*, for example, a landlord will lease a space to an arts organization for a specific rent amount with certain conditions regarding the length of the lease, security deposit, etc. If the terms are acceptable, then the contract can be signed as is, but if not the arts organization can submit a *counter-offer* with a different proposed rent amount and other details. The counter-offers can go back and forth between the parties until a final version of the contract is agreed upon. The same process can happen with performance contracts and purchase agreements.

A contract's language will be different depending on its purpose, and contract law depends on both federal and state regulations. State arts organizations and advocacy groups (for example, California Lawyers for the Arts, www.calawyersforthearts.org/) offer workshops on understanding and developing contracts for arts-related businesses.

Create a folder named Legal Protections. Write and file at least one page each describing situations where copyright, trademark, patent, trade secret or contract issues will affect your business. Identify legal counsel or other experts who will support your needs.

Tax Planning

Federal, state, and local taxes are an unavoidable necessity for any business owner, even an individual artist operating as a sole proprietor. There are ways to reduce your tax liabilities and meet your obligations, but they require careful record keeping and consistent filing of payments and reporting documents. Fortunately, there are some tools to help arts entrepreneurs stay on top of their tax situation.

Simple Tax Planning

For the individual tax filer organized as a sole proprietor, the main tasks for managing taxes are in documentation, record-keeping, and timely filing of required forms and tax payments. Over the course of a year, an independent artist might receive income from several sources. For example, a musician, photographer, writer or arts educator might:

- be paid by individual clients;
- receive a part-time salary from a school or other employer;
- earn income from the sales of original works through local or online transactions.

In addition to these *income* categories, the same individual will probably have several types of personal or business *expenses*, such as:

- rent, food, transportation, savings, and entertainment expenses that are *personal*:
- supplies, equipment, repairs, business travel, insurance, and educational expenses that are *professional*.

Here are a few of the important points about taxes that sometimes get overlooked by individual artists:

1. When you receive income from sources other than an employer – such as performance fees, sales of merchandise, or independent contractor work – you are taxed *twice*, once as the employer (because technically, you are your own employer), and again as the employee who receives the payments.
2. Deductible business expenses such as those listed above as *professional* must be carefully documented and meet certain criteria to be allowed for exemption. For example, deducting part of the cost of your personal living space because it is used for professional work (such as using a spare bedroom in your apartment for recording and mixing music) is only allowed if the space meets the *regular and exclusive use* regulations of the tax code.
3. All federal, state, and local tax obligations must be met every year in order to avoid problems with missed payments, which can quickly add up when penalties and interest charges are imposed.

How does the individual artist or owner of an arts venture manage tax liabilities and stay out of trouble?

- *Comprehensive record keeping* is the key to staying organized and having important data available when calculating taxes, filling out forms, and making timely payments. Some people use handwritten records on ledger paper, others design spreadsheets using Excel or other programs, and others use bookkeeping software such as Quick-Books to record income and expenses, generate reports, and file tax documents and payments electronically. However you choose to organize your income and expenses, make sure the records are consistent, easy to find, and backed up frequently if stored in an electronic medium.

- *Maintain separate bank accounts* for business and personal transactions. Although this may seem overly complicated for the individual business owner of a small organization, it is a much better option than combining personal and professional banking activity in one account because it allows you to track and document business income and expenses separately. Your two accounts can be within the same bank, allowing you to easily pay yourself with transfers between the business and personal accounts to cover personal expenses such as rent, etc.

- *Develop and follow a schedule* for the entire tax year. This is especially important if you need to make quarterly tax prepayments.

- *Get some help setting up your bookkeeping systems.* As with legal counsel who advise artists through support organizations such as California Lawyers for the Arts, there are qualified accountants who can work with an arts entrepreneur to evaluate tax obligations and help organize bookkeeping systems. If your business relies on QuickBooks, there are online forums and referrals to authorized individuals who can provide training and develop tax strategies tailored to your business. Classes on bookkeeping and tax management can be found in local university extension programs or community college departments. There are also a number of free or fee-based online learning opportunities worth exploring to learn or improve basic bookkeeping skills.

Moderate to Complex Tax Planning

For businesses organized as C- or S-corporations – or for any legal form where the tax obligations of the venture are significantly more than the owner can manage personally – it is essential to hire and regularly consult with an experienced accountant, preferably one who understands your type of business. Finding a good local accountant requires some effort, but it is well worth the time and expense. Start by inquiring through your network of advisors (partners, board members, investors, lawyers, bank officers, or insurance agents) or seek referrals from business development organizations such as the Chamber of Commerce or a nearby Small Business Development Center[19] (sponsored by the Small Business Administration).

There will be costs associated with hiring an accountant to organize your bookkeeping, provide strategic tax advice, and file your quarterly and/or annual taxes, but the expenses are more than justified because:

- you will know your tax obligations are being met on time;
- you will have representation if your business is selected for a tax audit;
- an experienced, professional accountant knows how the latest tax laws may affect your business – they can incorporate deductions, etc. into the calculations of your tax liability, often saving significant amounts of money.

In short, if your arts organization is large or complex enough, you should hire a qualified accountant to keep up with your tax liabilities.

Create a folder named Tax Planning. Write and file at least one page describing how your business will manage its bookkeeping and meet its tax obligations in an organized, timely manner. Identify a professional accountant and/or other advisors who will support the venture's tax planning and obligations for reporting and payments.

Limiting Liability: Insurance and Risk Management

The previous section on legal issues for artists presents the various forms of protection provided by corporate formation and intellectual property law. However, there is another category of protection that every business needs to consider: adequate insurance to protect property, minimize liability, and provide health coverage for owners and staff. Business insurance falls under a more general category known as *risk management*, which is an ongoing process designed to reduce the impact of potential losses while keeping the organization functioning in a safe, productive manner.

Risk management is all about preparing for unforeseen circumstances that could negatively impact your business. For example:

- an employee who gets injured on the job;
- a fire, flood, or earthquake that damages property;
- an auto accident that injures the owner and temporarily halts business operations.

The concept of risk management is not only about maintaining appropriate insurance to cover potential losses. It is also about incorporating processes (inspections of facilities, reviewing the physical demands within an employee's job description, providing safety and other training) designed to eliminate or reduce the possibility of an accident or other negative consequences. Arts organizations are just like other businesses: the ownership and staff all hope that none of these damaging scenarios will take place. Unfortunately, accidents do happen, and many business owners don't take the necessary steps to insure their property and personnel, or implement training and inspection programs to manage risk. Rather than postpone (or ignore) making risk management a regular part of your business, it is much better to evaluate and address your insurance needs while putting evaluation and training programs in place before the unexpected happens.

Insurance

The types of insurance needed by your arts organization may include:

- *General Liability Insurance*, covering a broad range of claims for injury or damage that occur during the regular operation of your business. Examples include a patron who is injured by slipping in the lobby of your performance venue, or damage to an invited photographer's work caused by a plumbing accident in your gallery.
- *Theatrical Property and Real Property Insurance* provide additional coverage for damage or loss to equipment such as lights, props, costumes, or audio gear.
- *Performance Interruption* and *Non-Appearance Insurance* are specialized products that provide protection in cases of lost revenue caused by natural disasters (earthquake, flood, fire), power outages or other interruptions, or the failure of a featured artist to make a contracted appearance.
- *Employment Practices Liability* protects employers against claims involving discrimination, wrongful termination, sexual harassment, retaliation, or other instances of inappropriate employment conduct. This area of coverage can be overlooked, but it is increasingly important for organizations with a significant number of employees or subcontractors. Business owners or members of the Board of Directors should evaluate the needs for this kind of insurance, along with *Directors & Officers Insurance*.
- *Workers Compensation Insurance* covers injuries to your employees that occur at the workplace. Different states have different laws about requirements for Workers Compensation Insurance, so you will need to investigate the regulations in your area.
- *Commercial Automobile Insurance* is required for vehicles owned by your business and used for commercial purposes.
- *Crime and Employee Dishonesty* protection covers losses caused by employee theft. It can also address risks such as forgery, computer fraud, or stolen data.

- *Tour Insurance* provides coverage during business operations involving domestic or international travel.
- *Life and Group Health Insurance* are especially important when your arts organization seeks to attract and retain key employees for the long term.
- *Disability Insurance* provides coverage in cases where a disabling injury or illness affects business operations and income.
- Specific insurance for *special events* or *serving alcohol* should be considered when your business hosts private receptions or sells/offers beer, wine or liquor to the public.

How will you decide what types of insurance are necessary for your arts venture and acquire appropriate policies from a reputable source? As with your search for an experienced accountant to assist with your tax planning, you can work through your network of friends, colleagues, advisors, and peer organizations to find a qualified insurance agent who can offer a range of suitable policies that fit your specific needs. You can also apply for insurance through organizations that support artists, such as the Annual General Liability Insurance program offered through Fractured Atlas (www.fracturedatlas.org/site/liability/Gl).

Risk Minimization

The way your organization operates on a day-to-day basis is directly connected with your ability to eliminate or reduce hazards and manage exposure to potential losses. You could hire a professional risk management consultant to develop a comprehensive plan (your insurance provider may be able to help with this), or you can develop and implement your own risk management program using common sense and consistent, scheduled inspections, procedural reviews and training.

- Conduct regular inspections (at least twice a year, more if needed) of the interior and exterior of your business location to look for risks, safety hazards or other liabilities: overloaded electrical circuits, improperly stored ladders or other equipment, fire extinguishers that are out of date, etc. Talk to every person associated with your business and ask about anything they have noticed that might be a cause for concern. Keep accurate records of any issues that are identified and act to resolve them as soon as possible.
- Develop and implement a safety-training program for all management, staff, and contractors who work on business property you own or lease.
- Keep up to date with inspections, surveys, and questionnaires required by local government agencies and your insurance provider.
- Update your insurance policies when your business operations expand or change to keep current with your actual needs. Consult with a risk management specialist to see if your insurance, inspection,

and training programs are providing sufficient protection against potential losses.

- Keep copies of your important documents (insurance policies, leases, contracts, financial records) stored offsite, away from the location where you normally conduct business.

Create a folder named Insurance and Risk Management. Write and file at least one page on each topic, describing how your business will manage its insurance needs and design and implement a risk management program. Identify an insurance agent who will help you address your venture's insurance obligations.

Corporate Organizational Structure

This chapter's previous sections on legal issues and insurance/risk management can be seen as part of the set of *external* relationships your arts organization will need to manage in order to become established and thrive. For example:

- corporate formation, accounting, and tax planning focus on the relationship between your business and government regulations;
- contracts and intellectual property issues are concerned with how your venture interacts with other individuals or organizations whose actions affect your business;
- risk management is about mitigating potential losses – including insurance claims and lawsuits brought by others – caused by unforeseen circumstances.

Other areas where external relationships impact your business include fundraising (interacting with donors, investors, and other supporters), competitive analysis (understanding where your venture resides within its context of similar organizations), and marketing (how you communicate and engage with consumers, the media, and other stakeholders). The larger issues related to the role of an arts organization within society – such as the benefits to individuals who create or participate in artistic projects, or the economic benefits delivered by the arts venture to its workers and the community – are addressed when choosing the purpose, form, and location of your business.

The following section on corporate organizational structure concentrates on the various *internal* relationships your business will need to develop and manage in order to achieve sustainable success. There is a wide range of potential configurations for an arts organization's structural design – from a sole proprietorship owned and operated by a single individual to a large business with multiple layers of executive, advisory, management, staff, and volunteer positions – but they all share the need to plan and execute an effective strategy for managing the venture's governance, operational and communications functions.

Corporate Administrative Structure: Who Does What, Who Manages Who

Consider the following examples of organizational design for an arts venture and the implications for management hierarchy:

- *One-person organization*: A single individual owns and operates the entire business, relying on hired consultants to manage accounting, legal, insurance, and other requirements. This one individual personally produces all of the art (or other deliverables such as arts education or arts-related services), raises money from a variety of sources, markets the business to consumers, manages all transactions that produce income or donations, handles bookkeeping, fulfills all obligations to customers (personally delivers the art or other product/ service), and maintains records of every aspect of the operation.
- *Partnership*: Three friends decide to set up and run a new venture dedicated to online distribution of digital media. The business is formed as a partnership, with equal shares of ownership and specific responsibilities for each partner to handle their part of the organization's functions and responsibilities.
- *A business owner with managers, staff, and volunteers*: An investor decides to purchase a building containing an established art gallery and turn the property into a multi-function business featuring a café, a community-based arts education program, a rentable venue for outside clients to hold private receptions and social events, a product design division that creates and sells merchandise featuring the gallery's well-recognized name and logo, and a year-round exhibition program that presents new works by local artists. The existing art gallery employs a manager, six part-time staff, and a changing roster of volunteers.

An examination of the possible administrative structures for each of these examples demonstrates some of the different approaches to management hierarchy available to the arts venture.

The *one-person organization* appears to have the simplest, most basic structure in terms of hierarchy: the owner manages his or her own time and effort while producing results based on self-designed and measured criteria. Although there are no other internal employees or volunteers to manage, there are a number of hired specialists whose contributions (legal, accounting, insurance, etc.) are crucial to the success of the business. The organization chart for this type of business would position the sole owner/operator at the center (with a comprehensive list of all the relevant responsibilities listed by category) surrounded by a group of consultants with their specific contributions.

Although this type of organizational chart is the least complex, it provides an important visual representation of the owner's concept for how the business will be structured and operated. This information is an essential part of the business plan for an arts entrepreneur, especially if the venture needs to raise money from donors such as foundations, corporations, or government programs (via fiscal sponsorship), from lenders such as banks under the Small Business Administration (SBA) program, from investors in the owner's network of family and friends, or from other supporters attracted during a crowdfunding campaign (see Chapter 4).

In addition to showing interested parties how the organization is structured now (or in the near future), it also provides a framework for the evolving business should it need to grow and expand its personnel. What if the sole owner/operator finds it necessary to hire an assistant, or bring in a manager and several part-time employees to keep up with demand and free the owner's time to concentrate on specific aspects of the business, such as new product/service development? What if the owner wants to sell the business to someone else, and the new owner wants fewer direct responsibilities and prefers to manage a small, dedicated team of employees? Organizational charts can be edited, revised, and updated as needed to reflect the changing circumstances of the business.

The organizational chart for a one-person organization provides an accurate portrait of how the venture currently operates while providing a foundation for future expansion.

Partnerships provide an opportunity to explore a horizontal or "flat" organizational structure. With each partner holding an equal share of ownership interest in the business, the three partners in our example have collective responsibility for running the operation successfully – there is no one supervisory figure directing the work of others. The organization chart for this type of business places the three partners on equal terms with one another, with each individual's responsibilities clearly indicated.

One of the challenges with horizontally structured organizations is the process for decision-making and planning. To move forward on key business issues such as product/service development and delivery, fundraising, marketing, financial management, and legal/tax issues, the three partners must evaluate, discuss, and compare a range of options until they reach a consensus on how and when to act. This deliberation process can slow down the venture considerably, especially if the business is expanding or if there are areas of disagreement between the partners on how to proceed. For example, the company may have an opportunity to provide online distribution of digital media for a new client who has considerable resources and content – however, for competitive reasons, the new contract requires the partnership terminate its relationship with a smaller client who is a friend of one of the partners and has been engaged since the formation of the business. In this scenario, the three partners would need to work together to find a solution that benefits both the company and their personal interests. The ability of an organization with a "flat" structure to navigate complex issues very much depends on the personalities of the partners and their skills in resolving potentially contentious issues that involve trade-offs and competing interests.

The positive aspects of horizontal organizations include the sense of involvement and control afforded to the partners. With no higher-level supervisor directing the operation, the partners get to exercise their range of knowledge and experience in nurturing the organization and helping it reach its full potential. As equal owners, the partners also reap the benefits of their participation in accordance with their stake in the company's profits. With the right mix of personalities and working methods, the horizontal organization can operate very efficiently and respond quickly to changing circumstances in their product/service market. Horizontal organizations can also work well when the partners live and work in different parts of the country, or even across international borders.

Like the one-person organization, the organizational chart for a horizontally structured venture provides a clear representation of how the business operates so that all the stakeholders – including the partners, their supporters, and customers – understand who does what, how decisions are made, and in what ways ownership and responsibilities are shared.

For an arts organization operated by a *business owner with managers, staff, and volunteers*, there needs to be a well-defined hierarchical structure that lays out lines of authority, communication, and coordination. Part of this is due to the sheer size of the organization: a more complex, multi-faceted business model relies on a greater number of people focused on specific aspects of the operation. The vertical organizational structure helps define responsibilities for all positions within the company – from owners and managers at the top to staff and volunteers at the bottom – while laying out the pathways for communications and decision-making.

In a vertical organization with an established hierarchy, communications flow in both directions: from the top management levels down to the staff and volunteers, but also up from the lower levels through the management structure to the top, including the owner. For example, the general manager might distribute a memo to all assistant managers and staff about a new company policy concerning employee flex-time and telecommuting. Or, a staff member in the arts education division might have an idea for a new class on digital photography: the proposal would be sent to the appropriate assistant manager, then the general manager, then the owner for review and approval.

Although vertical organizations rely on these clearly defined hierarchical pathways for efficient communications and operational decisions, there also needs to be communication *across* the organization horizontally in order to coordinate efforts for projects involving multiple departments. If an "open house" event was scheduled for the entire gallery business to highlight all of its programs and attract new customers, then all of the departments (café, education, merchandise, exhibitions) would need to synchronize their efforts toward a common goal. Likewise, if the education department wanted to host a reception for student artists to show and discuss their work in a public event, the café would need to be involved to provide refreshments. In cases where communications and planning work across the organization, the assistant managers and staff for each department would meet regularly to sort out the logistics and work together to plan and execute a coordinated effort.

Because artists – and people who choose to work in arts organizations – tend to resist the bureaucracy and excessive control found in some other forms of business, the amount of hierarchical division and conformity in an arts venture should be kept to a minimum: management should only impose as much organizational structure as is actually necessary to launch and sustain the company's programs. There should be many opportunities for employees and volunteers at the lowest levels to propose ideas and participate in decisions about the venture's strategic and operational functions. Having said that, it is clear that vertical organizations rely on upper management (usually the owner, or an executive director who reports to the board) for the final word on what the business will actually do and how responsibilities will be delegated. The goal is for management to use their experience and vision to make informed decisions that benefit the entire company. Employees at the assistant manager and staff levels should be supported in their efforts to run the operational details, with enough latitude to solve local problems and use their creativity to produce positive results.

Developing a Board of Directors

Some arts organizations find it necessary – or structurally advantageous – to have a board of directors overseeing the business at the highest level. For legal forms such as a C-corporation or a 501(c)(3) nonprofit organization, having a board of directors is a requirement, along with holding regular board meetings and taking minutes. For other arts ventures, creating and maintaining a board of directors serve to connect the business with the community while providing valuable experience, supervision, and financial support.

The Initial Board of Directors

When an arts business is being formed, it may be desirable to attract a group of engaged, committed individuals to serve on the board to provide guidance and help the venture raise start-up funds. This early phase of the business is where the leadership creates policies, establishes procedures, and sets the tone for the longer lifespan of the organization. During this formative stage, the experience, insights, and financial resources provided by a committed board of directors can make a lasting impact.

Some of the key contributions made by the board of directors include:

- hiring and evaluating the Executive Director;
- developing and approving plans for the organization's launch, with a view to anticipated business growth and sustainability;
- developing and approving the venture's budget, and being legally responsible for its financial reporting duties;
- directly contributing money or providing in-kind products and services, along with bringing in other potential supporters. Board members for nonprofits can make tax-deductible *donations*, while board members of for-profits can make *investments* in the organization;
- creating operational plans, policies, and procedures that lay out how different parts of the business will function, both independently and collectively. This includes the activities of the board itself, with guidelines on replacing members and recruiting future leaders.

As the list above indicates, the individuals invited to serve on the board should have significant business experience, along with possessing a real commitment to the successful realization of the organization's mission and purpose. The ability to donate money to the cause is important for several reasons: not only do board donations help the organization financially, they also signal each board member's level of commitment to internal stakeholders such as executives, managers, and staff. Having full participation of the board also allows fundraisers to invite prospective outside donors to "give with the board" when providing financial support.

Because the board's responsibilities are focused on governance (rather than daily management) of the arts organization, the qualifications for membership should include deep knowledge of accounting, marketing, law, fundraising, and organizational development practices. These attributes, along with having enough time to participate and the capacity to give money and provide access to other donors, are the key ingredients for an effective board member. The people invited to serve should have strong connections within the local community – they should also have a reputation for integrity, strong business acumen, and demonstrated stewardship of a successful venture.

As Your Business Evolves, So Does Your Board of Directors

Some boards have built-in term limits (one, two, or three years) that allow the business to recruit new directors and keep the leadership fresh, focused, and productive. Other organizations value long-term commitments by board members who serve indefinitely: they provide stability, continuity, and long-term institutional memory. However, even in the case of an open-ended board membership, there will be individuals who may decide to move on to other opportunities over time. These board members will need to be replaced.

The process of attracting new directors and developing a mature, effective board requires a good deal of tact and strong personal relationships with leaders in the community. It also requires running your business in a way that makes people *want* to join your board in order to support and participate in the governance of a successful venture. As your business grows and reaches a level of sustainability, there should be regular evaluations of the board's membership, productivity, and balance in terms of expertise, fundraising capacity, and community engagement.

Finding People to Serve on Your Board

Much like your process for hiring a suitable attorney, accountant, or insurance agent to help your venture succeed, your search for individuals to voluntarily serve on your board of directors should begin with recommendations from your closest advisors, colleagues, and staff. Look for a small number of directors to begin, maybe four to six in total, and set your priorities according to the needs of the organization. For example, the gallery business example mentioned earlier would benefit from a board member with experience in local real estate law to help advise on zoning, permits, and other property use issues. The underlying similarity for all board members is their understanding of – and support for – the business mission. The board of directors is legally responsible for the operations of the venture, but they are also key players in helping the organization stay on track financially and conceptually.

Structure, Management, and Resource Allocation

As discussed in the preceding section, the board of directors is made up of volunteers who offer their commitment, experience, and resources to serve the needs of the organization. Since the board directly supervises the Executive Director while developing, evaluating, and approving the venture's budget and operational features, there should be regularly scheduled board meetings (at least two per year, but typically more, especially in the start-up phase) to review business performance, make decisions on policies and procedures, and identify future work needed to resolve ongoing problems. Board meetings require a good deal of preparation beforehand to give managers and staff time to produce timely reports on the operation's financial health, programmatic successes, and challenges. The board also needs up-to-date information on possibilities for growth, outreach, or re-direction of some aspects of the business. Opportunities to contribute ideas for consideration at board meetings should extend broadly: from volunteers, interns, and staff through managers and executives, everyone should be able to have their concerns heard by the leadership. Giving everyone a voice in the analysis and planning process creates a sense of involvement and participation throughout the organization; it also brings attention to issues that require resolution by the board through their decision-making responsibilities. The board's actions are then put into practice by managers and staff as they implement the new policies and procedures.

For example, the gallery business may be experiencing unusually large crowds at some of its more popular events. Volunteers and staff who are present at these events would report the need for more crowd control measures, such as better routing of people as they enter and navigate through the gallery space and hiring a security firm to provide additional personnel and help maintain order. These concerns would be communicated to managers, the Executive Director, and ultimately considered by the board as part of both the financial and programmatic planning for the coming year. The board could then approve both a budget increase for future events to cover additional expenses for crowd control *and* work with other local performance spaces to move events with anticipated large attendance to a different, bigger venue nearby. In this way, the board reviews the issues and uses their decision-making responsibilities to produce both a budgetary result (increased funding for crowd control) and a programmatic result (negotiating with larger venues to host popular events in the future). The implementation of the board's decisions would flow through the organization from the Executive Director to managers, staff, and volunteers as they take actions based on the new policies and procedures. In financial terms, the board could designate selection and payment of the security firm to the manager of public events, while the staff and volunteers would find themselves working with additional help to keep operations running smoothly.

For smaller businesses with a horizontal structure (such as partnerships) or the single-owner/operator business, the lines of communication, decision-making, and implementation are obviously much simpler. Although these kinds of arts organizations don't require regular meetings with a designated board of directors, they should still develop a group of experienced advisors who can periodically review the venture's financial health, operational effectiveness, and strategic planning efforts. There is value in soliciting objective analysis and informed advice from experts in law, finance, marketing, fundraising, and other areas, even if these individuals are not directly contributing financial resources or held legally responsible for your business. Keep in mind that this group of close advisors may be able to refer you and your organization to other people within their network of associates who can provide donations, investments, or other support as your operation grows.

Create a folder named Board of Directors or Advisory Group, as appropriate for your business structure. Write and file at least one page describing how your business will attract, manage, and benefit from the advice and support provided by experienced, committed individuals with specific, valuable skills and strong ties to the local community.

Articles of Incorporation

For a business that is formed as a corporation, the first question is what state the organization will be incorporated in – different states have different laws and regulations pertaining to businesses that incorporate with their jurisdiction. After investigating the rules that apply to the business, it will be necessary to submit documentation to the appropriate state agency.

Articles of Incorporation

In most states, the document is known as the *articles of incorporation*, and in most states it needs to be filed with the Secretary of State. However, your particular state may have a different name for the document (for example, "certificate of formation") or a different state office where it needs to be filed (in Maryland, the State Department of Assessments and Taxation; in Arizona, the Arizona Corporation Commission). Virtually every state has a downloadable form that meets the state's minimum requirements for articles of incorporation.[20]

This document usually provides details about the business such as its name, location, purpose, dates of operation, names of officers and directors, and information about the types and amounts of stock the corporation will issue.

For an LLC (Limited Liability Corporation), there is a similar document called the *Articles of Organization*.

Bylaws, Operating Agreements, Memorandums of Understanding

An organization's *bylaws* spell out the specific actions followed by the board of directors to conduct their business. This includes the number of directors on the board, the roles and duties of each board member and officer (including the election, service, and rotation of the Chair), the frequency of board meetings, the procedures for appointing new directors, and other details focused on the venture's governance and operations. If your business is being formed as – or is converting into – a Benefit Corporation/B-Corp or an L3C Low-Profit Limited Liability Company, then the corporate bylaws are where language defining these attributes will be placed.

If you are operating a Limited Liability Company (LLC), you will need to have an *operating agreement* in place that describes the owner's responsibilities and the decision-making processes used within the venture:

According to U.S. Small Business Administration blog:

> An operating agreement is one of the most important documents used by LLCs because it structures the business' financial and functional decisions. The purpose of the document is to govern the internal operations of the business in a way that suits the specific needs of the business owners. Once the document is signed by the members, it acts as an official contract binding them to its terms.[21]

Like other contracts an organization enters into with external parties, the operating agreement clarifies the relationships between the people involved (the members of the LLC) along with laying out the operational features of how the organization conducts its business.

A *memorandum of understanding* (MOU) describes relationships between organizations in a way that allows the reader to understand how the entities work together and what the nature of their connection produces for each party. Although a memorandum of understanding is not legally binding in the way a corporation's articles of incorporation or an LLC's operating agreement are, the MOU serves an important function for lenders, investors, donors or other outside supporters who wish to understand the *dependencies* central to the organization's successful operation. For example, the gallery business in our earlier example may have a relationship with a local printing company that allows for the efficient, timely, and cost-effective production of catalogs, posters, mailers, and other materials. The printing company may also want to distribute and sell special editions of exhibition books that use content provided by the gallery. This kind of mutually beneficial relationship should be presented in a memorandum of understanding so people inside and outside the organization understand the nature of the relationship, how the organizations work together, and what kinds of benefits each derives from the synergy generated by their connection.

Other Business Requirements

Depending on the nature and location of your arts venture, it may be necessary to get certain permits or licenses in order to conduct business.

Check with your local Chamber of Commerce or visit the Small Business Administration's website[22] to learn about specific requirements in your area for the following documents:

Your business will need a *seller's permit* if you sell merchandise or taxable services. Most states require a seller's permit, which is also known as a *resale license* for businesses that buy goods at wholesale and mark them up to sell at retail.

A *business license* is usually issued by the city where your company operates. Local laws may also require a Fictitious Business Name (FBN) or Doing Business As (DBA) statement, which needs to be published in a local newspaper for a period of several weeks.

If your company has employees, you will need to apply for an *Employer Identification Number (EIN)*, which is provided by the Internal Revenue Service.[23]

For tax filings, your accountant can help with obtaining required documentation to comply with *state, federal and local tax* laws.

Create a folder named Required Business Documentation. Write and file at least one page each on the types of documents your business will develop, store, and update in order to comply with local, state, and federal regulations. Describe where the documentation comes from and who is responsible for keeping permits, licenses, and other paperwork up to date.

Chapter Summary

Like any other type of business, an arts organization needs to choose a legal form that fits its mission, goals, and operating processes. If your venture places public benefits at the top of its list of priorities, then forming as a 501(c)(3) not-for-profit corporation is a good choice, even though it takes some time to apply for and acquire this designation from the Internal Revenue Service. Not only does operating as a not-for-profit allow a business to qualify for funding from foundations, corporations, and government agencies, it also reduces sales, property, and income tax liabilities. To apply for grants and attract tax-deductible donations before attaining their not-for-profit designation, companies and individuals can work with a fiscal sponsor who will seek these funds on their behalf.

For the for-profit organization, there are a number of choices to consider. A sole proprietorship is the most basic, direct option for a business owned and operated by one person. A partnership allows small groups of people to collaborate and share in the organization's responsibilities and rewards, while a limited partnership provides an efficient structure that allows the venture to attract investors and replace partners as needed. As a company grows and becomes more complex in its relationships with customers, vendors, investors, and other stakeholders, incorporation can help limit liability for the owners while providing continuity for the organization. By establishing an independent entity (the corporation), business owners can create a separation between their personal assets and those owned and controlled by the corporation. Options for incorporation include the standard or C Corporation, the S Corporation, the Limited Liability Company (LLC), and the cooperative. New corporate forms have emerged recently that allow for-profit companies to include social benefits as part of their mission: these include the benefit corporation, or B Corp, and the L3C, or low-profit, limited liability company. An arts entrepreneur should seek the advice of an experienced attorney when evaluating different legal forms.

Qualified legal advice is also very important when navigating issues around intellectual property. Learning how copyright affects your organization, for example, is an essential step in developing a business around artistic production. Understanding trademarks, patents, and trade secrets is also mandatory for business owners whose product or service is connected with these issues. The different types of contracts encountered by an arts venture will also need to be evaluated with the help of a qualified, experienced attorney.

Tax planning is an area that some artists – or arts organization owners – tend to overlook, but managing tax liability is critical for launching and sustaining a successful business. Working with an experienced accountant, the arts entrepreneur should develop a comprehensive tax strategy that covers all aspect of the operation, from employment taxes to property, sales, corporate, income, and other tax obligations. Insurance is another area that is sometimes less thoroughly evaluated than it should be: make sure to understand and acquire proper business and other insurance based on your organization's specific areas of risk and potential liability.

Organizational structure refers to the way a business is designed in terms of supervision, communications, and responsibilities. Small organizations of one or two people should create an organizational chart that shows each person's responsibilities and the business relationships with external stakeholders (vendors or service providers). Larger, more complex businesses should develop a clear picture of their organizational structure that describes lines of authority, communications channels, and the implementation of policies and procedures. Many arts organizations have a board of directors as part of their structure. The benefits include using the valuable input and advice provided by established, experienced business leaders to help develop and run your organization, as well as directly raising money from the board and leveraging their relationships to increase access to outside donors and other supporters.

Creating, storing, and updating the required documentation are essential to the long-term viability of any business. For example, the corporate legal form requires articles of incorporation to be on file and the requirements for board meetings and minutes to be maintained. Bylaws, operating agreements, and memorandums of understanding are also critical components for starting and running a business. Depending on your organization's structure, location, and legal form, other mandatory documentation can include a seller's permit, a business license and Fictitious Business Name (FBN) or Doing Business As (DBA) statement, an Employer Identification Number (EIN), and other tax-related documents. Consult with your attorney, accountant and local Chamber of Commerce to make sure you have everything you need for starting and running a responsible, legally compliant business.

Discussion Questions

1. What are the reasons an arts entrepreneur might choose a not-for-profit legal form for a new business?

2. For-profit corporations have many benefits for owners and shareholders, but choosing the right corporate form depends on a number of factors. Describe how corporate liability and business continuity play a role in evaluating both the Limited Liability Company (LLC) and the S-Corporation as potential choices for an organization's legal formation.

3. For an organization that depends on frequent, new material produced by a popular artist, describe how copyright can help the business protect its interests. Include the specific methods for seeking legal protection for original work.

4. Name three different types of tax obligations an arts organization might encounter, and explain how to address each.

5. What is risk management and how does it relate to an arts venture?

6. Explain the differences between horizontal and vertical organizational structures, providing one example for each.

7. Imagine you are advising a new, arts-related business in its early planning and start-up phase. How will you recommend the business owners learn about and correctly implement policies, procedures, and documentation for their legal, tax, and insurance needs?

Notes

[1] See/www.irs.gov/Charities-&-Non-Profits/Charitable-Organizations/Exemption-Requirements-Section-501%28c%29%283%29-Organizations

2   Ibid.

3   See www.irs.gov/charities-non-profits/application-for-recognition-of-exemption

4   Ibid.

5   See www.fracturedatlas.org/

6   See http://theintersection.org/

7   U.S. Small Business Administration, *Choose Your Business Structure*, available at: www.sba.gov/content/sole-proprietorship-0

8   See https://smallbusiness.chron.com/s-corporation-operational-limitations-55768.html

9   Network of Bay Area Worker Cooperatives, see http://nobawc.org/

10   See www.nolo.com/legal-encyclopedia/benefit-corporations.html

11   See www.nolo.com/legal-encyclopedia/l3cs-a-hybrid-low-profit business-entity.html

12   Copyright Law of the United States of America and Related Laws Contained in Title 17 of the United States Code, available at: www.copyright.gov/title17/92chap1.html

13   See www.copyright.gov/title17/92chap1.html

14   Ibid.

15   Creative Commons, available at: http://creativecommons.org/licenses/

16   United States Patent and Trademark Office (USPTO) available at: www.uspto.gov/trademarks-getting-started/trademark-basics

17   Kweskin, Amy, Nancy Hytone Leb, Yesenia Sanchez, Greg Victoroff, Nancy Walch, and Richard Walch. *The business of art: an artist's guide to profitable self-employment*, 2nd ed. (Los Angeles, CA: Center for Cultural Innovation, 2012).

18   Cobb, Peter, Susan L. Ball, and Felicity Hogan. *The profitable artist: a handbook for all artists in the performing, literary, and visual arts* (New York: Allworth Press, 2011), p. 73.

19   For information on Small Business Development Centers, see www.sba.gov/tools/local-assistance/sbdc

20   See Nolo Press, available at: www.nolo.com/legal-encyclopedia/articles-incorporation.html

21   See www.sba.gov/blogs/operating-agreements-basics-0

22   Seewww.sba.gov/category/navigation-structure/starting-managing-business/starting-business/obtain-business-licenses

23   To apply for an Employer Identification Number, see www.irs.gov/Businesses/Small-Businesses-&-Self-Employed/Apply-for-an-Employer-Identification-Number-%28EIN%29-Online

6 Money Management and Entrepreneurial Finance

This chapter introduces concepts, tools, and techniques for managing the financial aspects of an arts venture. Some artists – and owners of arts-related businesses – are very experienced with budgets, forecasts, and financial analyses, while others are relatively new to the various strategies involved in money management. We will work through a number of key concepts such as budgets, documentation, financial planning, banking, and bookkeeping.

Although the scale and complexity of each business will determine the kinds of financial details required to launch and operate an arts organization, there are a few fundamental principles that apply to all businesses. For those who are new to money management practices, know that acquiring new proficiencies in this area is like adding another technique to your creative skill set in drawing, acting, or music composition. Artists are good at learning and applying new ideas and practices, so money management skills should be viewed as another area to expand your natural ability to learn and employ techniques that will help your career flourish.

Professionals such as bookkeepers, accountants, and financial advisors have extensive training and experience in important business matters such as tax strategies and financial planning. It is highly recommended that you develop relationships with financial professionals in the early stages of your business development and maintain them throughout the lifespan of your organization. Paid services for financial advice and tax preparation are not only tax-deductible as business expenses, they can save you considerable time (and money) by identifying potentially-overlooked financial issues and helping your venture stay on course for profitability and growth.

Financial Vision and Goals

Like the research and planning that help you clarify and organize your marketing and fundraising ambitions, laying out financial goals for yourself and your business will provide structure and direction while you pursue specific outcomes. Before constructing a vision for how your arts organization will perform financially, take some time to create a scenario for your personal finances.

Personal Expenses

One of the key steps in defining where you want your business to be financially in the future is to think about what kind of life you want to create for yourself and your family as a business owner and recipient of consistent funds generated by your business. Deciding how much you need – or want – to pay yourself, especially in the early years of running an organization, is an essential step in developing the overall financial picture for your growing venture. When thinking about your *personal expenses*, make a list of all the known and anticipated cost categories related to your basic living expenses (savings, housing, food, car, insurance, utilities, credit cards, etc.) for the next year and the following two years beyond that.

Some students will approach this step as a continuation of their current cost-of-living budget, keeping their location and expenses consistent as they move into their professional, post-academic lives. Others will plan on moving to another area (a different city/region, or even a different country) to pursue their ambitions. The reasons for this can include lower costs for housing and other essentials, but they can also include proximity to a specific market or potential support from family and friends, along with better connections with potential funding sources. Wherever your anticipated location turns out to be, start your personal budget with accurate figures for living expenses based on current conditions in that area.

Personal Budget

Use any or all of these categories – or others that might be appropriate – for expenses in creating your personal budget. Note that these expense categories are independent from the ones that will be used in your Business Budget, which will be discussed in this chapter's next section.

- Savings and emergency fund
- Housing
- Food & dining
- Groceries
- Auto & transport (car payments, repairs, bridge tolls)
- Bills & utilities (including phone, internet, cable, electricity, and other services)

- Shopping (clothing, electronics, sporting goods)
- Entertainment (concert tickets, books, etc.)
- Personal care
- Laundry
- Health & fitness (health club fees, also doctors, dentists, opticians, and prescriptions)
- Kids
- Education (including student loan payments)
- Gifts & donations
- Investments
- Travel
- Relocation (moving expenses and related costs)
- Service fees (from banks, credit cards)
- Taxes (federal, state, local, sales and property tax).

There are a variety of software programs available that can help you create and manage spreadsheets for your finances. An online search will produce several free or paid options for spreadsheet programs (such as Microsoft Excel). Or, you could create a paper-based budget with ruled or graph paper. In either case, start your document with a heading such as "Personal Expenses for (your name) (select a date range: year X through year Y)." Place each of the relevant categories from the examples above, plus others if you have them, in a list with one item per row going down and one column per year going across. Add the total of all anticipated personal expenses for each year and highlight that number at the bottom of each column. Create a folder named Budgets. Save this document with the name Personal Budget and place it inside.

The next section in your personal budget should be named Income, and it includes all the anticipated sources of money you will receive for each of the projected years in your budget. Typical income categories include wages received as an employee, financial support from parents or student aid programs, dividends from investments, income from rental properties, and payments for independent contractor work such as consulting. Note that this calculation of personal income excludes categories related to your arts-related business.

After the Income section, make a row named Excess/Shortfall and place the number calculated by deducting your total expenses from your total income for each year. Ideally, the difference between income and expenses should be zero – you can increase the amount for Savings and Emergency Fund if needed. Don't worry if this ends up being a negative number – we will address that in the next section.

There are two goals associated with creating a personal budget:

- to identify non-business income and expense categories and project future calculations based on these anticipated figures;
- to calculate a basic cost of living figure for yourself. This total amount will need to be addressed in your company's financial projections, typically as the annual Owner's Draw (the amount you pay yourself from the business) in your Profit and Loss statement.

An arts entrepreneur has several options when it comes to anticipating how much to pay themselves from their growing business. Some business owners will project no personal income for the first year or two as the business gets established – they cover their cost of living using funds from other sources such as a part-time or full-time job, investment income, or other resources. Another approach is to pay yourself a modest amount during the first few years and supplement it through these other means. Relying on a brand new business to pay for 100 percent of your cost of living is certainly possible, but this scenario needs to be realistically explained in both the Cash Flow projections and in the narrative portion of your business plan's financial section. In any of these cases, a convincing description has to explain how the business will be able to generate enough income to cover the Owner's Draw – in addition to all the other Expense categories. The people reading your business plan (investors, bank officials, potential partners, or other supporters) will want to see how you plan to pay *yourself* as part of your venture's regular operation. This is a sign that the founder has thought through the specifics of compensating themselves while running their own business (a detail that can sometimes be overlooked) and that the business itself can be expected to generate enough income so that the Owner's Draw can be included as a regular expense. Part of the process of describing a viable, sustainable business includes showing how the owner(s) will be paid. The reason why a personal expense calculation is important by itself is that it allows you to incorporate your basic cost of living into your overall business budget. You need to anticipate how much you need to pay yourself from your business in order to survive.

Business Budget

The budget for your business will include all of the anticipated expenses and income associated with running your venture. Each organization will have unique expense and income categories, so a good starting place for exploring the possibilities would be the Schedule C "Profit or Loss from Business" form provided by the Internal Revenue Service for tax filings.

Note that a Business Budget for future activity will be an approximation – you can only *estimate* income and expense figures if they haven't occurred yet. Creating a reasonably accurate financial picture for your arts venture helps clarify your specific income and expense categories while anticipating dollar amounts that *might* be realized in each area. Once the budget's time period has passed (for example, one calendar year), you can create a Budget vs. Actuals comparison that shows any variances between the expected and actual amounts. For example, a musician's Business Budget might indicate $20,000 in annual income from performances, but the Actual amount earned might end up being $28,500. The variance of + $8,500 would be shown on the Budget to Actuals spreadsheet, and the Budget for the upcoming year might be adjusted upwards in anticipation of higher earnings. Similar adjustments can be made for variances in all of the Expense categories. The two objectives of creating a Business Budget with anticipated dollar amounts – and then analyzing and adjusting with a Budget to Actuals variance spreadsheet – are: (1) to develop a reasonably accurate picture of financial activity that helps the business owner anticipate and make decisions based on realistic income and expense figures; and (2) to demonstrate to lenders, investors, partners, and other supporters the economic viability of the venture and the owner's ability to predict – and create – financial stability over time.

In the Income section of the IRS Schedule C form, you will see a row for Gross Receipts or sales. You should start with this income category for your own Business Budget and add specific sub-categories as appropriate. For example, a musician might have multiple sources of income from concerts, CD sales, music download revenue, fees for giving instrument lessons, and music publishing payments. A photographer might have income from commercial projects (work for hire), sales of original pieces in a gallery or other setting, licensing revenue from companies reproducing copyrighted images, and revenue generated by renting out studio space. Begin constructing your business budget by listing all of the possible sources of income associated with your venture. An experienced accountant can suggest income categories that are specific to your type of business, while online research (using "artists' income categories" and other terms specific to your organization) can yield possibilities for your particular budget.

The next row in the Income section of the Schedule C form is for Returns and Allowances, which is mostly for manufacturing, distribution or retail businesses, but may be relevant to your venture if you intend to accept (and provide credit for) returned merchandise. Line 4 of the form is for Cost of Goods Sold – this is an important item for any art-related business that uses physical materials to create its products: the clay used by a potter; the paper, developing chemicals, and frames used by a photographer;

the paint and canvas used by a painter ... anything that remains *part of the object* being sold. The tools and equipment used by the artist are not included here, but are itemized in the Expense section of the budget.

Using a software-generated or paper-based spreadsheet, begin creating a Business Budget for your arts venture. Place the business name at the top, indicate the time-frame the budget covers (for example, January–December, 2020) and create a category for Income, using separate rows for each income type that applies to your business. If appropriate, add rows for Returns and Allowances, as well as Cost of Goods. Sum these figures into a separate row named Gross Income.

After the Income section comes the Expense section. Referring again to the IRS Schedule C form, select each of the expense categories (from Part II Expenses) that are relevant to your business and list them on individual rows on your Business Budget spreadsheet. Some categories, such as Rent, Wages, Owner's Draw, and Travel will be common for many types of arts-related businesses. Others, such as supplies and insurance, will be specific to the type of organization you are operating. For example, a photographer might list auto expenses for business use of a vehicle, while a web designer might list the costs for computer hardware and software needed to create custom websites for clients.

How do you research and develop customized income and expense categories that are appropriate to your arts-related business before starting the venture? There are several resources beyond the general categories found on the IRS Schedule C form that you can pursue:

- Ask people in your immediate network to recommend a qualified book-keeper or accountant who has expertise in your particular field. A CPA who has other clients in your arts-related business category will have valuable advice on setting up an accurate budget for your venture.
- Local and regional unions, guilds, advisory boards and community support programs for artists can provide examples of budgets for individuals and organizations across a range of creative disciplines.
- Government agencies, foundations, and corporate programs that provide grants to artists and arts organizations often have budget templates available to assist in their grant application processes. Contact several of these funding sources to see if they can provide budget examples.
- Online research can yield many examples of budgets for arts-related businesses – try using different combinations of search terms that are specific to your venture.

Once you have designed a budget that lays out all of the anticipated Income and Expense categories for your business, the next step is to populate each category with dollar amounts that reflect reasonable estimates of your financial activity for the defined future time period. If you have some experience operating an arts-related business – or know someone who does – you can start with these historical figures and project future income and expenses based on what you already know.

If, however, you are starting from the very beginning with no background in real-world income and expenses for your proposed arts organization, some additional investigation will be necessary. Remember, the creation of a Business Budget is an approximate – and ever-evolving – exercise. You should be prepared to adjust your figures as your business grows and you learn more about how to accurately predict Income and Expense activity.

For Income amounts, do some comparative research within your target market to see what other companies are charging for their products or services. A ticket price for a local theater, a photographer's daily or hourly rate, a price per unit of custom-designed jewelry, a cost per download of a digital song or app installation ... there are many publicly available figures for arts-related businesses that you can target as reference points. Remember to adjust your own anticipated income by comparing the years of experience, established market presence, and brand awareness achieved by other comparable organizations. Also, don't forget to include only the income that actually comes to the artist or business owner after the sale – some transactions can have deductions such as gallery commissions or other reductions in revenue.

For the Expense amounts, start with the most basic categories such a space rental, materials, web hosting, and advertising. Keep your estimates in line with typical amounts found in your local area – space rental should be at the market rate for the location and size of the studio or office you will need. More detailed – and industry-specific – information on anticipated Expense amounts can be found using the resources listed above for researching and developing budget categories: a qualified bookkeeper or accountant, local community support programs for artists, funding sources for the arts, and online search results can all help paint a picture of your anticipated Expenses that will be tailored to your specific type of business.

Using a software-generated or paper-based Business Budget for your arts venture, create a category for Expenses (after the previously created Income category), using separate rows for each Expense type that applies to your business. Sum these figures into a separate row named TOTAL EXPENSES.

The examples in Figure 6-1 and Figure 6-2 show just two of the many types of Business Budgets that can be developed for an arts venture. Whether your business finances are simple or complex, it is highly recommended

Figure 6-1 Simple business budget.

Example: Simple business budget for a home-based graphic design company

Acme Graphic Design Agency
Business Budget, January 2020-December 2020

Income:
    Freelance clients
        Client 1   12,000
        Client 2   15,000
        Client 3   8,000
TOTAL INCOME: 35,000

Expenses:
    Computer hardware & software   4,000
    Marketing (web site, direct mail)   2,000
    Travel   1,000
    Meals   1,000
TOTAL EXPENSES: 8,000

TOTAL GROSS PROFIT: 27,000

Figure 6-2 Complex business budget.

Example: Complex business budget

Stellar Sounds Music Festival
Business Budget, January-December, 2020

Income:
    General admission tickets   85,000
    VIP tickets   25,000
    Concession income   14,000
TOTAL INCOME: 124,000

Expenses:
    Artist fees   35,000
    Hotel rooms, airfare   10,000
    Instrument rental (backline)   2,000
    PA (sound system)   2,000
    Lighting   750
    Production and event staff   7,000
    Security   1,000
    Fences and barricades   500
    Permits   500
    Insurance   500
    Backstage/green room refreshments   500
    Tents, tables, chairs   500

TOTAL EXPENSES: 60,250

TOTAL GROSS PROFIT: 63,750

Note: The simple business budget shows the *taxable* profit generated by one-person, home-based business. If the operation grows to include additional employees and a larger studio space, there would be other expenses such as payroll, rent, and insurance to incorporate into the budget. After deducting the appropriate federal, state, and local taxes, the remaining amount can be used by the business owner for personal expenses such as rent, food, phone, insurance and so forth. Later in this chapter we will examine how payments to the business owner should be recorded as an Owner's Draw expense as part of the Profit and Loss Statement.

that you work with an experienced bookkeeper or accountant to design your budgets and use them to address financial management, tax liability, and other critical issues.

Other Financial Documents

In addition to personal and business budgets, there are a number of other important financial reports and accounting tools that business owners use to run their organizations. In this section, we will discuss how to design, populate, and use these documents to explain and operate your business. Note that nonprofit organizations have somewhat different versions[1] of some of these financial documents.

Business Budget vs. Actuals Comparison

As an organization becomes established, it can be useful to compare how the anticipated income and expenses in its budget compare to the actual figures experienced over the year. Sometimes an unexpected – or previously unnoticed – variation in sales volume or a business expense category can be discovered and addressed using this type of comparison. Just like reviewing your strategic plan or marketing/fundraising goals vs. actual results, an objective analysis of your venture's finances can be a powerful tool for keeping the operation on track for profitability and growth.

To construct a simple Business Budget vs. Actuals comparison, copy your original Business Budget and add a column for Actuals to the right of the projected Budget figures, as in this example (Figure 6-3) for the Acme Graphic Design Agency:

You can also add other columns to the right of the Actuals column for Variance (the positive or negative difference in *dollars* between budget and actual for each row) and Percentage (the positive or negative difference in *percentages* between budget and actual for each row). As the business

Figure 6-3 Business budget vs. actuals.

Acme Graphic Design Agency
Business Budget vs. Actuals, January 2020-December 2020

	BUDGET	ACTUALS
Income:		
Freelance clients		
Client 1	12,000	11,000
Client 2	15,000	17,000
Client 3	8,000	4,000
TOTAL INCOME:	35,000	32,000
Expenses:		
Computer hardware & software	4,000	3,875
Marketing (web site, direct mail)	2,000	2,200
Travel	1,000	1,050
Meals	1,000	750
TOTAL EXPENSES:	8,000	7,875
TOTAL GROSS PROFIT:	27,000	24,125

develops over multiple years, you can produce year-over-year comparisons of Budget vs. Actuals financial performance to identify trends or understand and adapt to changing circumstances that are impacting your organization's sustainability.

Cash Flow Projection

The term "cash flow" refers to the movement of money into and out of an organization. Business owners use cash flow projections to anticipate future movement of funds within the operation and make adjustments to address anticipated funding shortfalls (or overages) before they happen. Constructing an accurate cash flow projection is obviously more feasible after the business has been in operation for some time, since the income and expense estimates can be based on actual data from previous years of running the organization. However, a brand new venture can (and should) construct a cash flow projection for future months and years of business operation by studying other similar businesses and making informed estimates about anticipated income and expenses. Like the business budget, a cash flow projection can demonstrate to an investor, lender, donor, or other supporter how the venture is expected to perform over time – and how the owner anticipates reacting to the company's anticipated financial activity.

Using the example of a simple business budget presented earlier for the Acme Graphic Design Agency, we can construct a cash-flow projection (Figure 6-4) that shows anticipated income and expense details for the first 6 months of the year 2021. This projection of *future* financial activity allows the business owner to predict instances of negative cash flow before they occur – and to prepare accordingly.

Figure 6-4 Cash
flow projection.

Acme Graphic Design Agency
Cash Flow Projection: January-June 2021

	Jan	Feb	Mar	Apr	May	Jun
Cash in						
Client 1	1000	1000	1000	1000	1000	1000
Client 2		5000			2500	
Client 3			2000			2000
Total cash in	1000	6000	3000	1000	3500	3000
Cash out						
Computer hardware & software	3000				1000	
Marketing (web site, direct mail)	500	500	500	500		
Travel			250		250	
Meals			250		250	
Total cash out	3500	500	1000	500	1500	0
Monthly cash flow (Cash in minus Cash out)	-2500	5500	2000	500	2000	3000
Beginning cash balance	5000	2500	8000	10000	10500	12500
Ending cash balance	2500	8000	10000	10500	12500	15500

During the month of January, the Acme Graphic Design Agency anticipates $1000 of total cash in (income) from client billings. However, there
will be an expected cash out (expenses) total of $3500 during the same
month, leaving a *negative* cash flow (loss) of -$2500. In this example,
the business owner has a beginning cash balance of $5000 in a busi-
ness checking account on the first of January, so the negative cash flow
created during that month can be deducted from this amount, leaving
an ending cash balance for January of $2500. This $2500 is carried forward as the beginning cash balance for the next month (February), where
the business generates $6000 in total cash in (income) but only $500 in
total cash out (expenses).This produces a *positive* cash flow of $5500 for
February, which can be added to that month's beginning cash balance of
$500 for a new ending cash balance of $8000, which is carried forward as
the beginning cash balance for March ... and so on.

Many art-related businesses have monthly or seasonal fluctuations in
their income and expenses, while others have a relatively consistent level
of positive cash flow throughout the year. Regardless of how your organization is expected to experience cash flow over future months and years,
a cash flow projection can help you predict variations before they happen
and keep the operation going. In the example of the Acme Graphic Design
Agency, having a beginning cash balance of $5000 in a business checking
account on January 1st helped the company through one month of *negative* cash flow, while the following months of *positive* cash flow repaid
that amount and continued increasing the cash balance going forward.

Many business analysts believe that lack of sufficient operating capital is one of the primary reasons why new small businesses fail. Having a beginning cash balance available in a business checking account or line of credit – plus a comprehensive cash flow projection – can help a new venture anticipate and survive financial fluctuations that might put a less well-prepared business into difficult circumstances.

Break-even Analysis

Businesses that produce and sell multiple units of products can use a break-even analysis to determine at which point the operation becomes profitable. For example, a gallery that makes and sells limited edition screen prints of unique pieces designed by invited artists can determine how many prints will need to be sold in order to reach profitability.

The first step in calculating this threshold between loss and profit (or the "break-even point") is to identify the company's fixed costs over a given time period. In this example (Figure 6-5), we will consider the case of the Westside Gallery, a business that anticipates producing and selling limited edition screen prints. Fixed costs are those expenses that will be incurred regardless of how many units (screen prints) are sold during the year – for example, rent, utilities, payroll, and insurance costs.

If the gallery sells the prints for $1000 each, that leaves a profit of $650 per unit after expenses. In order to cover the *fixed* costs of running the gallery, the owner would have to sell 12,800/650, or 20 prints per year, before reaching the point where the business becomes profitable: this is the *break-even point*. Every print sold beyond the first 20 would also

Figure 6-5 Break-even analysis.

Westside Gallery
Break-Even Analysis: January-June 2020

Fixed costs

Rent	6000
Utilities	500
Payroll	6000
Insurance	300
TOTAL	$12,800

Next are the variable costs, which are dependent on each unit produced and sold – for example, the expenses for each individual print such as the screen printing fee (from a local print shop) and framing materials and labor for each piece.

Variable costs (per unit)

Screen printing	200
Framing materials	65
Framing labor	85
TOTAL	$350

generate $650 of profit per unit. If the gallery sold an average of 4 prints per month, that would equal 48 prints for the year – the first 20 prints would generate the $12,800 needed to cover fixed costs, while the next 28 prints would generate $650 each in profit, yielding $18,200 in total profit for the year.

Profit and Loss Statement

The Profit and Loss Statement is similar to the "Statement of Activities" for non-profits. In this chapter's earlier presentation of Business Budget development, we considered the idea of using the Schedule C "Profit or Loss from Business" form provided by the Internal Revenue Service as a model for creating a *future* budget for your organization. The Profit and Loss Statement (or P&L) is a report of the venture's *actual* income and expenses, so it can only be created after the business has been running for some time. It includes a bottom line showing a net profit or loss based on how the business performed over the time period covered by the P&L, which is typically one calendar year.

Just like your Business Budget, the P&L statement can use the IRS Schedule C as a template to get started. Note that the final version of your P&L will include categories of income and expenses that are specific to your venture, so it will once again be useful to conduct online research, make inquiries within your network, and consult with an experienced bookkeeper or CPA to find examples of Profit and Loss Statements from companies similar in size, scope and concept to your own.

If you are considering using a bookkeeping software program such as QuickBooks (or similar products) to manage your finances, one of the key features will be the ability to automatically generate P&L statements and other financial reports from within the program: you simply select the type of report you are generating, set the date range for the report and in one click you have a complete snapshot of your income, expenses and net profit, organized by your specific categories. You can even generate P&L statements for multiple years to show increases/decreases in financial activity, shown both in dollars and in positive/negative percentages.

A simple Profit and Loss Statement for the Acme Graphic Design Agency would look like Figure 6-6.

Note that the amount paid to the business owner during the year ($24,000) is included as an Owner's Draw expense under Personnel. This is the typical method of recording and reporting payments made to the business owner – in this case, the Owner's Draw payments were $2,000 per month x 12 months. Since these figures are based on *actual* past income and expenses (not *projected* future amounts), it is preferable to show Owner's Draw payments in the P&L statement as expenses rather than part of the total Net Profit/Loss on the bottom line. This degree of accuracy in

Figure 6-6 Profit and loss statement.

Acme Graphic Design Agency
Profit and Loss Statement, January 2021-December 2021

Income:
    Contracted services   35,000
TOTAL INCOME: 35,000

Expenses:
    Personnel
        Owners Draw   24,000
    Total Personnel   24,000

    Project supplies and equipment
        Computer hardware & software   4,000
    Total project supplies and equipment   4,000

    Administrative
        Marketing (web site, direct mail)   2,000
        Travel   1,000
        Meals   1,000
    Total administrative   4,000

TOTAL EXPENSES: 32,000

NET PROFIT/LOSS: 2,000

reporting is especially important in preparing tax filings: your accountant (or accounting software) will rely on these income and expense details to calculate your tax obligations for quarterly or annual tax returns. Payments to individuals (such as the Owner's Draw amount) and the net profit or loss for the business might be subject to different deductions and taxed at different rates, so keeping precise records is essential for managing your tax liability.

If an organization receives donated income – either as a 501(c)(3) nonprofit or by working with a fiscal sponsor – these funds would be listed under an additional Income sub-category on the P&L called Contributed Income. Using the Westside Gallery (mentioned in this chapter's section on break-even analysis) as an example, imagine this business had generated funding for their arts education program by receiving grants and gifts through a fiscal sponsor. The resulting Profit and Loss Statement would look like Figure 6–7.

Again, notice the Owner's Draw is recorded under Personnel and outside services, not incorporated into the overall Net Profit/Loss of the business.

For the version of this financial statement used by nonprofits, do an online search for "statement of activities for nonprofits" and review some of the examples.

Figure 6-7 Profit and loss statement with contributed income.

Westside Gallery
Profit and Loss Statement, January 2021-December 2021

Income:
Contributed Income

	Grants	20,000
	Individual donations	5,000
Total Contributed Income		25,000

Earned Income

	Sales of prints	48,000
Total Earned Income		48,000

TOTAL INCOME:	73,000

Expenses:
Personnel and outside services

	Instructors for education program	20,000
	Screen printing for prints	9,600
	Framing labor for prints	4,080
	Gallery assistant	6,000
	Owners draw	12,000
Total personnel and outside services		51,680

Supplies and equipment

	Supplies for education program	5,000
	Framing materials for prints	3,120
Total supplies and equipment		8,620

Administrative

	Rent	6,000
	Utilities	500
	Insurance	300
Total administrative		6,800

TOTAL EXPENSES:	67,100

NET PROFIT/LOSS:	5,900

Balance Sheet

The Balance Sheet is similar to the "Statement of Financial Position" for nonprofits. While the previous financial reports show activity over the course of one year (or longer), the Balance Sheet shows a snapshot of the business as of a specific date. This report lays out the full picture of the business in terms of assets, liabilities, and owner's equity. As shown in Figure 6–8, the business assets include Current Assets such as cash on

Figure 6-8 Balance sheet.

Westside Gallery
Balance Sheet as of December 31, 2020

Current Assets	
Cash on hand	10,000
Accounts receivable	3,000
Inventory	2,150
Total Current Assets	15,150
Fixed Assets	
Furniture and fixtures	1,200
Total Fixed Assets	1,200
TOTAL ASSETS:	16,350
Liabilities and Equity:	
Current Liabilities	
Accounts payable	1,400
Credit card debt	600
Total Current Liabilities	2,000
Long Term Debt	
Bank loan	5,000
Total Long Term Debt	5,000
Total Liabilities	7,000
Owner's Equity	
Invested capital	5,000
Retained earnings	4,350
Total Owner's Equity	9,350
TOTAL LIABILITIES AND EQUITY:	16,350

hand, accounts receivable (amount owed to the business), and inventory (unsold merchandise), along with Fixed Assets such as furniture, fixtures, and equipment. An experienced bookkeeper or accountant can help you set up your first Balance Sheet (Figure 6–8) and provide figures for details such as accumulated depreciation to keep everything complete and up to date.

The formula for calculating net worth on a Balance Sheet is:

Assets - Liabilities = Net Worth (or Equity).

For the nonprofit version of this financial document, do an online search for "Statement of Financial Position for nonprofits" and review the results.

Using software-generated or paper-based spreadsheets, create a complete Personal Budget, Business Budget, Cash Flow Projection, and Break-even Analysis for your new venture. For existing businesses with a history of financial data, also create a Budget vs. Actual comparison, Profit and Loss Statement and Balance Sheet for the previous and current years. Create a new folder named Financial Documents and place these files inside.

Using Financial Reports to Keep Your Business on Track

Designing, populating, and maintaining financial reports are just the beginning. How does a business owner use these tools to help their business thrive? The Business Budget, Budget vs. Actual comparison, Cash Flow Projection, Break-even Analysis, Profit and Loss Statement and Balance Sheet each have specific roles to play in operating a successful business.

The *Business Budget* provides the foundation for understanding how the organization expects its future income and expense activity will develop, typically for one calendar year. Assembling an accurate budget takes some time and effort, especially for a new venture with a limited number of comparable businesses to study as models. The recommended strategy for a new business in creating financial statements – working with an experienced bookkeeper or CPA, conducting research online and via other resources, and seeking input from a network of knowledgeable advisors and colleagues – should produce enough information to generate a reasonable budget for the first year of operation. Calculating future expenses such as rent, payroll, and marketing may be easier than correctly predicting income from the organization's various sources of earned and contributed revenue, so keep in mind that the initial budget is both flexible (subject to change during the year covered by the document) and meant to be used as a business analysis tool over time.

After an arts organization launches and begins producing actual income and expense figures, these numbers should be incorporated into the *Business Budget vs. Actuals* comparison to study how accurate the estimates in the original Business Budget are relative to the historical data. A comparison report should be produced and analyzed at the end of each quarter (every three months) in the early years of a new venture, and into future years as well to watch for any unanticipated changes in income or expense categories that need attention. A monthly review of the Business Budget vs. Actuals comparison can provide an even more timely picture of the organization's financial performance, allowing the owner to respond quickly if needed. For example, if the Acme Graphic Design Agency signed up two additional clients in the fourth and seventh months of its first year, the Business Budget should be updated immediately to reflect both the additional income (from client billings) and expenses (hiring an assistant to help with the additional work) for the current year. An unexpected increase in expenses (such as rent) or decrease in income (loss of revenue) should also be immediately incorporated into the revised Business Budget. In this way, both the Business Budget and the Business Budget vs. Actuals comparison can help the organization plan its financial future and respond quickly to changing circumstances as they develop.

The *Cash Flow Projection* is another important tool for predicting financial activity, analyzing real-world data and making adjustments to keep the operation on track. Rather than only looking at the balance in your business checking account from time to time, the Cash Flow Projection shows you how much cash you have on hand to get through the upcoming month – and future months beyond that – before problems develop. If an unanticipated reduction in sales volume occurs or expenses suddenly increase, these numbers should be incorporated into an updated Cash Flow Projection. The business owner can then take action to compensate for *current* changes by adjusting *future* income and expense figures. For example, the Acme Graphic Design Agency might need to borrow some funds from its business line of credit to cover additional payroll expenses in March and April to produce work for a new client who might not finish paying for that project until June and July. In its Cash Flow Projection for the entire year, the agency would add a row under Cash In for Business Line Income and show the borrowed amounts for March and April, along with a new row for Payroll under Cash Out to record those payments for the same months. When the client finished paying for the project in June and July, that income would be put into a new Client 4 row under Cash In for those months, and the expenses to pay back the business line of credit would be recorded under a new Business Line Expense row under Cash Out.

Client invoices are often paid 30–60 days after their receipt of a bill: this is known as net 30-day or net 60-day terms. It is important for the business owner to anticipate future expenses and income and compensate for the time lag between them – for example, compensating an employee to work on a project this month and receiving client payments for that project several months in the future. Although there are some risks involved in maintaining an "accounts receivable" relationship with your sources of income, there are ways to limit this risk by requiring references and credit checks for new clients, using signed contracts, purchase orders, and change orders to document the transactions, and scheduling payments at the beginning, middle, and end points of the project.

There are several ways to use a *Break-even Analysis* when developing a business idea or running an actual organization. In our example of the Westside Gallery, we determined that the organization needs to sell at least 20 prints per year to cover its fixed costs – the 21st print and beyond would generate a profit of $650 per unit sold. Suppose the gallery owner negotiated a lower cost per piece from a different screen printing company, say, $125 per unit instead of $200 each. If the gallery's retail price remained $1000 per print, then the profit per unit would be $725 each: the gallery would only need to sell 17 prints to cover its fixed costs and achieve profitability of $725 each for the 18th print and beyond. Lowering expenses while maintaining consistent income is one way to modify the break-even point; another way is to maintain consistent expenses and increase the income. For example, the Westside Gallery could raise the price per print to $1250 each while maintaining consistent fixed and variable costs. Or, imagine the business became successful enough that the owner decided to open a second location, called the Eastside Gallery. By doubling the organization's overall sales volume with a second location, the owner could negotiate not only a lower price per unit from suppliers such as the screen printer, but also lower costs for framing materials and other expenses. The Break-even Analysis allows the business owner to experiment with different scenarios for achieving profitability and forecasting growth associated with operating and expanding the organization.

Because the *Profit and Loss Statement* is a depiction of the venture's financial condition over a defined time period it can be a very useful tool for analyzing the overall performance of the organization as it evolves. How much money has the business made or lost in the past month, quarter or year? The Profit and Loss Statement has the answers, along with other vital information about specific income and expense categories that help the owner monitor – and react to – financial activity as it occurs. Generating a monthly P&L gives the business owner a clear picture of where the income and expense figures stand at that moment. Quarterly or annual P&L Statements can be used, respectively, for a view of accumulated seasonal or yearly data. The P&L report can also provide basic information about taxable income and tax deductions for a given month, quarter, or year – these figures will be essential for your accountant (or accounting software) to properly calculate your company's tax liabilities, reporting, payments/refunds, and other obligations. Accounting software packages make it easy to produce a P&L for a specific date range – you can also create a comparative P&L to evaluate business activity over multiple months, quarters, or years and spot trends in financial increases or decreases that warrant a closer look.

The *Balance Sheet* tells the story of the entire organization on a given date, including cash on hand and money owed to the company in accounts receivable, the value of its assets (adjusted for depreciation), its current liabilities, and long-term debt obligations, and its current owner's equity as invested capital and/or retained earnings. Seeing these accumulated totals by category, as well as understanding the current "net worth" of the organization, can help the owner evaluate the past performance of the operation and make key business decisions about how to address issues such as:

- offering (or cancelling) net terms to clients carrying accounts receivable balances;
- implementing debt reduction or debt restructuring strategies;
- increasing investment in the organization to grow the business by expanding into new markets.

Financial Reports for Lenders, Investors, and Donors

In addition to helping the business owner (and a qualified accountant) analyze and respond to the organization's financial activity, the statements described above are required by banks, funding agencies, and investors who might be interested in supporting the venture. For organizations in a pre-launch stage, the Business Budget, Cash Flow Projection and Break-even Analysis are especially important, along with a Balance Sheet for the owner's personal finances and possibly a Personal Budget as well. For an established business, there will be the additional requirements for a Profit and Loss Statement and Balance Sheet, along with possibly a Budget vs. Actual comparison. Lenders, investors, and donors view this financial data as essential components in approving – or refusing – funding and other support for a new or growing company, so it is imperative that the business owner keep accurate, up-to-date records that demonstrate the venture's current conditions and prospects for the future.

Banking

Most people have experience with a local bank for their personal checking account, savings, auto loan, mortgage, and other products and services. Business owners need to develop additional relationships with the banking system in order to set up, run, and monitor their organization's financial activities. The development of new products – such as online banking, cloud-based systems for managing income and expenses, and mobile apps for point-of-purchase transactions – have increased the number of options available to keep track of money as it moves into and out of the venture.

Although it may seem easier for a small, one-person business to simply incorporate their business-related income and expense activity into an existing personal checking account, this approach is strongly discouraged by professional financial advisors. Business income and expenses need to be tracked in a separate *business checking account*, which most banks are happy to provide for their customers. There are two main reasons for keeping independent personal and business checking accounts: first, your regular business bookkeeping and accounting will be much simpler – and more accurate – if it is separated from the transactions in your personal account. Second, when it comes time to work with your accountant (or accounting software) for monthly, quarterly, or annual tax reporting and payments, it will be much easier to identify business income and expense activity from a separate business account, rather than trying to extract this data from your personal account. Plan on opening a business checking account with your local bank (such as one you already have a connection with) or ask your advisors for a recommendation.

It will be beneficial to compare different terms for business banking accounts to see who has the best mixture of minimum balance requirements, interest rates, and fees for merchant services and other products. Some banks will prefer, or even require, that a business owner open multiple accounts with them – for checking, savings, merchant services, credit cards, and lines of credit – in order to qualify for their best rates and services, so it is worth some time to investigate a variety of local banking options.

With the recent availability of online-only banks (with no physical locations to visit for deposits, withdrawals, or other transactions), a business owner can investigate even more options for setting up and using business banking accounts. The factors involved in choosing the "right" bank for your venture will depend on the full range of banking needs that are specific to your organization. Many of the traditional banking tasks that used to require a physical bank – such as depositing checks, requesting a cashier's check, or moving money between accounts – can now be accomplished online. However, there are some transactions – such as depositing cash or making change for a cash drawer – that can be better served with a physical bank. There is also something to be said for developing an ongoing relationship with local business banker who can answer questions, analyze account activity, and suggest beneficial strategies and products for your venture, in addition to recommending other valuable business contacts such as a local insurance agent, bookkeeper, accountant, or financial advisor. Watch out for the extra fees charged by some online-only banks, such as additional ATM charges for accounts ... although some physical banks are also starting to charge for *in-person transactions* involving a bank teller. Compare rates among several different banks, and types of banks, to find the best business checking and other accounts that fit your company's needs.

A *business savings account* can be linked to your business checking account for overdrafts and to accumulate funds for future shortfalls, such as an expected seasonal decrease or an unanticipated drop in sales volume due to extreme weather. As with your business checking account, investigate several options for setting up and using a business savings account, either with your current bank or another company.

To accept credit card payments from customers, you will need to set up a *merchant services account*. This is the intermediary between your customers, the issuer of their credit card (Visa, MasterCard, American Express, etc.) and the bank account you have identified to receive the funds. Many banks offer merchant services (for a fee) as part of a business package that bundles together business checking, savings, and other products. Some business owners will stay with one bank for all of their needs, while others will shop around for better rates or for access to special services, such as accepting mobile credit card payments using a smart phone or tablet.

Like other products offered by banks and financial institutions, *business credit card accounts* can be a convenient option for making and tracking purchases related to your organization. It pays to research the many credit card types (with reward programs such as cash back, points, airline miles, etc.) and different interest rates to get the best deal. Keeping a separate business credit card account makes it much easier to manage the venture's bookkeeping, since personal purchases will not be mixed together with business transactions. Opening a business credit card account at the same bank that provides your business checking, savings, and merchant services makes it even easier to manage your money by transferring funds between accounts and generating financial activity reports on a monthly, quarterly or annual basis. As with other revolving debts, make sure to pay off business credit card balances frequently to avoid ongoing finance charges.

A *business line of credit* is another type of revolving debt offered by banks to their established business customers. Often featuring a lower interest rate than credit card accounts, the line of credit can be useful for financing occasional improvements (such as purchasing major equipment) or to cover temporary shortfalls in the business checking account. As with the business credit card account, regularly repaying the business line balance will help reduce finance charges and keep the operation's debt in check.

Investments

Most small businesses will not have access to large amounts of capital that need investing, unless they have a substantial endowment or other funds that aren't needed for regular operational expenses and are therefore able to produce interest income through stocks, bonds, real estate, or other investments. Some large cultural institution such as museums or performing arts centers will show investment income on their profit and loss statements – this may be the sign of the organization managing a large gift (or accumulated donations) by investing the principle and using the dividends and interest income to cover operational expenses. If your arts venture needs to invest an endowment or other large amount of accumulated funds, it will be necessary to seek the advice of an experienced financial planner or investment banker to evaluate the different choices for managing risk and receiving optimal interest income while preserving and growing the principle.

One form of investment that all business owners should consider is a retirement account to set aside money for their future. Your accountant or bank can recommend – and help you evaluate – different investments such an IRA (or Roth IRA), annuity, closed-end fund, or other account to build towards a financially stable retirement.

Loans

As mentioned earlier, temporarily borrowing – and repaying – funds from revolving credit lines, such as credit cards or a business line of credit, can be a good strategy for covering anticipated shortfalls in seasonal revenue, getting through unexpected downturns in income or to finance major purchases. For working capital during the business development and start-up phase – or to purchase an existing organization and build on its reputation, customer base, and facilities – some business owners seek funding from a loan provider via the Small Business Administration (SBA) programs.

Founded in 1953, the SBA is a US government agency that helps entrepreneurs get loans, counseling, and other support. The agency doesn't lend money directly to consumers – instead, it makes capital available through banks and non-bank lending institutions. The lenders provide the loans and the SBA provides underwriting, along with other services to help the business owner develop, operate, and expand their venture.

There are several different SBA loan types to consider. The *General Small Business Loan 7(a)* is one of the more popular choices. Loan funds provided under this program can be used for long-term or short-term capital needs, to purchase inventory, equipment, or real estate, to establish a new business or acquire an existing one, or to refinance certain business debt. The SBA also has a micro loan program, as well as disaster loans and specialized real estate and equipment loans.

The application process for an SBA loan requires a high degree of preparation and organization on the part of the borrower. Along with an SBA Loan Application, the required forms include most of the financial documents covered earlier in this chapter:

- Personal financial statement
- Profit and Loss Statement
- Cash Flow Projections
- Balance Sheet
- Income tax returns
- Other documents depending on the type of loan and intended use of the funds.

Individuals seeking loan approval from the SBA (or other sources such as a local bank) need to demonstrate their creditworthiness. This is typically done using credit reporting agencies such as *Equifax, Experian,* or *TransUnion.* Maintaining good credit is an essential part of owning and operating a business, so take the necessary steps to keep your credit score as high as possible with these reporting agencies.

In addition to financial support, the SBA provides mentorship and guidance through their regional offices and counselors from a local Small Business Development Center (SBDC). The Small Business Administration website (www.sba.gov/) has a wealth of information to help you learn techniques for business development, manage an existing company, apply for funding, and connect with experienced advisors.

Borrowing and repaying money from loans and credit lines require recording these transactions as income and expenses on your financial projections and analysis statements. For a revolving credit line, drawing funds during the early spring would be recorded as income, while repayments in the summer months would be recorded as expenses. Loans have a fixed payoff schedule and pre-determined monthly principal and interest payments – the current debt balance is reported on the Balance Sheet and the monthly payments are shown on the Cash Flow Projection and Profit and Loss Statement. Loans and credit lines can help a business stabilize and grow over time, but the associated debt management must be handled carefully: a large business loan can help a business owner purchase major equipment or real estate, but the sizeable monthly payments can have a significant impact on the company's net profit.

Here are some examples of how arts-related businesses borrow and repay money from loans and credit lines:

- The Stellar Sounds Music Festival has its annual concert series in mid-September, but the organization needs to pay deposits in March to reserve the venue (a local concert hall) and finalize contracts with catering, sound production, and security companies. In January, the owners work with a local bank to open a business line of credit large enough to cover these and other anticipated near-term expenses. The company takes a draw from the credit line in March to pay the deposits, then pays back the balance in October after profits have been realized from tickets sales, concessions, and other revenue received during the fall festival.
- An important new client has been acquired by the Acme Graphic Design Agency, but the client's corporate headquarters are in a different state. Since maintaining the account will require regular travel to meet with the client, the design agency owners decide to open business credit card accounts with an online bank that offers low interest rates and customer rewards for travel-related purchases. The agency owners use their business credit cards for all travel-related purchases needed to work with the new client, including airfares, hotel, rental car charges, meals, and incidental expenses, such as parking and bridge

tolls. The new client pays a quarterly retainer for the design agency's services, so every time a payment comes in the agency pays off its credit card balances. The agency owners use their monthly credit card statements to record business transactions in their bookkeeping software, and their bookkeeper uses the Annual Credit Card Activity Report for tax liability calculations.

- After years of renting space in a desirable commercial district, the Westside Gallery has the opportunity to purchase the building they occupy. The gallery has an established track record as a successful venture, so the owners decide to apply for an SBA loan through their local bank. After meeting with a loan officer and submitting their application and other required documents, the Westside Gallery is approved for an SBA loan to purchase the property. The funds are allocated at the close of escrow, the building ownership is transferred to the gallery owners (with the bank placing a lien on the property to secure the financing), and the loan payments are made on schedule. Eventually, the SBA loan is paid off and the Westside Gallery owns their building free and clear of any associated debt.

Create a file named Banking and list all of your business accounts: checking, savings, merchant services, credit cards, lines of credit, investments, and loans. Describe the need for each type of account, where it will be located and how it will be used. Place the file in your Financial Documents folder.

Other Forms of Financing

In addition to personal savings, bank credit lines and loans from the SBA or similar bank-based lending programs, arts entrepreneurs can consider pursuing investments from other outside sources looking to support – and ultimately benefit financially from – creative businesses. There will likely be significant competition for these funds, especially from tech startups and serial entrepreneurs from other industries looking to launch their next venture. However, depending on the type of business you are developing, the strength of your business plan and the qualifications of the company's founders, your organization might be a good candidate for one the following types of funding opportunities. Be aware that investors are looking for business opportunities that have the potential for rapid growth and significant return on investment (ROI), usually in an exit phase where the company has expanded to a stage of significant success and then sold. Professional investors and venture capital firms may also seek a percentage of the organization's ownership and expect control via seats on the board of directors, along with some degree of management authority. In some cases, the founder him or herself may be end up being replaced by one of the venture's investors – or someone they designate – as part of the business development strategy. The arts entrepreneur may or may not be comfortable with these types of founder/investor relationships – but it is worth investigating some of the possibilities.

Business investment is a rapidly developing area that is constantly changing in terms of who offers what kinds of support, with new investment types and sources being developed and offered on a regular basis. The suggestions below are just a starting point for your explorations – keep up to date on business investment trends and opportunities by studying publications like *Forbes*,[2] *Entrepreneur Magazine*,[3] or the *Wall Street Journal*,[4] in addition to conducting frequent research online and through your network of contacts.

Start-up launch platforms, such as startups.co[5] and Gust,[6] provide a range of services to entrepreneurs. Startups.co has a group of products for founders and offers training, planning, mentorship, funding, and other support, while Gust connects investors with entrepreneurs who are looking to launch and grow their own companies.

Angel Networks are regional or otherwise affiliated groups of individual "angel" investors who seek opportunities to invest their money in potentially profitable businesses. Each "angel" will have a different preference for the type of company he or she will invest in – they will also have different styles of interacting with the business owners and expectations about the venture's management, growth, control, exit strategy, and rate of return. Sometimes an "angel" investor can be found among the entrepreneur's network of friends and family.

In Chapter 4 on fundraising, we examined crowdfunding as a potential source of financial support for an artist or arts organization. There is an additional type of crowdfunding known as *equity crowdfunding* that allows entrepreneurs to attract investments and help their startup businesses launch, develop, and become profitable. In standard crowdfunding, the "backer" provides financial support (at low, medium, or high levels) to the campaign's creator in exchange for a reward (depending on the level of money provided) and a sense of involvement in the project. In equity crowdfunding, the backers get ownership shares in the company they are investing in, along with a sense of participation in the venture's mission and goals. Like other forms of investment, the investor assumes all the potential upside and downside risks of placing their money in a company – they may realize significant profits if the venture does well, or lose everything if it doesn't. There are a number of strict regulations that apply to both crowdfunding investors and to business owners who receive their investments. If this idea sounds appealing for your concept for an arts venture, try an online search for "equity crowdfunding" and investigate the many options.

Business *incubators* and *accelerators* provide a supportive environment for a newly forming – or to ready to expand – startup. Incubators allow founders to refine their concepts and settle on a business plan, while accelerators help early stage ventures evolve into their next stages of growth and success. Some business incubators and accelerators are based in universities, while others are associated with government agencies. The International Business Innovation Association website[7] has information for its members on these (and other) opportunities for business startups.

LinkedIn is a very popular platform for connecting all kinds of individuals and companies to each other – it can also be a powerful tool for raising awareness about an arts entrepreneur's professional profile and business ambitions. By creating an engaging LinkedIn presence, reaching out to a wide range of connections and building up recommendations, a business owner can develop an ever-expanding network of supporters and collaborators.

Friends and family can offer advice, recommendations, referrals, and introductions to help the new business owner develop and launch their venture. They can also, in some cases, provide financial resources and in-kind contributions. Carefully consider the many implications of seeking and accepting investment funds from immediate family members or close friends – these relationships can be affected in both positive and negative ways, depending on the company's financial performance over time.

Bookkeeping, Accounting, and Taxes

Like other business owners, arts entrepreneurs are responsible for maintaining up-to-date records of their financial activity, filing required tax reports for income, expenses and payroll activity, and paying their personal and company taxes on time. Managing an individual's – or an organization's – bookkeeping can be simple or complex, depending on the nature of the business, the corporate form it operates under (sole proprietorship, LLC, C Corp or S Corp, etc. – see Chapter 5 on legal issues, for more information) and the number of employees and independent contractors its supports. The development of accounting software such as QuickBooks, along with payroll management tools such as Intuit Payroll, has made it possible for business owners to handle data entry, reporting, and tax filings by themselves, especially if the company is small and structured in a compact, straightforward way. As businesses grow and their accounting needs become more complex, it can become necessary to hire a professional bookkeeper and/or accountant to keep track of the organization's income and expenses, especially when payroll, depreciation, and other tax-related issues become more prominent. Tax law is a complex, continually evolving field, so it pays to have professional advice and support when running a business. Bookkeeping and accounting services do represent a (deductible) business expense, but the time they save the business owner – together with the accuracy they provide and the potentially overlooked tax deductions they can uncover – can more than pay for the cost of their services over time.

Record-keeping, Archives, Filing Documents, Searchable Financial History

Regardless of whether you manage your own finances using bookkeeping software or hire a professional to manage your books and file your organization's tax forms and payments, it will be necessary to set up an accessible, ongoing system for retaining your financial records. Software accounting systems, including cloud-based services, have an advantage over paper-based systems when it comes to searchable financial history, reporting and archiving official documents. Bookkeeping software also provides easy access to business analysis and planning documents such as Profit and Loss Statements, Balance Sheets, and Cash Flow reports.

Good quality record-keeping systems help keep the business on track with tax and reporting requirements while providing these and other documents for analysis and planning. Note the IRS has requirements for records retention for different categories of business documents, such as accounting, personnel, contracts, and taxes. Work with an experienced bookkeeper or accountant who can set up your company's accounting system and give you advice on records retention, tax filings and other key financial requirements.

Chapter Summary

To develop a vision for how your arts business will become part of your personal financial support system, develop a personal budget that lays out all of your anticipated expenses such as rent, food, phone, and other monthly and annual costs – along with your expected income sources. Bookkeeping software such as Excel can help with this exercise, but a hand-written spreadsheet works as well. A personal budget can help you calculate how much you need to live, and how much your business will need to pay you as the owner. Next, create an outline for your business budget, using the income and expense categories found on the IRS Schedule C form. Add more details depending on the type of business you are creating – you can discover specific income and expense categories for your particular venture by asking a local bookkeeper or accountant, checking with local arts support organizations or conducting online research. After your organization has been in operation for some time, create a Budget vs. Actuals comparison to see if your predictions have been accurate ... and to adjust any operational features of the venture that need attention. The Cash Flow projection is another tool to analyze financial performance and help you identify areas where future income and expenses can be adjusted based on recent activity. Artists and arts organizations that produce goods using materials and labor from outside sources can benefit from a Break-even Analysis to determine profitability while seeking efficiencies in their spending patterns. A Profit and Loss Statement shows the business's income and expense details over a specific time range. This financial report – along with a Balance Sheet showing the organization's assets, liabilities, and equity – are essential when seeking funds from investors, donors, or lenders such as the Small Business Administration (SBA). To keep personal and business accounting separate, open independent checking, savings, credit card, and line of credit accounts (if needed) for the company. Bank loans are one source of funding for start-ups, but there are others such as launch platforms, "angel" investors and equity crowdfunding. Be thorough and timely in all financial record keeping for your venture, and seek the support of a professional bookkeeper and/or accountant to keep current with your taxes and other document filings.

Discussion Questions

1. How would you describe your financial goals in five years, both for yourself individually and for your company?

2. How much will your venture need to pay you in "Owner's Draw" compensation during the first, second and third years of operation?

3. List the anticipated business income and expenses for your specific type of organization. How do they compare with other similar businesses found in your research?

4. How does an arts organization use a Business Budget vs. Actuals report to analyze financial performance and adjust its future plans?

5. Explain how a Cash Flow Projection helps a venture evaluate its current cash position and make changes to its anticipated spending.

6. Name two ways a company can improve profitability, using a Break-even Analysis.

7. What are the purposes of a Profit and Loss Statement, for the business owner and potential lenders or investor?

8. Why should business bank accounts – such as checking, savings, and credit cards – be kept separate from personal accounts?

9. Describe how a professional bookkeeper or accountant can help an arts entrepreneur meet their venture's tax obligations and keep the business on track.

Notes

[1]   See http://nonprofitinformation.com/understanding-nonprofit-financial-statements/

2   See www.forbes.com

3   See www.entrepreneur.com

4   See www.wsj.com/

5   See https://www.startups.co/

6   See http://gust.com/startups

7   See https://inbia.org/

Further Reading

Adelman, Philip J., and Alan M. Marks. 2014. *Entrepreneurial finance.* Upper Saddle River, NJ: Prentice Hall.

Cobb, Peter, Susan L. Ball, and Felicity Hogan. 2011. *The profitable artist: a handbook for all artists in the performing, literary, and visual arts.* New York: Allworth Press, Internet resource. See Chapters 3, 4, 5, 6, and 7.

Luttrull, Elaine G. 2013. *Arts & numbers: a financial guide for artists, writers, performers, and other members of the creative class.* Chicago: Agate Publishing.

7 Cultural Policy and the Arts Entrepreneur

> Cultural policy represents the decisions (by both public and private entities) that either directly or indirectly shape the environment in which the arts get created, disseminated, and consumed.[1]

This chapter looks at the policy context within which an artist or arts-related business operates. *Cultural policy* is a term that describes a range of factors that can influence how arts entrepreneurs plan, run and evaluate their businesses – these can include governmental (public) rules, regulations, and programs, as well as institutional norms and practices found in the private sector. In addition to exploring the impacts cultural policies have on an arts organization, we will consider how cultural policy has been developed in the US and other countries to identify how and why different approaches have evolved, especially in terms of government subsidies for art-making and appreciation. Cultural policy refers to much more than government grants for cultural institutions or individual artists: it also covers legal frameworks such as tax codes, intellectual property regulations and federal, state and local rules for everything from labor laws to zoning ordinances.

The areas of cultural policy covered in this chapter include:

- the history of cultural policy in the US. and other countries;
- government grants and loans for culture and art;
- other government programs that can support cultural activities;
- cultural policy expressed through laws;
- how cultural policy is made and applied;
- institutional norms, practices and trends.

The Origins of Cultural Policy

Before examining the history of cultural policy in the US it helps to review earlier instances of state support for culture to see how and why other countries approached the issues surrounding arts policy formation and implementation. The origins – and evolutions – of cultural policies have followed different paths in different countries, and a comparative view serves to lay a foundation for understanding each instance relative to the others. Looking at the cultural policy frameworks found elsewhere also prepares those arts entrepreneurs who are seeking an international presence by establishing their organization with multiple locations in different countries, or who are developing projects that cross borders.

History of Cultural Policy in Other Countries

Historical Overview of French Cultural Policy

The earliest instances of French arts support can be found during the reign of François I during the Renaissance.[2] An office overseeing royal art treasures and architecture was established in 1535 as part of the monarch's mission to make France the next Rome. Cardinal Richelieu expanded on this idea in 1635 by creating the *Académie Française* as guardian of France's "official" conception of art. Members of the *Académie* held their first exhibition in 1667 – later these became "salons" where official art was displayed. In 1680, the *Comédie Française* was established under Louis XIV as an official theater company with federal support, a status it has in some ways preserved to this day. During this period, the state commissioned art from members of the academy, who were licensed suppliers of artwork to the King. Exercising the power of the monarchy through artistic patronage was a vital part of regime building and establishment of a legacy. Much like erecting statues and memorials, supporting art salons and an "official" theater promoted the ruler's artistic judgment and taste, especially as representative of the entire nation's cultural vision.

In 1789, in the French Revolution, the royal academies were dismantled and the self-governing *Commune des Arts* was organized with the help of prominent painter Jacques-Louis David – a friend of Robespierre and strong supporter of the French Revolution. The group expanded to become the *Société Républicaine des Arts* and eventually came under the newly formed Education Ministry (1793) and Ministry of the Interior (1795). A national arts institute was formed, which was organized by Napoleon in 1803 into four divisions, including the Beaux Arts. State support for the arts was established during this period. Along with providing patronage and enforcing censorship, the government now sought to "democratize" or widen access to culture. State subventions for culture became linked to the idea of public education, and music and art schools were established.

Ultimately the Third Republic distanced itself from the notion of state management of French culture. Neither the left-wing Popular Front of the 1930s nor the Vichy regime of 1940–1944 under the Nazi Occupation supported an expanded role for the French government regarding the arts. A centralized federal arts program in France would not re-emerge until after World War II.

After the end of World War II in 1945, "cultural rights" were incorporated into both the new French Constitution and the Universal Declaration of Human Rights of 1948. When President Charles de Gaulle initiated the Fifth Republic in 1958, France was still in the midst of a major reconstruction effort, both to rebuild the country and to revitalize the spirit of the French people. In 1959, focus was brought once again to the question of how to "democratize" culture. At this moment, de Gaulle appointed the first Minister of Cultural Affaires, and his name was André Malraux.

Malraux was a celebrated novelist, hero of the French Resistance and political figure. Despite limited funding and ongoing rivalries with other ministries (education, foreign affairs), Malraux ambitiously sought the creation of cultural centers, or *maisons de la culture*, in each of the twenty *départements* or regions of the country. The two major themes of French cultural policy, democratization (or access to the arts) and quality (or official standards of excellence) are embodied within the Ministry of Culture from this point forward: access and excellence. One of de Gaulle's objectives was to promote the "glory and grandeur of the French State," hence the close relationship between political power and culture. The new Ministry of Culture project sought nothing less than the construction of a new sense of national identity.

Although "access and excellence" were dominant themes during the Malraux/de Gaulle period of the early 1960s, "high culture" continued to be the only segment of society's creative output deemed worthy of public subsidy. Access to culture had been opened up, but only to a culture defined as "noble" and therefore deserving of attention. The events of the late 1960s, and the student revolution in May 1968 in particular, caused a number of voices to be raised against the notion of an "official" unified national culture imposed from above. Malraux's *maisons de la culture* were attacked, and the student uprising demanded government support for newer, more popular art forms. The socialists put these ideas into practice in the next major milestone in the development of French cultural policy. The iconoclastic politician Jack Lang was culture minister under President François Mitterand from 1981 to 1986, and again from 1988 to 1993. Lang, who had a background in theater, put cultural policy at the forefront of the government's political agenda.[3] In 1982, with the French Socialist Party in power, the state budget for culture was increased 79 percent over the previous year. Lang opened up access to government subsidies for popular art forms, as well as works that challenged traditional notions of appropriate public art.

The funding increases and inclusive, populist agenda of the culture ministry under Lang mark the last major expansion of arts support by the French government. The late twentieth and early twenty-first centuries have seen relatively stable funding levels, which are actually net reductions of support when increased demand and rising costs are factored in. The state has implemented a decentralization of power and administration from the federal level to the regions, although the Ministry still controls the overall budget and allocations. Recent trends in French cultural policy indicate a willingness among nationalized institutions to embrace the concept of donations from private businesses, as evidenced by the corporate supporters of the *Musée du Quai Branly*.[4]

Historical Overview of Cultural Policy in the United Kingdom

In the 17th edition of *Compendium: Cultural Policies and Trends in Europe*, authors Rod Fisher and Andrew Ormston cite the creation of the Council for the Encouragement of Music and the Arts (CEMA) in 1940 as "the first national body to support the arts" in the UK.[5] Organized to provide public and private funds to keep culture thriving during World War II, this agency became the Arts Council of Great Britain in 1946. The Arts Council's mission resembled the post-war ambitions of France's Ministry of Culture in that both sought to preserve their national heritage and revitalize artistic expression as part of a campaign to rebuild their country. In the 1970s and beyond, regional and local arts associations supported less traditional art forms and engaged "alternative" artists in contrast to the more "traditional" classical work supported by the Arts Council. The 1980s saw increases in private/public funding under a still-active charitable organization known as Arts & Business, while the 1990s saw the unified Arts Council of Great Britain split into the individual Arts Council of England, the Scottish Arts Council and the Arts Council of Wales. The relationships between regional or local arts organizations and the national programs remain a notable structural feature of UK cultural policy, as does the ongoing impact of budget cuts implemented since the worldwide economic recession of 2007–2008. Author Anna Rosser Upchurch's 2016 book, *The Origins of the Arts Council Movement: Philanthropy and Policy*[6] provides a detailed look at national arts policies in the UK, Canada, and the US.

History of Cultural Policy in the US

Unlike other countries, the US does not have a long history of government support for the arts at the federal, state, or local levels. In his 1969 booklet on US cultural policy for UNESCO, author Charles C. Mark points out that the formative goals of the National Endowment for the Arts were "not significantly different from the stated policy positions of France or the United Kingdom."[7]

Cultural institutions in the US – such as museums and orchestras – were initially private enterprises founded by wealthy families to promote the arts and provide social occasions for their family and friends. The earliest libraries and museums were created to house the collections of individuals. For example, the Museum of Fine Arts in Boston, founded in 1870, was based on a collection from the Boston Athenæum, which began in 1807 as a library and reading room for members of the Anthology Society.[8]

Great concentrations of private wealth are an ongoing part of American history, as is the tradition of philanthropy toward social causes such as alleviating the effects of poverty and encouraging access to education and the arts. Private foundations have served to support and promote culture, even if most of America's artistic products (classical opera, literature, painting and sculpture) were inspired by or directly imported from Europe during the seventeenth and eighteenth centuries. Some family foundations eventually embraced goals for cultural access and excellence that resembled the model developed in other countries, such as France: the Solomon R. Guggenheim Foundation was created to open up its collection for "promotion and encouragement and education in art and the enlightenment of the public."[9]

The earliest instances of direct US government support for the arts can be found in President Roosevelt's New Deal programs of the 1930s. Initiatives such as the Works Progress Administration (WPA) and the Federal Arts Project (FAP) were designed to employ writers, visual artists, actors, and other workers in the creative sector. The US was at the lowest point of the Great Depression in the early 1930s, with 13 million citizens unemployed. Work relief was central to Roosevelt's overall recovery strategy, and many new American theater companies, public art projects (such as murals), musical works, and published manuscripts were made possible by the New Deal.

When President Kennedy was elected in 1960, the US was emerging from the rabid anti-communism of the McCarthy era that had lasted from the late 1940s through the late 1950s. Hope, change, and a renewed sense of opportunity and optimism were emblematic of the Kennedy campaign and administration, although issues such as civil rights and the Cold War divided the electorate. President Kennedy – and even more so the First Lady, Jacqueline Kennedy – championed the arts in the White House as a way to bring the country together around a sense of creative spirit that was uniquely American. Art forms such as Abstract Expressionism, modern dance, and jazz were dynamic, contemporary examples of America's ability to lead the world in cultural production. Much like the advances in science and technology that were driving the space program, the arts were viewed as a rallying point for the American public, as well as a signal to other nations of America's emergence as a dominant force on the world stage.

Kennedy and his team developed an Executive Order establishing the President's Advisory Council on the Arts, but it remained unsigned on his desk after his assassination.[10] It was President Johnson who ultimately pushed through a Congressionally approved federal arts program that would become the National Endowment for the Arts (NEA). The NEA offered federal dollars to the states on the condition of locally sourced matching funds, increasing arts support dramatically overall and inspiring widespread participation in the program. From modest beginnings in the late 1960s, the NEA's funding levels grew rapidly through the 1970s and 1980s, only to be cut back severely in the conservative political backlash over federal support for controversial artwork during the 1990s. The twenty-first century has seen gradual increases in the NEA's budget, although the current level is still below that of the early 1990s. The US presidential election of 2016 inspired a resurgence of conservative viewpoints about public funding for the arts, with politicians once again arguing in favor of the elimination of NEA funding from the federal budget. The federal budget for Fiscal Year 2017 included a slightly increased allocation of $149.8 million for the NEA, while Fiscal Year 2018 saw a modest increase to $152.8 million. There have been recent attempts by conservative political leaders to shut down the NEA, but Congress has been able to rebuff[11] those efforts – for the time being.

Despite these threats to government arts programs, there have been several important studies and initiatives that point towards a more optimistic future for US cultural policy. In his book *Performing Policy*,[12] author Paul Bonin-Rodriguez cites three important developments that have grown in opposition to conservative criticisms of federal arts support:

- Held in 1997, "The Arts and the Public Purpose"[13] was the 92nd meeting of the American Assembly, a think tank at Columbia University in New York. The resulting publication of that meeting, which included many prominent artists and policy specialists, offers recommendations that provide a framework for the future of cultural policy in the US – these include Achieving Collaboration and Partnership, Improving Financial Support and Investment, Making the Arts More Accessible, Preserving the Nation's Heritage, Improving Education and Training, Meeting Research, Information, and Evaluation Needs, and Strengthening Advocacy.
- The Creative Capital Foundation[14] was founded in 1999 to support challenging work by adventurous contemporary artists. Their "venture philanthropy" model combines direct funding with mentorship, training, and advisory services to help selected artists achieve and maintain successful, sustainable careers – with the hope that supported artists will "give back" to the program through reinvestment and in-kind support.
- *Investing in Creativity: A Study of the Support Structure for U.S. Artists*[15]was published by the Urban Institute in 2003. This data-driven report analyzes the support environment in the culturally vibrant communities of Boston, Chicago, Cleveland, Houston, Los Angeles, New York City, San Francisco, Seattle, and Washington, DC – along

with a composite profile of rural communities. Its conclusions and "Priorities for action" identify areas of critical importance, such as encouraging better public understanding of artists and their work, strengthening artist-focused organizations, establishing broad-based networks of stakeholders, creating an information infrastructure to monitor the big picture, strengthening the capacity of artists to advocate on their own behalf, cultivating existing and potential diverse markets for what artists do and make, encouraging changes in artists' training and professional development, and strengthening the awards and grants system.

The current cultural policy landscape in the US includes a wide range of governmental and non-governmental agencies, programs, and practices. Our exploration of this topic begins with a look at public funding sources.

US Government Grants and Loans for Culture and Art

The U.S. system is comprised of public and private entities, tax policies, legislative allocations, donated bequests, restricted endowments, education mandates, and social agendas. The hierarchy of government agencies, composed of city, county, state, regional, and federal strata, is itself a dizzying scheme, especially to people whose own nations have highly centralized, state-directed systems.[16]

As the NEA's own publication indicates in the quote above, the array of government funding sources for art and culture in the US is complex and multi-faceted. Focusing separately on each category of public support provides an introductory picture of the funding landscape.

Federal Arts Programs

Founded in 1965, the National Endowment for the Arts (NEA) supports art creation and engagement for a wide variety of disciplines. The range of artistic practices and communities served by NEA programs are a reflection of the agency's commitment to "providing all Americans with diverse opportunities for arts participation."[17] NEA funds are allocated in categories such as Creation of Art, Engaging with Art, Promoting Knowledge and Partnerships for the Arts. Grant opportunities can be found for nearly every type of artistic practice or focus area, including arts education, creative placemaking, dance, design, folk and traditional arts, literature, media arts, museums, music and musical theater, opera, multidisciplinary works, theater and visual arts. The agency also supports work in research and analysis, accessibility and the development of artistic communities. Project funding opportunities listed under the NEA's Grants for Organizations will be of particular interest to the arts entrepreneur, although it is important to note that these awards require matching funds. For example, an organization receiving $10,000 in grant finding from the NEA must demonstrate an additional $10,000 raised from other sources. If your arts enterprise does not have non-profit 501(c)(3) designation from the IRS, you can still apply for NEA grants by working through a fiscal sponsor (see Chapter 5, Legal issues, for more information). This strategy is also possible when seeking funds from other public programs. In addition to directly supporting projects, the NEA also partners with state, jurisdictional, and regional arts agencies around the country.

State Arts Agencies

> State arts agencies exemplify government by, for and of the people. Each state arts agency is governed by a council of citizen leaders that oversees its work. Broad public engagement is central to state arts agency planning, grant decisions and programs that respond to local needs.[18]

Cultural grants at the state level vary depending on location and funding levels. In addition to distributing resources allocated by the NEA, the budget for a state arts agency can include funds provided by their legislature and other sources. However, the availability of arts funding found in each state is dependent on the political and economic conditions of the moment. For example, after an all-time high of $32 million in 2000–2001, the California Arts Council lost 94 percent of its arts funding in 2003–2004 due to a fiscal crisis. In 2016–2017, the budget rebounded to $21.1 million, but with the NEA's future in question, there is much uncertainty about funding levels – and the organizations they support – going forward.

Despite these fluctuations in resources, state arts agencies are exceptionally good candidates for creative enterprises focused on community development, arts education, diversity, historic preservation, economic growth, and other public benefits.

Regional Arts Organizations

There are six Regional Arts Organizations in the US that receive funds from the NEA and other sources and distribute them to state agencies, organizations, and individuals in their territories.[19] Representing a group of states in each area of the country, the Regional Arts Organizations (the New England Foundation for the Arts, the Mid-Atlantic Arts Foundation, South Arts, the Mid-America Arts Alliance, the Arts Midwest, and the Western State Arts Federation) resemble one another in their relationships to the NEA but are unique in their individual structures, programming, and focus areas. For example, the New England Foundation for the Arts has grant programs in dance, international engagement, music,

Native American arts, presenting, public art, and theater, while Arts Midwest features programs in education, conference development, folk music, touring, world music, research/training, and reading.

Like their partners at the federal and state levels, Regional Arts Organizations are committed to issues such as community engagement, diversity, and inclusion. Arts entrepreneurs should investigate their Regional Arts Organization for financial support as well as workshops, information, and networking opportunities – they also have programs for domestic and international touring artists.

County, Cities and Neighborhoods

Arts councils at the county, city, and neighborhood levels exist in many areas of the US, although their funding levels and program focus areas are different depending on their location and sources of support. Some city arts programs, for example, are very active in directly funding local artists and arts organizations, while others concentrate on education or arts marketing efforts.

Interacting with Government Arts Agencies

The arts entrepreneur has a number of choices to consider when engaging with local, state, regional, and national programs for culture. Applying for grants – either directly as a 501(c)(3) nonprofit or indirectly through a fiscal sponsor – is a natural first step in developing relationships with public arts agencies, especially for a growing venture focused on issues such as community development, diverse audiences, or at-risk youth. Note that some public programs are geared toward established arts organizations or individual artists, while others target individuals just launching their careers or businesses in their formative stages.

In addition to financial support, many government arts agencies offer professional development training, research publications, and networking opportunities. City and county arts programs often provide services such as listings or directories for local arts organizations to help them become better known in their area. An arts business can also offer support *to* their state and local arts agencies, either through financial contributions or in-kind donations such as providing space for events or volunteering labor for a project.

For an even closer relationship with their local arts agency, the owner of an arts organization can join the agency's advisory council or become an appointed member of the governing board. This is especially important when, after becoming well-established in the community and recognized as a leader, the arts entrepreneur is able to offer expertise and guidance for the agency's policies and programs. Although government arts agencies are tied to regulations at the local, state, and federal level, they are also led by individuals who have significant influence over how their cultural programs are designed and implemented. Over time, the owner of an established arts business can participate in – and to some degree shape – the structure and impact of public programs for the arts.

Exploring Arts Agencies and Making Connections

How does one go about researching and developing relationships with the various arts agencies that may be of interest to the arts entrepreneur? There are several avenues to consider, either individually or in parallel with one another:

- Use online research to find the federal, state, regional, and local arts agencies that apply to your venture. This includes studying the websites of the NEA, the National Assembly of State Arts Agencies, the Regional Arts Organizations and the county, city, and neighborhood agencies near you. After developing a list of target government programs, examine each opportunity to evaluate productive connection points with your business, including grant programs, training sessions and research publications. Follow links to all instances of the agency's social media to read current postings and learn about the organization's recent history.
- Sign up for each agency's newsletters, email notifications, and other announcements, including social media postings. Interact with each agency by offering comments, likes, questions, or other input.
- Ask your network of advisors for their views on the background, current activities, and future prospects for each arts agency and the specific programs you have identified. Seek connections with individuals *within* each of these target programs by working through your network or introducing yourself at events where they appear.

The aim, over time, is to develop productive, mutually beneficial links with all of the government programs for arts and culture that relate to you and your business. Establishing and maintaining these relationships takes time – to raise awareness, to increase understanding, and to develop trust – but with tact, perseverance, and genuine common interest, there can be productive results for everyone involved.

Create a folder named Cultural Policy Interactions. Create a new document named Government Arts Agencies and list all of the relevant federal, state, regional, and local programs for your venture. Include targeted funding programs, as well as training, research, and networking opportunities. Indicate deadlines for grant proposals, event participation and other points of contact. Place the Government Arts Agencies document in the Cultural Policy Interactions folder.

Cultural Diplomacy: the U.S. Department of State

In addition to the National Endowment for the Arts, there are other federal programs that support creative enterprises, especially for projects involving cultural exchange with other countries. The U.S. Department of State's Bureau of Educational and Cultural Affairs (ECA) offers a range of cultural programs[20] in different artistic disciplines (film, dance, music, writing, etc.) designed to promote American culture abroad and bring foreign artists to US audiences. The State Department also manages study abroad programs for students (including Fulbright Fellowships and travel grants) and professional development programs for established artists, educators, and administrators. The purpose of these programs is to encourage international awareness, dialogue, and appreciation of cultural activities in the US and overseas – the term "cultural diplomacy" refers to the exchanges, interactions, and relationships that can further the cause of mutual understanding between nations. Many other countries besides the US offer similar programs, so arts entrepreneurs with an overseas presence should investigate cultural exchange opportunities there as well.

Federally Funded Cultural Institutions

Unlike other countries that provide direct financial support to a large number of national museums, galleries, and performing arts venues, the US has a relatively modest list of federally funded arts institutions: the National Gallery of Art and the Smithsonian Institution in Washington, DC, and the John F. Kennedy Center for the Performing Arts in New York. Each of these well-established organizations offers fellowships and internships that deserve consideration as professional development programs for the evolving arts entrepreneur. They also provide opportunities for contributing financial and in-kind resources – a good strategy for developing relationships between an established arts venture's leadership and these high profile cultural institutions.

Preserving US Cultural Heritage

Maintaining the legacy of a nation's cultural heritage is one of the most common themes of cultural policy found in countries around the world – it is also one of the key objectives of the United Nations Educational, Scientific and Cultural Organization (UNESCO). In the US, the Library of Congress – and its affiliated programs such as the National Recording Preservation Foundation – collects a wide range of materials from domestic and foreign sources for research and other purposes. Other federal programs, such as the cultural heritage programs[21] managed by the National Park Service, protect and promote important landmarks around the country. Arts organizations focused on history, interpretation, and cultural legacy should explore relationships with these federally supported institutions to expand their networks of information and influence.

Arts Education

Initiatives aimed at training student artists, supporting arts educators, and broadening awareness and appreciation of culture have always been key elements of cultural policy, both at home and abroad. The benefits of arts education include greater understanding of one's own culture (as well as cultures claimed by others), opportunities for experimenting with art-making techniques and discovering one's affinities and aptitudes, and increased enthusiasm among future patrons for traditional and contemporary art forms. Arts education serves multiple cultural policy goals, from preserving and extending cultural heritage to creating new practitioners – and audiences – for innovative modes of cultural expression.

Like government programs at different levels for professional art making and distribution, there are a number of arts education programs at the federal, state, and local levels. For example, the NEA lists Arts Education under its Art Works program, while the U.S. Department of Education has, under its Office of Innovation and Improvement,[22] support for arts instruction, services for students with disabilities or from low-income families, and professional development for arts educators. Many state, regional, and local government arts agencies also have programs specifically for arts education, as do some foundations and corporate programs.

The arts entrepreneur who is interested in arts education has a number of options to consider. Some business founders see opportunities for launching an arts education venture that produces public benefits by offering supplemental arts training for K-12 schools that lack extensive arts programs, sometimes due to budget reductions. Others concentrate on teacher training projects or new technologies for cultural awareness courses and innovative art skills. There are also government scholarships for students in higher education arts programs – these can be leveraged as part of one's academic/professional development plans.

As with the exploration of public resources for amateur or professional artists, the arts entrepreneur should investigate opportunities in arts education by conducting online research (including social media), joining relevant email lists and newsletters, and consulting with advisors to find links within your network that lead to people and programs in your area of interest.

Create a new document named Government Arts Education Programs and list all of the relevant federal, state, regional, and local programs for your venture. Place the document in the Cultural Policy Interactions folder.

Humanities Grants

In addition to the federal support for the arts found under the NEA, there is another government agency dedicated to research and scholarship in the humanities known as the National Endowment for the Humanities (NEH).[23] This agency supports projects focused on areas such as language, literature, history, philosophy, archaeology, comparative religion, and ethics. NEH grants have cost-sharing requirements, meaning their awards will cover some (but not all) of the total budget for any given project. Like grants from the NEA and other programs that require matching funds, receiving an NEH grant can be a catalyst that inspires additional contributions from internal or external sources, such as board members, individual donors, foundations, or corporate sponsors. Although continued government funding for the NEH is also in question, the agency has strong support from its allies in education, historic preservation, research and institutions, and programs at the state level.

Other Government Programs

In its introductory publication, *How the U.S. Funds the Arts*,[24] the NEA lists a number of programs that have a history of providing grants and other support to arts-related projects. These include:

- U.S. Geological Survey (Earth as Art)
- Department of Defense (military bands)
- General Service Administration (art in architecture, fine arts)
- Department of Housing and Urban Development (sustainable communities)
- National Forest Service (Cultural Resource Stewardship, Artists-in-Residence, Expressions of Freedom).

There are also government programs that can support cultural activities in areas such as:

- economic development (businesses, neighborhoods, counties, regions);
- job training;
- transportation (airports, rail stations, public transit systems, etc.);
- commercial/residential real estate development;
- public housing;
- cultural tourism;
- repurposed military bases, brownfield remediation, urban and rural renewal projects;
- international collaborations, exchanges and other initiatives promoting US businesses abroad.

The availability of these and other programs to the arts entrepreneur changes over time, with new opportunities being introduced and existing programs undergoing modifications or being terminated. The method previously described for investigating government arts agencies and arts education programs applies here as well: conduct online research, join relevant email lists and social media instances, and consult with advisors to discover possibilities for public support and mutually beneficial relationships with these and other public programs for culture.

Cultural Policy and the Law

In addition to arts-related government grants and support programs, there are different legal structures that can have an impact on businesses focused on cultural production or presentation. Laws affecting an arts entrepreneur can come from several sources, including constitutional law, statutory law (from Congress), regulations (from the executive branch and federal agencies), executive orders and directives (from the President), case law (from the court system), and state and local laws. We now turn to ways of understanding, navigating, and shaping the laws for arts and culture.

Federal Programs

At the national level, federal arts programs such as the National Endowment for the Arts are created by Congress – they are also funded by Congressional approval of the annual budget. The executive branch can intervene via executive order, while the judicial branch can have influence via decisions in lawsuits – see *National Endowment for the Arts v. Finley*, 524 U.S. 569 (1998) for a case involving "decency" and publicly funded art projects. If your arts venture wants to seek funding from the NEA or another federal program, it is advisable to investigate the specific program you are interested in (for example, Art Works or Our Town for organizations, or Creative Writing Fellowships for individuals) by studying the agency's website and using online research to find instances of successfully funded projects similar to your own. Your grant application or other proposal can target a specific federal funding program while demonstrating your awareness of that agency's history and previous grant-giving activity.

Influencing cultural policy at the national level requires a commitment to working with an elected Congressional official and his/her staff to initiate or modify statutory laws affecting businesses in the creative sector. Other forms of applying influence can include providing testimony in public hearings, creating or working with lobbies and special interest groups, and publishing influential works that become cited by lawmakers in their deliberations. For more direct involvement, there is always the option of seeking office as a Member of Congress in the Senate or the House of Representatives. Running an election campaign to become a Representative or Senator can be a daunting task, especially if one of your intended goals is to increase federal support for the arts or reshape

US cultural policy. However, there may be opportunities to attract voters to your views depending on your local environment. Some business-owners-turned-politicians reach national prominence by starting at the local level as a member of their city council, mayor of a town or as a state senator or representative. Another way to join the government and engage with cultural policy is to find a job in one of the federal agencies involved in arts and culture, such as the National Endowment for the Arts, the National Endowment for the Humanities, the Institute of Museum and Library Services, the Corporation for Public Broadcasting, the Library of Congress, the Smithsonian Institution, and the John F. Kennedy Center for the Performing Arts (among others). Many of these organizations also have advisory boards and public programs that can provide opportunities for input. Although employees of federal agencies don't typically have direct influence over the legal frameworks that affect arts entrepreneurs, they can certainly play a role in the *interpretation* and *implementation* of the many regulations, guidelines, and policies that matter to artists and arts organizations.

State and Local Laws

The legal frameworks for arts organizations at the state and local levels operate in many of the same ways as the federal system. There are state, regional, and local arts agencies that receive legislative appropriations and partner with the NEA – they also attract support from other sources such as corporations, foundations, and private donations. These agencies distribute funds through a wide range of programs aimed at increasing cultural awareness and production. See this chapter's previous section on "Interacting with Government Arts Agencies" for an introduction to working with government programs at the state and local levels. The strategies for influencing local cultural policies are the same as those operating at the national level: work with elected officials (or become one yourself) to introduce legislation that benefits artists and arts-related businesses, join an arts-advocacy group as a supporter or advisor, make your views heard through writing or speaking at public hearings, or seek employment in a regional, state, or local government agency to participate in the interpretation and application of laws affecting the arts entrepreneur.

At either the federal or state/local levels, exercising your right to vote is another key element in shaping the cultural policy landscape. Find and support candidates whose positions represent your interests on issues affecting arts entrepreneurship, and share your views with elected officials who depend on public support for their continued employment. Organizing with other artists and business owners in your area can produce even more leverage – there is power in numbers, especially when seeking media coverage and offering (or withholding) endorsements and financial support for politicians.

> Create a new document named Cultural Policy Engagement and Influence. List all of the ways you and your arts venture will respond to – and exert influence on – the federal, state, and local laws affecting your business. Place the document in the Cultural Policy Interactions folder.

Taxes, Including Charitable Deductions and 501(C)(3) Status

> To an extent unknown elsewhere, the American government through its tax code has delegated broad policymaking powers to private institutions in the pursuit of various eleemosynary (charitable) goals.[25]

There are two main areas where tax laws affect artists and arts organizations: (1) compliance, which involves carefully following the many tax rules and regulations relevant to a specific artist or arts-related business; and (2) revenue, where financial benefits are realized through tax incentives, or funding available from sources created by federal, state, and local tax codes.

Compliance

When an employee of a company files federal, state, or local tax returns, there has typically been an amount withheld from each paycheck that reduces the annual total tax owed or generates a refund. When a business owner or independent contractor files his or her taxes, the process can include a much more complex set of calculations and documentation for income, expenses and deductions. (NOTE: For any owner of an arts-related venture, it is essential to work with a qualified accountant and/or bookkeeper to set up an accurate bookkeeping system and stay on top of tax-related issues such as filing deadlines, payroll and sales taxes, standard and itemized deductions, and business vs. personal income.) Online research about "taxes for artists" or "taxes for arts organizations" will produce a number of specialty accounting firms, books, and web articles on topics of importance to the arts entrepreneur, regardless of the size or nature of the venture. Try narrowing your web search using your location (state, county, or city) for more targeted local results. A customized tax strategy needs to be developed by the business owner and their experienced financial advisors so that all tax obligations can be anticipated and met. For example, scheduling an annual "tax check-up" with your accountant can draw attention to your organization's prior year tax issues while responding to new developments in the tax code or anticipating changes in your various income and expense categories.

Revenue

> Since 1917, contributions made to 501(c)(3) nonprofits have been tax-deductible, in part as result of wide recognition of nonprofits' benefit to the public good.[26]

The US has a long history of tax deductions for charitable giving, a feature not found in some other developed countries. Originally conceived as a way to encourage donations to charities during World War I, the laws for tax deductions have played an important role in attracting financial support for arts organizations. The "public benefit" provided by eligible arts-related businesses is in the area of education – this can include not only instructional programs but also performances and exhibitions of artistic works. The *sale* of cultural products or services is not usually considered a viable main business activity for an arts nonprofit, unless the proceeds are used to support the organization's primary program that is educational in nature. Becoming a nonprofit corporation requires approval from the Internal Revenue Service for 501(c)(3) status. To qualify, an organization must become established as an ongoing business and be able to demonstrate – through documentation – its legitimate claims to an educational "public benefits" purpose, along with its history of well-managed finances and other requirements. Once nonprofit status is acquired, it must be maintained with regular reporting and more documentation. Despite the challenges associated with getting and keeping nonprofit 501(c)(3) status, there are a number of benefits beyond the ability to offer tax deductions to individual donors – these typically include exemptions from state and local sales and property taxes. A designated nonprofit can also apply for funding from foundations and corporate support programs that restrict their access to arts organizations with the official IRS status.

Another pathway to attracting tax-deductible charitable gifts is to work with a fiscal sponsor. In this case, the for-profit arts venture partners with an organization such as Fractured Atlas (www.fracturedatlas.org) to receive grants and gifts from donors, using the fiscal sponsor's 501(c)(3) nonprofit designation in lieu of its own, See Chapter 4 on fundraising for more information on working with a fiscal sponsor to raise money for your arts-related business.

As described in the quote at the beginning of this chapter's section on taxes, the tax code can be viewed as delegating *policymaking powers* to private institutions. The tax benefits enjoyed by nonprofit arts organizations – and the individuals, foundations, and corporations that fund them – are not tied to any specific results, other than the core mission of "public benefits" pursued by the business. The donors and recipients of financial support have flexibility in creating and implementing their own policies and programs. For example, The Andrew W. Mellon Foundation's Arts and Cultural Heritage program "supports the work of outstanding artists, curators, conservators, and scholars, and endeavors to strengthen performing arts organizations, art museums, research institutes, and conservation centers."[27] The recipients of grants under this program would necessarily have priorities and specific projects that align well with the foundation's charitable goals. The funder's grant guidelines, along with the recipient's institutional focus and targeted use of grant funds, constitute an *extra-governmental* cultural policy that influences the actions and impact of both parties. Understanding and navigating this particular cultural policy landscape require awareness of the factors that determine availability and use of contributed funds. Shaping this environment requires direct participation in designing and implementing either the foundation's grant program(s) or the recipient's intended application of the associated financial and other support. Other instances of extra-governmental cultural policy can be found in corporate programs focused on the arts, as well as gifts by major donors who offer significant amounts of cash and other assets to organizations whose mission and goals align with their own. All of these methods of private or institutional giving have associated tax laws that provide a variety of deductions for charitable donations.

Other Ways Tax Laws Can Provide Financial Benefits to Arts Organizations

- *Tourism taxes*: Special taxes on businesses frequented by tourists (such as hotels, car rental companies, and restaurants) are applied at the state and/or local level to provide funding for a range of programs, often in support of the arts or to encourage cultural tourism. For example, San Francisco has a 14 percent Occupancy Tax (applied to hotels, motels, and short-term rentals such as Airbnb) plus a 1–1.5 percent Tourism Improvement District assessment. Revenue from these sources was expected to exceed $400 million in Fiscal Year 2016–2017. This income was allocated not only to the General Fund (which in turn supports the San Francisco Arts Commission and the Grants for the Arts Program), but also the War Memorial and Performing Arts Center, the Neighborhood Arts Program, and the Cultural District Stabilization Fund. Most states and major cities – and some smaller towns – have similar mechanisms that collect tourism taxes in order to fund cultural programs and projects in their communities.
- *Property taxes*: Owners of residential and commercial real estate pay property taxes, which provide the majority of funding for local governments. State, county, and city arts commissions use this income to support community-based arts organizations, arts education programs, and individual artists. Public art projects are often recipients of property tax-funded grants, as are local museums and libraries.
- *Sales taxes*: Sales of products and services are often taxed, both at the state and local level. In addition, there can be taxes that target entertainment consumers (with the revenue going to support the local

entertainment industry) and "cultural district" taxes that collect income from – and provide resources to – entire neighborhoods. Some counties or cities use voter-approved measures to levy a special additional sales tax (0.5 or 0.25 percent) that is applied to community development, cultural heritage, or other arts-related projects.

- *Percent-for-Art*: Another popular method for funding public arts projects in major cities involves ordinances that require a percentage (typically 1 percent) of the total construction budget of a public building project to be used for commissioning or purchasing artwork, which is then displayed at the location of the new structure.
- *Cultural districts*: In addition to direct government support from the NEA's grant program for creative placemaking (Our Town), there are local programs aimed at increasing the vitality of neighborhoods through engagement with the arts. Incentives can include tax exemptions for artists who commit to living and working in cultural districts, and marketing support for arts organizations that locate their businesses in developing areas and collectively promote their unique features through architectural tours, art walks, "open studio" weekends, and other public events.

Create a new document named Taxes. List all of the ways you and your arts venture will address the tax compliance and tax-related financial benefits issues for your venture. Place the document in the Cultural Policy Interactions folder.

More Examples of Government Policies and Regulations that Can Have an Impact on an Arts Venture

Zoning

Zoning is the term used for planning and control of land use within a city or county. Examples include residential, commercial, industrial, or mixed-use "zones" or designated areas. Zoning, permits, and use restrictions are some of the ways local governments manage how neighborhoods or individual properties are developed and used by their occupants.

Zoning restrictions are sometimes implemented to maintain a certain quality of life within a given area. For example, a quiet residential neighborhood would have restrictions prohibiting some commercial businesses within its boundaries such as live-music venues or manufacturing facilities. Likewise, an area zoned as industrial may have regulations prohibiting residential or "entertainment" related uses of warehouses or abandoned factories. An arts entrepreneur wishing to establish a physical presence for their venture must consider the relationship between their business activity and the allowances or restrictions in place at the intended location. There are sometimes opportunities to request an exception (or variance) to the existing rules associated with zoning. For example, a theater company might be able to get permission from the local city planning department to temporarily occupy an "alternative" space such as a storefront, warehouse, or vacant industrial building for performances of an experimental play. Permits are another way that municipalities control access and use of certain properties within their boundaries. A concert promoter looking to present a music festival in a public park would need to get the required permits for sound reinforcement, security, vendors, and other aspects of their event. A café or bar owner wishing to present live music on the weekends may need to acquire the necessary permit (sometime called a "cabaret license") to comply with local laws.

Although zoning can sometimes be perceived as a way to prevent arts organizations from becoming established in certain neighborhoods, there are instances where zoning actually encourages cultural use of areas or specific spaces. An *overlay district*, for example, can create a special zoning district over the existing one that allows development, occupancy or limited access for artistic purposes. A neighborhood zoned as commercial or industrial might have an overlay district that allows live/workspaces, or the creation of temporary or permanent galleries or performance venues. Many major cities have *special use districts* (such as the Special 125th Street District[28] that supports Harlem's "Main Street" in New York) that encourage development or use by artists and arts organizations to enhance the cultural vibrancy and livability of their neighborhoods. An *adaptive reuse* ordinance might allow the rehabilitation of an historic building (or an entire neighborhood) and encourage businesses in the food, beverage, and entertainment industries to become established and revitalize the area. These programs can also support small business development in these same districts, especially ventures in the creative fields that generate employment (and tax revenue). Your local city planning department is a good place to inquire about zoning restrictions – and zoning opportunities – for the emerging arts venture.

Zoning, permits, use restrictions, overlay districts, etc. are forms of cultural policy that are locally developed and implemented. An arts entrepreneur evaluating locations for a new business should investigate selected neighborhoods and specific properties to discover where zoning either inhibits or encourages arts-related activities. Like the strategies for shaping other state and local laws that affect an arts venture, directly influencing the local environment for zoning and permits involves working with – or becoming – an elected official with responsibilities for creating and implementing regulations. By joining the city council, becoming a member of the state house or senate, or working as an elected official's advisor or employee, artists and owners of arts organizations can have a hand in creating the local policy regulations that impact the entire cultural economy.

Intellectual Property, Copyright

The laws covering copyright, patents, trademarks, and fair use are complex and subject to interpretation depending on the case. Arts entrepreneurs with potential issues around intellectual property should seek advice from a qualified attorney with experience in their field. Information can also be found online from organizations such as the College Art Association[29] and Chicago Artists Resource.[30] Recent examples of cultural policy developments in the US that focus on intellectual property concerns include the The Digital Millennium Copyright Act (DMCA)[31] and the Orrin G. Hatch–Bob Goodlatte Music Modernization Act.[32] See Chapter 5, Legal Issues for more information on arts organizations and the law.

The artist Shepard Fairey sued the Associated Press in 2009 over their claims that he infringed on the copyright of one of their photographs in his creation of the popular "Hope" poster featuring former President Barack Obama. During the extended legal battle, he felt compelled to destroy some pieces of evidence and fabricate others, for which he was found guilty of contempt and sentenced to two years probation and a $25,000 fine (Fairey and AP settled the copyright case out of court). Although this saga illustrates some of the possible outcomes for an artist appropriating and modifying an image in the creation of his own work, it doesn't begin to clarify the intellectual property issues for artists who claim *fair use* of materials they find on the internet, via publications or through other sources. Fair use is a legal doctrine that allows one person's original work to be used by someone else, as long as certain criteria are considered – such as the amount of the original work used, the impact of the secondary work on the marketability of the "original" piece, and the intended use of the secondary work for educational or research purposes. Whose legal claims are stronger – the original creator and copyright holder, or the artist who modifies source materials or uses appropriation to comment on iconic cultural images and messages? Copyright law has different implications for the arts entrepreneur depending on the art form (music, video, painting, live theater), the medium (digital, non-digital, some of both) and the original copyright holder's willingness to pursue damages over perceived infringement.

As a form of cultural policy expressed through the legal system, the rules and regulations covering intellectual property should be of paramount concern to an arts entrepreneur, especially if there are any plans to use "borrowed" or appropriated material as part of the business, or if there are concerns about enforcing copyright infringement claims against someone else who uses *your* original works. The emergence of widely available digital video, music, text, photography, illustrations, and other content only makes the landscape more complicated for artists looking to promote, monetize, and protect their work. Have a qualified attorney advise you as needed while you develop, launch and maintain your arts-related business. See also Lawrence Lessig's book *Freeculture* (available as a free pdf)[33] for an in-depth look at the evolution of copyright law and the issues surrounding ownership and control of creative works.

Media Regulations: Distribution of Content, Digital Rights

Traditional media outlets such as newspapers, magazines, television, and radio each have different regulatory environments that affect their operations. TV and radio stations need to acquire and maintain operating licenses from the Federal Communications Commission (FCC). Print media outlets are not regulated by the government and have free speech protections under the First Amendment, but they must abide by defamation laws covering libel. In some cases the government will undertake criminal proceedings against journalists who refuse to identify their sources, especially when sensitive national security information has been exposed. Launching a new business in the world of traditional media is also a financially risky venture, since many print newspapers and magazines have struggled to remain viable in the age of digital information and internet distribution. The old business model for traditional print media companies surviving on subscriptions and advertising revenue has been challenged by the onslaught of "free" news, editorial, and other content that is available online.

Digital media and "digital rights" are areas of intense debate and controversy. Some corporations and government regulators favor Digital Rights Management (DRM) schemes that control access to digital content and penalize people (and companies) who freely distribute digital material. Their argument is that copyright infringement is illegal and DRM technologies protect the owner's interests in fair compensation for use of their original work. Opponents to DRM laws – such as the Electronic Frontier Foundation (EFF) and the Free Software Foundation (FSF) – claim that DRM technologies only serve to enrich large media corporations, don't effectively limit copyright infringement, make protected content inaccessible when DRM technologies become obsolete, and inhibit innovation and competition by imposing technical restrictions on access to digital content.

The legal issues relevant to your business will naturally depend on your venture's specific products and services. Legislation, case law, technical innovations, and accepted business practices are constantly changing – even more reason to work with a qualified legal expert as you develop and run your organization. For the arts entrepreneur looking to operate their business outside of the US, work with a law firm that specializes in that country's legal framework for intellectual property issues. Likewise for the arts venture involved in international trade between two or more countries, as some foreign governments have very different views on topics such as copyright law, fair use, and protections for originators of creative content.

Ownership of Cultural Property, Repatriation of Foreign Art and Antiquities

Art dealers, gallery owners, and museum curators work in an environment where antiquities, art, and culturally significant objects have historically been removed (sometimes illegally) from their places of origin and traded in the lucrative worldwide market for rare, valuable works. The attitudes – and international legal frameworks – toward ownership and display of artworks from other cultures have undergone some important changes in recent years, with major museums returning significant pieces to where they were taken from. Examples include the return of the Euphronios krater (an ancient Greek bowl from 515 BC) to Italy by the Metropolitan Museum of Art in New York in 2006 and pledges by the French government in 2018 to return their museum-held artifacts back to Africa. These efforts align with the evolving contemporary views against historical imperialism and colonization: looted art and antiquities rightfully belong to their culture of origin and should be returned. There are, however, arguments against repatriation, including claims about the number of people over time who might be able to view a given art object (greater in the major museums in New York, London, and Paris than in the smaller institutions found in the item's "home" country), questions about the legitimacy of the originating country's current political and legal system claiming ownership of art made by ancient peoples and cultures, and promotion of the idea that "art belongs to everyone" and should be freely shared and exchanged among nations for research and appreciation.

For an arts entrepreneur interested in art history and antiquities, there may be opportunities on either side of the repatriation debate. Individuals and companies who specialize in art conservation or undertake investigations into an object's provenance (ownership history) will be in demand by museums, galleries, and private owners to help settle claims of ownership and determine the artwork's source. Storing, moving, or displaying rare, historical art objects requires valuable skills and experience – which can be the basis of a local, national or international business.

Investment Regulations

The policy environment around investments contains a number of implications for artists and arts organizations. At the wealthiest economic levels, there are investors operating individually or in groups who buy and sell high-end art in order to extract profits from a volatile but potentially lucrative international market. For example, the list of rare, collectable paintings that sell privately or at auction for tens of millions – or even hundreds of millions – of dollars continues to grow each year. The competition for investment-grade fine art includes well-funded speculators from around the world, and the laws pertaining to ownership, taxation, and (sometimes) repatriation need to be understood and followed carefully to avoid legal complications between the buyer, seller, and government regulators.

Program Related Investment (PRI) Rules for Foundations and Eligibility of L3C Corps

Another policy area of interest is focused on Program Related Investment (PRI) rules for foundations. The Internal Revenue Service (IRS) requires private non-operating foundations to distribute at least 5 percent of their previous year's assets for charitable purposes – this can take the form of low (or no) interest loans, investments in organizations pursuing high-risk projects with social benefit outcomes, and community investments aimed at spurring economic revitalization and growth. If a foundation's purpose includes support for the arts, then a Program Related Investment (PRI) is one way to direct financial support to the recipient. For example, in 2011, the real estate developer Artspace received a $3 million dollar low interest loan from the Ford Foundation as a PRI.[34] This is a rare, but not entirely uncommon, method of financing for arts organizations. The L3C corporate form (see Chapter 5, Legal Issues) allows organizations to qualify as recipients of PRI funding without having to acquire and maintain 501(c)(3) nonprofit status from the IRS. Although this feature of the L3C corporation has not yet inspired substantial increases in art-related PRI funding from foundations, there may be possibilities for more investments of this type in the future for organizations located in states[35] that recognize L3C as a corporate form.

Equity Crowdfunding Regulations

A relatively recent development, equity crowdfunding allows a *backer* of an art-related project (like a film, original music release or graphic novel) to become an *investor* in the business formed by the creator of a cultural product. Public interest in making equity crowdfunding available has been driven by experiences such as the well-known Oculus Rift project,[36] a virtual reality product that raised over $2 million on KickStarter in 2012 while attracting donated labor from programmers to help develop its "open source" system. When Oculus Rift sold the company to Facebook for $2 billion in 2014, many of the product's supporters (and volunteer developers) were disappointed by both the impression that "their" revolutionary start-up had sold out to a big corporation and the recognition of a lost opportunity to reap financial benefits themselves had they been allowed to invest in the company in its pre-acquisition phase.

In the United States, the Securities and Exchange Commission (SEC) regulates the sale of securities such as stocks and bonds. As equity crowdfunding was being introduced as an accepted form of investment, the SEC imposed restrictions on who could participate in order to protect inexperienced investors from losing their money to fraudulent business owners. At first, only experienced, high net worth individuals could invest in equity crowdfunding ventures. In recent years, the SEC has opened up participation for other individuals as long as they adhere to investment limits based on their net worth. The overall goal has been to gradually introduce opportunities for equity crowdfunding to more people without exposing inexperienced investors to high levels of risk.

For the arts entrepreneur considering equity crowdfunding for their new business, a thorough investigation of the history, current policy environment, and likely future conditions should be undertaken. As with other rapidly evolving conditions for arts organizations, a multi-faceted approach involving online research (including social media), joining relevant email lists and newsletters, and consulting with experienced advisors will produce a good foundation for understanding and, perhaps, using equity crowdfunding as a source of capital.

Import/Export Duties and Fees, Restrictions

The US does not impose duties for personal or commercial imports of handmade artworks such as paintings, drawings, and lithographs. There are also exemptions that apply to sculptures, hand-painted fabrics or ceramics and drawings for architecture, engineering, or industrial projects. The export of cultural material *from* the US is also largely unregulated. However, importing cultural objects that were unlawfully removed from other countries is prohibited under US law and the conventions enacted by the United Nations Educational, Scientific and Cultural Organization (UNESCO). An arts venture planning on importing artworks from abroad should work with an experienced legal team to investigate and follow both US laws on import allowances/restrictions and the export laws of the foreign nation(s) where the cultural objects originate.

Outsourcing

Some arts entrepreneurs develop and launch their business as a one-person operation, doing all of the work themselves. This includes not only the *creative* aspects of the organization – such as product/service design and making and delivering original work – but also all of the *administrative* tasks such as bookkeeping, marketing, fundraising, facilities management, and handling legal obligations. These multiple levels of responsibility can become overwhelming, especially as the business grows and attracts more interest and involvement by customers, suppliers, and media contacts. To reduce the workload and maintain focus on keeping the operation creatively alive and engaged, business owners may turn to outside services for help. This strategy can be as simple as hiring a local bookkeeper, maintenance service, or marketing consultant to provide support for your business. It can also include shifting manufacturing, web design and other operational needs to a place where labor is significantly cheaper, which can sometimes be found overseas. Delegating parts of your business to an outside service, or *outsourcing*, is not in itself a good or bad choice for an arts venture ... it all depends on the nature of the relationship between the business owner and service provider and the degree of compliance with the legal environment at home and abroad.

For example, the Columbus Association for the Performing Arts (CAPA) in Columbus, Ohio, handles finances, marketing, ticketing, and fundraising for a number of established performing arts organizations in the area.[37] By taking over the "back office" operations for their clients, CAPA can provide essential business functions using their own experienced staff. The owners and managers of the local performing arts companies can rely on CAPA for administrative support on an "as-needed" basis, rather than hiring full-time or part-time employees to be available year round. This approach may work for some arts ventures but not others, depending on the volume of work, the scheduling of the organization's critical tasks and the cost-benefit realities of paying an outside service vs. hiring, training, and nurturing productive relationships with in-house staff. These types of business practices and norms are examples of non-governmental cultural policy – arts organizations using hired services for administrative needs to save time and money. Of course, an individual artist, or owner of an arts-related business, could start their venture by initially working with a centralized service provider (for payroll, accounting, web design, etc.), then shift to directly hiring skilled administrative personnel as the business grows.

Another form of outsourcing follows the model used by some manufacturing and consumer products companies where cheap foreign labor is relied upon to increase efficiency and boost profits. Examples include tech companies building – or contracting with – overseas factories for fabrication and assembly of consumer electronics, such as cell phones, and athletic footwear and apparel manufacturers who rely on low-cost workers in countries with relatively lax environmental regulations and labor laws. An arts venture focused on manufacturing and distributing products may find some attractive features in outsourcing some of their business operations to inexpensive production opportunities found overseas. However, the potential increase in profitability can come with some risks. Using a foreign factory that exploits workers, ignores environmental laws, or exposes employees to dangerous conditions can generate some strongly negative attention for the business in the media and among the general public – your outsourcing partners' questionable behavior can (and probably should) reflect on your organization's willingness to tolerate practices that would be considered illegal and unethical at home. When considering outsourcing for either products or services, investigate the foreign provider's reputation for fair labor practices, environmental responsibility, and overall financial health before making any commitments that may temporarily increase profits but damage your venture's image, prospects in the consumer market and operational sustainability for the longer term.

International Organizations and Foreign Ownership

Some arts ventures are launched as – or grow to become – an international business with locations in two or more countries. This is true for both for-profit and nonprofit organizations, although acquiring and maintaining consistent corporate status in multiple countries requires a fair amount of consultation with legal experts. Issues such as tax status, regional and local laws, intellectual property protections, labor regulations, and risk management strategies need to be carefully considered for each location where the business operates.

Foreign ownership of US assets, including corporations, has drawn considerable attention in recent years. Some companies seek tax advantages through *corporate inversion*, a controversial tactic that transforms a US-based parent company with a foreign subsidiary into a foreign-based parent company with a US-based subsidiary, thereby reducing (sometimes substantially) its tax liabilities. In other cases, a US corporation will sell some of its ownership to foreign investors, both to raise money and expand the organization's international presence. The pros and cons of each of these practices need to be weighed carefully with respect to the arts venture's brand, image, financial solvency, and legal standing.

Labor Laws for Employees, Owners, Contractors

The legal framework for employers and employees includes federal, state, and local regulations that must be understood and carefully followed to avoid complications or conflicts. Laws covering minimum wage, working hours, trade unions, and health and safety codes will directly affect your business if you hire staff for your venture. Hiring independent contractors, on the other hand, carries other responsibilities for wage reporting and intellectual property ownership. See Chapter 5, Legal Issues, for more information on this topic.

Censorship

According to the Merriam-Webster online dictionary,[38] a censor is:

> 1 : a person who supervises conduct and morals: such as
>
> a : an official who examines materials (such as publications or films) for objectionable matter "Government censors deleted all references to the protest."

b : an official (as in time of war) who reads communications (such as letters) and deletes material considered sensitive or harmful.

The relationship between an artist's right to unrestricted creative expression (covered by the free speech protections found in the US Constitution's First Amendment) and the public's right to object to art that is broadly recognized as obscene highlights the multiple roles played by cultural policy when controversial art is involved. Censorship, as indicated in the definition above, implies a moral position where offensive art is subjected to government regulations. Morals, of course, are shaped by an individual's religious, political, and other views – collective morals are harder to identify and employ as regulators of "good taste" or "decency" because one person's outrage over unacceptable art is another person's commitment to making bold, challenging creative works that focus on issues such as gender, race, and inequality. Government policies both enable controversial artwork (by providing funding and other support) and regulate offensive content through court decisions and congressional statutes. Examples of law suits[39] include:

- *Miller v. California*: A 1973 Supreme Court case involving pornographic material distributed by mail. The Court's decision redefined obscenity as that which lacks "serious literary, artistic, political, or scientific value."
- *Serra v. General Services Administration*: A lawsuit brought by artist Richard Serra over the removal of his sculpture "Tilted Arc" from Federal Plaza in lower Manhattan. Serra's site-specific piece was commissioned by the General Services Administration and installed in 1981, but was later found to be unacceptable in its location. Serra eventually lost the case and his work was dismantled and removed in 1987.
- *National Endowment for the Arts v. Finley*: This 1998 Supreme Court case focused on public funding of controversial art. It upheld a congressional statute that requires the NEA to consider "general standards of decency" when selecting artists for financial support.

How should an arts entrepreneur navigate the policy landscape for obscenity laws and the public's tolerance for controversial work? The first step is to honestly evaluate your ambitions with respect to the organization's stakeholders and target market. What do your board of directors, outside advisors, and market analysis results tell you about exposing the local population to challenging, potentially offensive artwork?

Producing, displaying, or distributing art that addresses controversial issues in a direct, uncompromising way can be an essential part of the business concept, so don't be reluctant to pursue that strategy if it is central to your beliefs and intentions. However, what works as a business concept in an urban, socially progressive environment might be not be as successful in a rural, socially conservative setting. Staying true to one's ideals is important, but so is operating with an awareness of the sentiments and beliefs held by local consumers and critics.

If your creative product or service *depends* on raising eyebrows and inspiring some degree of controversy, it will be especially important to find compelling, outspoken allies to represent your viewpoint and publicly support your business. Seek out media contacts (editors, journalists, critics), sponsors, government officials and other prominent individuals who can promote the values of your organization's brand and offerings. Consider accommodating a diversity of opinions in your organization's offerings. For example, a theater company staging highly political works can schedule panel discussions or public Q&A sessions after each performance to encourage dialog and enable the community's entire range of attitudes and beliefs to be heard.

Chapter Summary

Cultural policy covers a wide range of factors that can influence an arts-related business, including government funding, legal frameworks at the local and national levels, and industry norms. Understanding the history of cultural policy development and implementation – both in the US and in other countries – allows the arts entrepreneur to both navigate the current policy environment and participate in creating its future. Older civilizations such as France and the UK developed their cultural policies out of their historical patronage systems. The US government first experimented with federal funding for the arts during the Great Depression as a way to increase employment and encourage economic growth. After World War II, federal arts programs such as the National Endowment for the Arts (NEA) were launched to encourage cultural production and appreciation across many arts disciplines, including music, dance, literature and theater. In addition to the NEA, there are other federally funded programs and venues for art and culture such as the Department of State's Bureau of Educational and Cultural Affairs, the National Gallery of Art, the John F. Kennedy Center for the Performing Arts, and the National Endowment for the Humanities. There are also many cultural support programs at the regional, state, and local levels that are worth investigating for a new arts venture.

The legal environment for artists and business owners includes federal, state, and local legislation, tax regulations, and court decisions. Influencing cultural policy in these different areas requires participation in the legislative process, either through voting and public dialog, as a consultant/advisor, by working for an established politician's organization or by becoming an elected official. Government arts agencies, especially those at the local level, are attuned to the needs of their local populations and can be influenced in their decision-making processes by public involvement in city council meetings, special elections, and ballot initiatives.

Tax law is another key area that deserves close attention by an arts-related business. In terms of compliance, there are many tax rules that may affect an organization's regular operations, including deductible business expenses, payroll taxes, and distribution of profits (or maintenance of nonprofit status). Working with an experienced bookkeeper or accountant is the best way to keep on top of the many tax issues relevant to an arts venture. In addition to these and other tax compliance issues, there are a number of ways that tax policy provides financial and other benefits. Acquiring and maintaining nonprofit 501(c)(3) status from the IRS is one example – there are also programs that distribute funding raised from tourism taxes on hotels and restaurants, property taxes, sales tax, and assessments for special cultural districts.

Zoning is yet another facet of the cultural policy environment for an arts organization to examine, especially for a performing arts business looking to become established in a restricted neighborhood. While some zoning laws appear to inhibit certain types of arts-related businesses from operating in specific locations, others actually encourage the development of properties for cultural uses in overlay districts and adaptive reuse programs.

Other laws that need close attention by the arts entrepreneur include intellectual property rules, media regulations, free speech laws, and digital rights. Ownership of imported cultural property and repatriation of antiquities are areas of special concern for art dealers and gallery owners. Investment regulations will be important to organizations raising money via Program Related Investment funds from foundations or from equity crowdfunding projects. Instances of cultural policy found in industry norms include outsourcing the organization's operational needs to external (and well-qualified) services. Censorship laws need special consideration, particularly in cases where the art-related business produces and distributes highly controversial works or pursues unusually provocative activities that inspire oppositional reactions from consumers and critics.

Discussion Questions

1. How does the development of cultural policy in the United States compare with that of other countries?

2. What are the current grant-making programs provided by the National Endowment for the Arts (NEA)?

3. How might the owner of an arts-related business influence the state and local regulations affecting their organization?

4. Besides the NEA, describe some of the other federally-funded programs and venues for art and culture.

5. What kind of support should an arts entrepreneur seek to responsibly handle all of the company's tax liabilities?

6. Describe some of the revenue opportunities made possible by federal, state, and local tax codes.

7. How might zoning regulations affect a performing arts organization?

8. How could an instance of artistic appropriation be legally allowable under copyright law?

9. Describe the arguments for and against Digital Rights Management (DRM).

10. How might your business pursue equity crowdfunding as a form of investment?

11. What are the reasons in favor of outsourcing an arts organization's operational activities, such as bookkeeping, marketing and fundraising?

Notes

[1] Grantmakers in the Arts (Organization). *Grantmakers in the Arts reader* (Seattle, WA: Grantmakers in the Arts, 2002).

[2] Lebovics, Herman. *Mona Lisa's escort: André Malraux and the reinvention of French culture* (Ithaca, NY: Cornell University Press, 1999).

[3] Looseley, D. "Jack Lang and the politics of festival." *French Cultural Studies* 1 (1990): 5–19.

[4] See www.quaibranly.fr/en/support/you-are-a/company-foundation/

[5] See www.culturalpolicies.net/web/unitedkingdom.php

[6] Upchurch, Anna Rosser. 2016. *The origins of the Arts Council movement: philanthropy and policy* (London: Palgrave Macmillan).

[7] Mark, Charles Christopher. *Reluctant bureaucrats: the struggle to establish the National Endowment for the Arts* (Dubuque, IA: Kendal/Hunt, 1991), p. 12.

[8] The Proprietors of the Boston Athenæum, "History of the Boston Athenæum," available at: www.bostonathenaeum.org/node/38 (accessed October 26, 2010).

[9] The Solomon R. Guggenheim Foundation (SRGF), "History: 1920s to 1940s," available at: www.guggenheim.org/guggenheim-foundation/history/1920s1940s (accessed October 26, 2010).

[10] Mark, *Reluctant bureaucrats*, p. 15.

[11] See www.nytimes.com/2018/03/23/arts/nea-and-neh-spared-in-spending-bill.html

[12] Bonin-Rodriguez, Paul. *Performing policy: how contemporary politics and cultural programs redefined U.S. artists for the twenty-first century* (Basingstoke: Palgrave Macmillan, 2015).

[13] See http://americanassembly.org/publications/arts-and-public-purpose

14 See /www.creative-capital.org/

15 Jackson, Maria-Rosario. *Investing in creativity: a study of the support structure for U.Ss. artists* (Washington, DC: Culture, Creativity & Communities Program, Urban Institute, 2003).

16 NEA. *How the United States funds the arts* (Washington, DC: National Endowment for the Arts, 2012).

17 See/www.arts.gov/

18 See https://nasaa-arts.org/state-arts-agencies/

19 See http://usregionalarts.org/

20 See https://eca.state.gov/programs-initiatives/cultural-diplomacy

21 See www.nps.gov/nr/travel/cultural_diversity/Preserving_the_Places_and_Stories_of_Americas_Diverse_Cultural%20Heritage.html

22 See https://innovation.ed.gov/what-we-do/arts/

23 See www.neh.gov/

24 NEA. *How the United States funds the arts.*

25 Mulcahy, K.V. "Cultural policy: definitions and theoretical approaches." *The Journal of Arts Management, Law and Society* 35 (4) (2006): 319–332.

26 See www.americansforthearts.org/by-program/reports-and-data/legislation-policy/legislative-issue-center/charitable-giving-tax-reform

27 See https://mellon.org/programs/arts-and-cultural-heritage/

28 See www1.nyc.gov/site/planning/zoning/districts-tools/special-purpose-districts-manhattan.page

29 See www.collegeart.org/programs/caa-fair-use/best-practices

30 See www.chicagoartistsresource.org/articles/law-artists-fair-use

31 See www.copyright.gov/reports/studies/dmca/dmca_executive.html

32 See www.copyright.gov/music-modernization/

33 http://www.free-culture.cc/freeculture.pdf

35 See http://createquity.com/2011/08/artspace-receives-3-million-program-related-investment-from-ford-foundation/

35 See https://nonprofithub.org/starting-a-nonprofit/jargon-free-guide-l3c/

36 See https://alj.orangenius.com/equity-crowdfunding-art/

37 See www.npr.org/templates/story/story.php?storyId=127039922&ft=1&f=1008?storyId=127039922&ft=1&f=1008

38 See www.merriam-webster.com/dictionary/censoring

39 See www.law.harvard.edu/faculty/martin/art_law/public_art.htm

8 Organizational Design, Career Development, and Future Trends

This chapter focuses on three separate areas of interest to the arts entrepreneur:

1. *Organizational design* refers to the structure of an arts-related business. The relationships between owners, managers, and staff can be formalized to define everyone's roles and responsibilities, maximize operational productivity, and enable effective communications throughout the company.
2. *Career development* explores some of the ways job seekers approach the employment market and what kind of tools they use to get hired. This section also considers how the experience of working for an existing company can help an arts entrepreneur develop skills and cultivate relationships as part of the process of conceiving and launching their own venture.
3. The section on *future trends* looks at some emerging business concepts in the arts and cultural areas that are relevant to arts entrepreneurship students and established business owners. Founders looking to grow or modify their company and its offerings need to continually inform and educate themselves about developments in consumer behavior and product design/delivery in order to remain viable for the long term.

Organizational Design

It is part of the arts manager's job as an organizer to decide how to divide the workload into manageable tasks, assign people to get these tasks done, give them the resources they need, and coordinate the entire effort to meet the planning objectives[1]

In Chapter 2 on Planning and Assessment, we examined the techniques for producing a strategic plan that guides the efforts of a specific project or the entire organization. When implementing the strategies and tasks identified within the strategic planning process and laid out in the resulting timeline, the assignment of roles and responsibilities within the organization becomes increasingly important. Who is responsible for each area of the company's operations? Who has responsibility for decision-making when problems or conflicts arise? How will resource allocation issues be addressed, especially when income and expense projections differ from actuals? Organizational design helps answer these and many other questions for the arts venture as it works through its design, launch, and sustainability phases.

Some organizations are created with very few participants. The owner may also be the producer of all original creative content and responsible for its distribution, marketing, and related financial activity. Other businesses rely on small teams that plan, collaborate, and interact as equals, especially when there is a shared ownership model in place such as a collective. Still other companies are structured with dozens of positions (or more) located within a single facility or spread out geographically across the region or around the world via telecommuting arrangements.

For example:

- An independent artist (such as a musician, painter, or actor) could run their business by themselves using available technologies such as a portable laptop computer or smart phone and cloud-based applications for financial transactions, communications, and contracts. Although this type of venture has only one individual working as both the business owner and producer of all creative content, it is important to identify external consultants and service providers to properly describe the organization's structure. Individual artists must rely on accountants, attorneys, web hosting services, insurance agents, and other individuals and companies. For this type of business, the organizational chart would show a single individual at the center (who is responsible for running the entire company) with connections to external supporters who provide specific services as needed.
- A small company with 5–10 employees or partners can create an organizational structure that suits the needs of the business and reflects the relationships between the individuals. For example, an interior design firm with five equal partners could produce an organizational chart that shows all five people with equal responsibilities for attracting/retaining clients, managing projects, tracking income and expenses, researching sources for equipment and supplies, and keeping the overall operation running. This would be considered a horizontal, or flat organizational structure. On the other hand, a design firm with an owner/principal designer at the top and several subordinate staff members responsible for scheduling, bookkeeping, marketing, and office management would use an organizational structure that is more vertical or hierarchical, with the founder at the top of the organizational chart and staff members positioned below and reporting to the owner.

- A larger organization with 20–30 (or more) employees might have multiple layers of management, starting at the top level with the Board of Directors and CEO, then branching downwards to other roles such as the managers of various departments and, ultimately, the staff and volunteers. A theater company might have a board of directors who appoint and supervise the Executive Director, who in turn manages the department heads for production design, ticket sales, fundraising, facilities maintenance, and other key areas. These department heads would have staff reporting to them, as well as volunteers helping with various components of the operation.

No matter how small or large the organization, it is important to define the roles and responsibilities for each position in order to clarify expectations and encourage transparency and understanding throughout the organization. It can be useful to think of a job within your company as a *position*, rather than something defined by the person occupying that particular role – in this way the job description is tailored to the needs of the organization, not tied exclusively to a single individual. When a new position is being created, or an existing position is being filled after an employee leaves, the job description can be refined or revised to suit the evolving needs of the company.

Use an Organizational Chart to Define the Roles and Communicate the Organizational Structure

To begin the process of creating an organizational structure that accurately reflects all aspects of your business, answer the following questions with enough detail so that a non-expert (such as an individual unfamiliar with your business category) can understand your intentions in developing the venture's concept and how your company will be built around it:

- *Who* is involving in operating the business?
- *What* product or service is being offered to consumers?
- *When* will the business begin operating (then maybe expand...)?
- *Where* will the business be located?
- *Why* is this business likely to succeed?

Create a new folder called Organization Design. Start a new document and answer the five questions above in a way that expresses your idea for an arts-related business so a non-expert can understand what is being created and how it will succeed. Pay particular attention to the first question about *who* is involved in operating the business. Name this document Organizational Structure and place it within the Organization Design folder.

Using the information about the roles and responsibilities you have identified for your business, create a drawing that graphically represents the organizational structure. This document can be made using a word processing program such as Microsoft Word or a page layout program such as Adobe InDesign. Place each job title, along with the name of the person occupying that role, in a box. The business owner should be at the top of the overall diagram and a Board of Directors should be located above the Executive Director if appropriate for the organization. Continue developing the organizational chart by placing additional job titles (and the names of people associated with them) in boxes located below the top level. Draw lines between the boxes to show reporting responsibilities and lines of communication. Use a horizontal (or flat) organizational structure if that represents the relationships within your business. Or create a vertical (or hierarchical) organizational structure with as many layers of responsibility and management as necessary. You can do an online search for "organizational charts for arts organizations" to see some examples, then use those references – plus the information above – to create an Organizational Chart for your own venture. Name this document Organizational Chart (org chart) and place it within your Organization Design folder.

For a business run by a single individual, remember to include the external advisers, consultants, and service providers in the org chart to help the reader understand how the business will handle all of its functional responsibilities, such as bookkeeping, legal support, marketing, and fundraising. For the medium to large organization, the external sources of support can also be included in the org chart. The more detail you provide in the written and graphic representations of your venture, the easier it will be for the reader to understand the interrelationships within your organization and how connections with external services and people serve the various needs of the company.

Communication

Communications between Management Layers, across Departments, and with the Public

Once the business structure has been established and the relationships between managers and staff have been defined, the lines of communication should be clarified so that everyone in the company understands what is expected in terms of receiving and sending information throughout the company. Does the owner want to receive email and voice mail directly from everyone in the firm, or is it more productive and efficient to channel messages through the company's management layers? Is there proprietary or sensitive information that needs to be separated from regular communications and shared only with specific individuals? Does the venture need to archive some communications as part of its product development history and project management analysis and planning efforts?

Consider some of the following options for managing communications within the organization:

- *Email* is now the most popular tool for one-to-one communications or one-to-many announcements. The ability to track conversations using email threads, along with search functionality within large collections of email from different sources, can help with decision-making and retrieval of valuable historical information. However, many people are increasingly experiencing email overload in their daily lives and find it difficult to keep up with the never-ending increase in unread messages waiting in their Inbox. Email management tools have improved the ability to filter messages and reduce, to a degree, the amount of time a business owner must dedicate to managing email. Most arts entrepreneurs will want to create an email account that is branded with their venture's identity, both for interactions within the company and for communications with external organizations and individuals.
- *Collaboration tools* such as Slack[2] have become increasingly popular due to their many expandable, customizable features. Although these services come with a fee, they do provide valuable functionality in terms of team development and interaction, messaging, data security, and integration with other software tools and services.
- *Software development platforms* such as GitHub[3] are very useful for version tracking and collaborative project management. Although primarily intended for the development of computer source code, these services can also be used to create repositories for other kinds of information and to track projects or assign tasks.

Communications Transparency and Public Access to Company Information

Some arts organizations are making strategic decisions to expose detailed information about their company's activities, such as the number of visitors to a museum or the amount of money raised towards a capital project. Many startups, along with the customers they seek to attract, value transparency as a key element in pursuing an open, honest approach to interactions of all kinds. The degree of transparency a company is comfortable with will depend on the founder's interest in sharing key business information with the outside world.

Communications with Government Agencies, Banks, Foundations, Investors, and Accrediting Organizations

Another issue involving communications has to do with the assignment of responsibility for submitting mandatory reports, payments, and official document filings. A new business needs to produce and deliver a range of different forms in order to become established within its community, such as:

- an application for a business license (including a fictitious name statement if appropriate);
- a request for a Federal Tax ID Number (EIN);
- a resale license (if re-selling merchandise purchased from a wholesaler, manufacturer or other source);
- an application for membership in the local Chamber of Commerce;
- tax filing documents for quarterly/annual reporting, or on another schedule, depending on the type of business;
- initial application and subsequent reporting documents to acquire and maintain nonprofit status;
- mandatory paperwork for banks, foundations, government programs, and individual investors who provide financial and in-kind support;
- applications and reports for agencies providing accreditation, licensing, or other externally approved status;
- other documents necessary for the continued successful operation of the business.

Some applications and reports can be submitted electronically, while others require paper forms with original signatures in ink. Although the owner is ultimately responsible for producing and submitting all official business documents, the organization can turn to an experienced bookkeeper, accountant, lawyer, or consultant to help prepare the paperwork and stay on top of filing deadlines. A good strategy is to plan out the entire upcoming fiscal or calendar year in advance, with deadlines noted for each upcoming submission. A glance at a well-prepared calendar will inform the founder about upcoming document submissions and help avoid late charges, penalties, or loss of approved status from an important government agency or other entity.

Communications and the Marketplace: Who Is Responsible for the Organization's Public Image and Voice?

Like an art venture's products and services, the company's brand and public messages can be developed and distributed with the goal of inspiring a positive impression among consumers, critics and advocates. Starting with corporate identity, a skilled graphic designer can craft a logo, website, printed matter, and other materials that convey the desired image and "personality" of the company. Likewise, an experienced copywriter can develop messages for advertising, email, social media postings, and text campaigns that drive consumer awareness and help build the brand into a known – and sought-after – source for its products.

In the case of a single-person operation, the founder may initially need to take on responsibilities for all of the visual and written materials used by the venture. Sometimes a barter arrangement with a local designer, photographer or writer can be developed to provide professional content for a new company's brand, especially if the creative service wants or needs access to the arts organization's offerings. Many small businesses begin by developing their own communications materials, then contract later with professionals as they expand and generate more activity and income. Hiring a full service design, advertising or marketing agency can always be introduced once the organization achieves a greater level of business growth and operational need. The same is true with media relations, press releases and launch events: the founder and/or core team can organize and implement strategies for media relations in the early days, then delegate the work to other staff or outside services as the company grows.

Documentation and Records Retention

The Internal Revenue Service (IRS) has rules about the length of time a company is required to retain its business records, including tax returns and documentation showing income and expenses. Consult with a qualified accountant – or refer to the IRS website – for specific information related to retention of your business records.

Create a new folder called Communications Management. Start new documents for Internal Communications and External Communications, and describe in each how your arts organization will manage its responsibilities in these areas. Place these documents within the Communications Management folder.

Assigning Responsibilities and Managing People

Once a company's organizational structure has been designed and its policies for internal and external communications are established, the important processes for hiring and working with employees must be addressed. Creating job descriptions that suit the needs of the venture – and recruiting, training, and managing talented staff – are all essential ingredients in building a successful arts organization. The quality of any business is very much dependent on the quality of its workforce and the ability of managers to properly support and direct the company's employees.

The first step in building an effective, dedicated staff is to carefully develop job descriptions that are both tailored to the company's current requirements and designed to anticipate future needs as the venture grows. Some organizations produce highly detailed job descriptions for each position that must be filled, with clearly defined expectations for the position's responsibilities and the necessary levels of skills and experience.

For example, an arts venture needing to hire a marketing person would develop a job description that spells out the responsibilities for marketing concept development, budgeting, content creation, and the management of internal staff or outside services. This job description would also indicate the number of years of experience expected for an individual who might fill this particular job, which can range from a beginner with one year or less of documented work experience to a seasoned professional with five or more years in the field.

Job descriptions should be created for each position the company needs currently – or will require in the near future. The process of writing and publicizing a job description serves several purposes. While drafting and revising a job description, the business owner must deliberate carefully to design positions that accurately reflect the operational needs of the venture. Once it has been finalized, a job description serves as a template for advertising the opportunity to attract potential candidates. Finally, when interviewing and hiring an individual to fill a position, the job description works as a key document for developing a mutual understanding about the job expectations and how the employee and manager can work together to accomplish the company's overall goals. To maximize a sense of mutual respect and shared interest – and to demonstrate the company's dedication to transparency and openness – business owners and managers should share their ideas about *their own* positions' responsibilities and contributions to the organization's success.

Managing Employees

Whether the company culture is informal and loosely organized around roles and responsibilities, or highly structured with strict rules about supervision and authority, it serves the interests of both owners and employees to have a clear sense of job performance expectations and reporting relationships. Using the job description described earlier, a business owner or manager can schedule a performance review with each employee once or twice a year to discuss the job's responsibilities, the employee's accomplishments during the past year (or other time period), the expectations for job performance in the future, and any suggestions or comments from either party to help clarify misunderstandings or resolve conflicts. As the founder of a new arts organization, it can be helpful to think back on your own experiences as an employee and reflect upon instances of good interactions with your manager – or negative experiences that you would want to avoid repeating. A good manager should enable each employee to do their best work and feel a sense of accomplishment by making job expectations clear, providing regular feedback, allowing for dialogue and interaction to resolve issues, and thinking ahead to anticipate – and provide – management support as needed.

Company Meetings and Identification of Individuals for Specific Deliverables

Organizing – or participating in – a workplace meeting can either be an efficient, productive use of one's time or a waste of everyone's availability, attention, and effort. Some managers set strict limitations on meeting length, such as a 30- or even 15-minutes maximum, in order to impose a sense of urgency and focus and to produce results quickly. Other meetings are necessarily lengthy in order to give enough time for a thorough consideration of the complex, interrelated issues that need attention. No matter what the purpose of a meeting might be or the preferred schedule, it helps to prepare and distribute a meeting agenda in advance so all the participants can come prepared and ready to contribute.

Most company meetings try to end with a shared understanding of the decisions that have been made and agreements about the actions that need to take place. These final points can be organized into a list of *action items* that are associated with individuals or teams. The person running the meeting can assign tasks to specific individuals. Or, meeting participants can volunteer to assume responsibility for one or more of the action items. After the complete list of action items is reviewed and each task is associated with an individual or team, the meeting can come to a conclusion and the participants can move on to accomplishing their assignments.

Scheduling and Project Management

Once an organization's managers and staff have a clear understanding of what needs to be done, the process of scheduling the work and producing deliverables needs to be addressed. For large, complex organizations, investment in project management software may become necessary in order to keep track of all the details involved in running the company. However, for a smaller organization it may be enough to use a simple online scheduling system (such as Google Calendar) to keep projects on track and make everyone aware of upcoming deadlines and their associated responsibilities. In order to make key decisions and keep the venture moving forward to accomplish its overall goals, the business owner needs to have a complete overview of all present/future projects and their status on the timeline. As individual projects are completed, they can be moved to an archive for easy reference to prior work. The project archive can also be a valuable source of information for evaluation and assessment of the company's performance during a prior time period.

Proposals, Reports, and Working Documents

Every organization has a collection of documents – either on paper or in an electronic format – used to share information and accomplish its many planning, production, and assessment tasks. And arts education firm needs to publish its upcoming list of classes and workshops to enroll students. A photographer needs to develop and present a proposal for a new client's project. A musician needs to create and distribute marketing materials to attract interest from presenters and develop a booking schedule for the coming year. A designer of custom jewelry needs to track all the production steps involved in ordering and receiving raw materials, producing a collection of pieces, delivering the finished products to customers, and receiving final payments. For a one-person arts venture, creating and storing documents using commonly available software such as Microsoft Word or Apple Pages is a simple, reliable way to generate a wide range of production and communications materials. For companies with multiple participants involved in document generation and distribution, an online platform such as Google Docs can help teams of writers and editors contribute to shared documents and collectively finalize their work. As with all other business-related documentation, it is important to follow commonly accepted data security protocols and make backup copies of all essential information in two locations, one at the business site and another offsite using cloud-based storage or a portable/remote hard drive.

Maintaining Communications and Document Integrity

As a business matures and its staffing needs evolve, employees may join or leave the organization depending on their career path and their suitability for the company's ambitions. To minimize the risks associated with loss of intellectual property or to protect important business documents and communications, a centralized document storage plan should be implemented. When a new employee joins the venture, they can be provided with a company-owned computer, along with a login to the organization's data storage and backup accounts. By storing critical business documents on a centralized server instead of keeping them on an employee's laptop or desktop computer, the organization can maintain some continuity and historical recordkeeping as staff members come and go. Maintaining archives of business-related email can be more challenging, since most people expect their email accounts to be accessible only by themselves. One possible solution is to establish an email account for a staff position, rather than for the individual who is filling that position. For example, a marketing manager could use "marketing@businessname.com" instead of their own name for all business communications. The login and password for that account could be set up by the manager or owner of the company – that way, the next person in that position can have access to previous communications, as well as the account's address book and related attachments.

Designing Positions for the Company, Recruiting and Training Staff

Like any other organization, an arts-related business will have different needs for staff depending on the type of venture it is and how the owner chooses to structure the team. Some companies will need highly skilled professionals in order to launch and become established, while others can rely on novices, interns, and volunteers to run the organization. No matter what experience level the founder requires for the company's employees, it is important to recruit carefully in order to make the best match between the venture's needs and the background and skills of its staff. After developing a detailed job description for each required position, the business owner or manager should advertise through the best channels available for attracting the right kind of candidates. These can include using online platforms such as LinkedIn or indeed.com, as well as retaining the services of a specialized employment agency. Sometimes good prospective employees can be found through word-of-mouth by announcing the job opportunity through the founder's personal network of contacts in the industry.

Once a candidate has been identified and a job offer has been accepted, the employer must provide training and guidance to the new hire. The early stages of a new employee's involvement with a company are very important for clarifying expectations and providing opportunities to ask questions and learn about the organization's operating procedures and culture. Specialized training should be provided to new employees as needed. Also, professional development opportunities should be made available to encourage staff to continue learning and growing as they become increasingly valuable participants in the venture's success.

The steps below describe the process for recruiting, hiring, and retaining staff. (For more information, see Chapter 7, "Human Resources and the Arts" in *Management and the Arts* by Byrnes.[4])

1. Develop a detailed job description.
2. Advertise the job opportunity using online platforms (such as LinkedIn, indeed.com or others). If appropriate, work through your network of contacts to get recommendations for suitable candidates.
3. Invite applications (including resumes, letters of interest and references with contact information) for the position to be submitted through a web portal, via email or through surface mail.
4. Work with other managers and consultants to review the application materials.
5. Select a number of candidates (three to five) for interviews.
6. Check the references.
7. Consult with the hiring team, choose a candidate, and make the job offer.
8. After negotiating salary, benefits, start date. and other details, prepare to welcome the new hire and schedule time for orientation and training.

9. Schedule performance evaluations once or twice a year, focusing on the job description, past accomplishments, and expectations for future job performance.
10. To keep employees motivated and productive, consider offering incentives, rewards, and bonuses for exceptional job performance.
11. Employees will appreciate the possibilities for promotions and/or salary increases as time goes by. Consider developing and implementing a medium- to long-term plan for career advancement goals that staff can look forward to achieving.

Termination

Unfortunately, there are some occasions when an employee is no longer suitable for continuing in their position with a company. This can happen for a number of reasons. Sometimes it is a case of employee burnout and loss of interest in their position or the mission of the organization. In other cases, it is the company that changes focus and finds itself no longer needing a specific position. Economic downturns or changes in the organization's financial performance can also affect the ability of a company to retain its staff. When considering laying off an employee, it is important to be aware of the legal implications, especially if the individual was hired under a contract that contains specific language about termination. Work with your legal adviser to prepare hiring documentation, develop a formalized process for termination actions and keep all signed agreements with staff and contractors up-to-date.

Labor Unions

Large, well-established cultural institutions – such as opera companies, museums, or theaters – often have relationships with unions. Labor unions exist to represent the rights and interests of workers as they negotiate contractual agreements with their employers. One example is the American Guild of Musical Artists (AGMA), a "labor organization that represents the Artists who create America's operatic, choral and dance heritage."[5] On its FAQ page, AGMA presents the following information to prospective members:

> AGMA protects its members. We negotiate contracts, called collective bargaining agreements, that provide guaranteed wages, safe working conditions, rehearsal and overtime pay, regulated work hours, vacation and sick pay, resolution of disputes and protection against discrimination and abuse in any form. We enforce those contracts. We assure that our collective bargaining agreements provide for health insurance, pension coverage, and protection against unreasonable working conditions and unsafe workplaces, and we make sure that employers live up to their contractual obligations. We protect the

legal, civil and artistic rights of our members, through an aggressive, litigious constant vigilance.[6]

If your idea for an arts organization includes working with labor unions, you should consult with an attorney who specializes in labor law to plan out your strategy and develop workable contractual relationships with represented staff.

Creating a Corporate Culture that Inspires All Stakeholders to Be Productive, Supportive, Focused, and Committed to the Company's Mission

> Businesses create their own social systems. Typically, these social systems evolve around the shared values, beliefs, myths, rituals, language, and behavioral patterns of the leadership and employees.[7]

An individual who chooses to create their own business will often have very clear ideas and expectations about how the organization will be run and what type of corporate culture will develop over time. However, other stakeholders in the organization – such as its employees, consultants, volunteers, and other supporters – are also involved in defining and participating in the company culture. Business owners can greatly improve their chances of creating a positive, productive work environment by doing the following:

- explicitly communicating their *own* values, beliefs and goals as they relate to the formation and continued operation of the business;
- inviting input from staff, consultants, volunteers, and others and acting on their suggestions;
- setting clear, reasonable rules and boundaries for workplace behavior and enforcing company policies fairly and consistently;
- being responsive to changing conditions both inside and outside of the organization and adapting to the circumstances facing all stakeholders, both during their work hours and outside of the workplace;
- informing themselves, through research and educational opportunities, about the latest tools and techniques for launching, growing and sustaining a well-regarded business that attracts and retains talented, dedicated workers.

Create a new folder called Employee Relations. Start new documents for Job Descriptions, Employee Management Policies, Project Management, Documentation, and Corporate Culture, and describe in each how your arts organization will manage its responsibilities in these areas. Place these documents within the Employee Relations folder.

Career Development

Being an Employee

Although the primary focus of this textbook is the creation of a new arts-related venture, the financial realities facing many students are such that finding employment during and after their educational commitments may be necessary. Although working for someone else may not seem like an obvious pathway to becoming an arts entrepreneur, there are in fact many good reasons for choosing to become an employee first and then work toward becoming a business owner later.

Some of the benefits associated with being an employee in someone else's business can include:

- Gaining valuable experience on the job in an area that interests you. If you are able to find employment in a field that it is closely related to your idea for a new venture, job training and work experience can be important sources of inspiration and practical knowledge as you develop your readiness for launching your own company. Workplace experience is especially valuable when it gives an employee the opportunities to practice problem-solving and use their creativity to engage with challenging business situations.

- Working for and with other people in a business environment can help the aspiring entrepreneur discover ways of communicating and interacting with others that will be useful once they launch their own venture.

- Concentrating on specific aspects of business operations – such as marketing, fundraising, or creative production – can greatly increase knowledge and understanding of the many practical issues involved in running an arts-related organization.

- An employee's manager or supervisor can become a valuable reference in the future when the arts entrepreneur is ready to seek funding or other support for their new business.

- Developing connections with co-workers, consultants, and customers can be a way to expand one's network of contacts. It may be possible to hire a former co-worker – or develop a contract with the former consultant – when the arts entrepreneur is ready to form a team for their own business.

- Earning a regular paycheck and responsibly managing your finances (especially with timely payments to credit cards, car/student loans and other debts) is an excellent way to build your credit rating and demonstrate your viability as a borrower for future business loans. By setting aside some of your salary in a savings account, you can begin to create a business startup fund. Using your own financial resources to develop your business concept is an exceptionally good strategy, even if this represents only a fraction of the capital needed to launch and run your venture.

Preparing to Enter the Job Market and Finding Employment

Some readers will already have experience as a paid worker, intern or volunteer. Others will be approaching the job market for the first time and are just beginning the process of developing application materials, connecting with job opportunities, preparing for interviews, negotiating terms of employment, and getting hired. Regardless of your prior job experience, it is a good idea to review the processes involved in preparing yourself as a prospective employee and finding job opportunities that suit your interests and experience.

Note that it can be important to create both paper-based and digital/online versions of your resume, other written materials and work samples in order to be ready to apply to a range of different jobs as they become available.

Create a Resume

Working on your resume before applying for a job allows you to organize your education, employment history, and related skills into a well-structured document that you can present to prospective employers. An online search for "resume examples" will provide a number of commonly accepted layouts to follow when preparing your own. (A search for "artist resume" will also produce some useful results.)

Two of the most common versions of resume design include:

- *Chronological resume*: This type of resume presents your education and employment history in chronological order, with the most recent instances first and previous experiences further down the list. For each entry under the Education heading, include the name of the institution, the date range, the type of degree earned, the academic major, and a brief description of any honors or awards. Under the Employment heading, include each position's title, the name and location of your employer, the date range, and a brief description of job responsibilities. It can also be appropriate to mention specific job accomplishments, such as an increase in company sales figures, the design and implementation of a new fundraising program, or the number of new accounts established during your employment. After your education and employment history, you can add descriptions of specific job-related skills (such as graphic design, foreign languages, or software programming) and specialized training. Make sure to list any publications you contributed to or conferences you participated in that relate to your area of interest.
- *Functional, or skills-based resume*: In this type of resume, your previous experiences are organized around specific themes rather than listed in chronological order. For example, a photographer might group together skills such as concept development and art direction,

photo editing and retouching, or experience with location-based projects. Because you can include course-related work and other experiences acquired as a student, this type of resume can be effective for individuals who do not have an extensive employment history. Instead, you can present a well-organized document that demonstrates your interests and skills and communicates your qualifications as a potential employee.

There are a number of other resume formats to consider, including those that combine the chronological and functional designs described above. To explore some possibilities, gather a collection of potential resume types by conducting online research, visiting a local library and working with a reference librarian, and consulting with established professionals within your network. Once you have created a resume that includes your qualifications and skills in a generic format, your resume can be customized later to suit the specific job opportunity you are pursuing.

Develop other written materials

- *Biography*: Developing a clearly written, compelling biography can help the job seeker communicate their unique background, life experiences, and career pathway. An employer may find some of your biographical details interesting enough that, along with your resume and work samples, they decide to offer a job interview. Keep your biography brief and detailed – some good examples can be found on book jackets (see About the Author, usually on the back) in the fiction or nonfiction sections of your local library or bookstore. Your written biography can also be used on your website, in your social media profile or distributed in a publicity packet to the media for use as background material for profiles and interviews.

- *Artist Statement*: The Artist Statement is different than either a resume or a biography in that it conveys the influences, concepts, and intellectual framework underlying the artist's work methods and final results. Although it may be challenging to explain in written prose the artist's *meaning* in producing a specific piece or series of works, the reader of such a document will benefit greatly through increased understanding and appreciation of both the artist and the artwork. To discover some examples of well-written Artist Statements, look through museum catalogs, gallery publications, and online at your favorite artists' websites or social media accounts. As with other written materials used to promote your work and your career, you should develop a first draft of your Artist Statement and share it with friends and colleagues to get feedback and improve the document before sharing it with the wider public. An Artist Statement might be appropriate to include in a job application, but it is more commonly printed in an exhibition catalog, distributed in a press release, or used on a website or social media platform.

- *Cover letter*: Most job opportunities request that applicants submit a resume and cover letter in order to be considered for a position. The cover letter is a specific opportunity to communicate with the prospective employer about your interest in the job and your qualifications as a candidate.

Before starting the draft of your cover letter, carefully review the job description and make notes about particular areas where your skills and interests intersect with the position. Start the letter by addressing the recipient (such as the human resources department or hiring manager of the organization), then provide a precise, convincing statement of your qualifications. Next, mention specific areas of the job description that interest you and the ways in which your skills and experience align with the *employer's* needs. Finish with an expression of interest in arranging an interview and mention the inclusion of your other application materials, such as your resume, work examples and references.

An effective cover letter – of up to one page in length – should provoke interest in the reader and make a compelling case for you as a candidate for the job. Once you have completed a first draft, ask someone to read you the letter and listen as if you were the hiring manager of the organization you are contacting. Keep refining the cover letter until it presents you and your qualifications in the best possible manner.

Create a Portfolio Featuring Examples of Your Creative Work

Visual artists – such as painters, illustrators, graphic designers, and photographers – typically develop a portfolio that demonstrates their range of skills and highlights work created for themselves or their clients. However, it is also important for artists in other disciplines to create examples of their past projects to convey their unique talents and attract the interest of potential employers.

For the visual artist, generating high-quality image files are the first step in developing a portfolio. In some cases, you can use the original digital source to make a high-quality print, especially if the final product was developed using Photoshop, InDesign, or a similar software program. However, if your preferred medium is oil paint, watercolor, pen and ink or any number of other media for drawing, sculpture, or product design, then it will be necessary to photograph your work in order to include it in the printed and online versions of your portfolio. If you have access to high-quality photographic equipment – such as cameras, lenses, lighting, and professional backgrounds – as well as the skills and experience required to produce high-quality results, then you can take on the responsibilities for producing photographs of your own work for your portfolio. However, in many cases it may be necessary to work with an experienced photographer in order to get the best images. Sometimes a visual artist can barter with a professional photographer by offering an original piece or a commissioned work in exchange for photographic services. Remember that the goal is to generate the highest quality images possible for the visual representations of your work. This is also true when selecting pieces for inclusion in your portfolio: always choose quality over quantity when choosing representative samples, and include newer pieces (while removing older, outdated examples) whenever possible.

For the performing artist, developing a portfolio of video or audio examples is an excellent way to present your talents and stylistic interests to prospective employers. Musicians, actors, dancers, multimedia artists, and others should document their projects using their own equipment and skills, or by making arrangements with a professional videographer. Remember to carefully edit the final result when mixing audio and visual materials and incorporating titles, credits, and other graphics.

Artists working in either visual media or performance-based art forms should produce portfolio pieces that can be presented directly to a potential employer (using a DVD, CD, in a printed brochure or organized in a portable portfolio case) or stored online on a personal website, social media account or employment service such as LinkedIn.

Develop a List of References

Many job announcements will request submission of three or more references along with your other application materials. Employers check references for selected candidates because they want to hear from someone (other than the candidate) who is knowledgeable about the applicant's skills, work habits, personality, and ability to interact with others in the workplace. Your References document should include the name, title, employer, mailing address, phone number and email address for each individual.

Cultivating references is an ongoing process. Early in your career, you can ask professors and other professionals in your academic world if they might consider making themselves available as a reference for your future job searches. Many people in academia will be happy to support you in your career ambitions. You can also contact former supervisors from your work history and ask if they might offer to serve as references on your behalf. Of course, you want to develop positive, professional relationships with professors and employers while you have the opportunity and while your qualifications and skills are still fresh in their minds. By applying yourself effectively both in school and at work, you should be able to gather a list of quality references that you can use when applying for jobs when the opportunities arise.

Create an Online Profile for Job Hunting

Online employment services – such as LinkedIn or indeed.com – provide opportunities to create an identity for the job seeker and develop a network of connections to help attract the interest of potential employers.

In particular, LinkedIn allows the user to develop a highly detailed profile that includes their educational background, work experience, general interests, and professional contacts. As with other social media platforms, the jobseeker should carefully craft their online identity by curating their postings and background information with the goal of presenting a positive, engaging presence. You might consider deleting your old social media accounts and starting fresh with the new online identity that conveys a more professional image to prospective employers. Users of online employment platforms should also interact regularly with other people and organizations in their network by making recommendations, posting comments, and promoting employment opportunities as they arise.

Conduct a Job Search and Find Opportunities

How should you go about researching job opportunities that align with your interests and skills? For an individual with extensive work experience, the sources of job announcements in their area of expertise may already be well known. However, for the first-time job seeker the process of identifying and applying for employment can seem daunting at first.

Searching for Employment Online

In the past era of printed job announcements in the classified advertising sections of local newspapers, a job search would entail daily or weekly examination of the local listings. This method has been almost entirely replaced by online job searches, using websites such as monster.com, indeed.com, idealist.org, or online employment services such as LinkedIn. To pursue job opportunities available on these and other sites, use the following steps:

- Study the policies and procedures for each website carefully to understand the most efficient and effective ways to use their services.
- Investigate the profiles of existing jobseekers to discover the different approaches used in communicating one's background, skills, and interests.
- Consider doing an online search for articles and how-to guides that discuss strategies for using specific web-based employment services.
- Start creating your own accounts on several employment platforms, beginning with those that are free or low cost. Experiment with different formats and develop descriptive content for yourself that promotes your qualities as a potential employee.
- Ask for feedback from your family, friends, and professional contacts about your online profiles and how to improve them.

Once you have produced one or more profiles using the web-based employment services described above (and others you can discover), you can then conduct online research for open positions that suit your interests and experience level. Try using search terms – either in Google or directly within an employment website such as indeed.com or LinkedIn – to see what kind of results are produced. You can also post your resume online and let employers find you, although this technique sometimes requires a service fee. To apply for a specific position, carefully follow the guidelines posted in the job announcement and make sure to include any requested materials such as your resume, cover letter, work examples, and references.

Universities and Colleges as Employers

Don't overlook opportunities to apply for open positions in a local university, college, or other educational institution. There can be jobs in academia that align with your interests and skills, especially in programs focused on the arts. Examples include museums, performing arts venues, academic programs in visual art, dance, theater, music, digital media, or other disciplines, and administrative positions within student arts groups or alumni organizations.

While you are still enrolled as a student, don't forget to take advantage of the career development or job placement services available at your college or university. Many employers work through established school programs to attract qualified students and hire them into positions.

Note that *internships* are also a desirable first step toward becoming employed and, eventually, launching your own business. Most schools have internship programs designed to connect students with jobs that are offered by established companies in the area. It is advisable to research the internship opportunity – and the company associated with it – in order to select the best fit for your interests and experience. Like becoming an employee in a company, becoming an intern can turn out to be a positive or negative experience, depending on the nature of the position and the willingness of the internship sponsor to invest time and energy into making the relationship productive and educational.

Ask Your Network for Help

Another approach is to post your employment availability and interests on your social media accounts, such as Facebook, Instagram, or other platforms. Promote your job-seeking in a professional, direct manner and encourage others to support you by sharing your announcement through their network of contacts.

Use an Employment Agency

In most major cities, there are employment agencies that offer job placement services. Look for those organizations that specialize in areas of interest to you, especially in art, design, or performance. Employment agencies typically receive their compensation from the company that hires a candidate found via their services. However, there may be some agencies that want to charge the job seeker as well. Evaluate the options in your immediate area and ask your network of contacts for recommendations of reputable, productive employment agencies nearby.

The Job Interview

From the employer's point of view, the process of recruiting, selecting, and hiring an individual usually includes one or more interviews, conducted either in person, via phone or online using Skype or another online communications service. If you are presented with the opportunity to interview for a job, it does not necessarily mean that you will be chosen to receive a job offer. It *does* mean that you have been selected for consideration from the pool of applicants and are in the running for the position, along with several other candidates. As a result, you should take time to prepare carefully for any job interview, as it may very well be the deciding factor in whether or not you are offered employment.

Here are some suggestions on how to prepare for, and participate in, a job interview:

- Study the job announcement carefully and make notes about specific areas where your skills and experience connect directly with the requirements of the position.
- Research the company you are interested in – including the individuals in their leadership and management positions – to develop an understanding of the organization's mission, specific products and services, staff structure, and the functions of the job opportunity you are pursuing. The goal is to learn as much as possible about the business and the relationship of the available job opportunity to the overall company.
- Anticipate interview questions that you will be asked to answer. These can include questions about your background, interests, skills, and experience. You may also be asked about why you are interested in the position, or to articulate your thoughts about the overall company and how you might fit in with their corporate culture. Some interviewers will request responses to prompts such as, "Describe a difficult situation in your previous job and how you resolved it," or "Tell us about your greatest weakness as an employee." These kinds of interview questions are designed to elicit an honest, revealing response from the candidate that indicates their willingness to address challenges or acknowledge shortcomings.
- Prepare some of your own questions about the position and the company. For example, you can ask if this is a new job or if the position was held previously by someone else. You can also ask about future

prospects for someone in the job and about the organization's overall ambitions for the future. Keep the number of questions to a minimum when participating in an interview over the phone or online, but bring a longer list of detailed questions when being interviewed in person.

- Practice interviewing before your scheduled appointment. Ask someone from your network of family, friends, and consultants to conduct a mock interview with you as the candidate. Consider recording the practice interview and listen to how well you interact with the interviewer and answer questions. Use the practice interview to work on your interviewing skills, to improve your answers and gain experience in the overall process.

By preparing yourself with information and practicing before the actual interview, you will be much more confident and relaxed when interacting with a potential employer. If you know anyone who is currently working for the same firm, or who has worked there in the past, you can consult with them about the inner workings of the company and learn more details about the position you are pursuing. Make sure to arrive at the interview on time, dress appropriately, and interact with interviewers in a professional manner.

Receiving a Job Offer and Negotiating Employment Details

After your preparations creating a resume, biography, Artist Statement, portfolio of work examples and a list of quality references, and once you have successfully applied for a job opportunity and been interviewed, the next step (hopefully) is receiving an offer of employment and negotiating some of the specifics of the position. If this is your first job, then you may not have much leverage in requesting a higher salary or other benefits – it may be best to accept the terms offered by your new employer and work toward building your career over time. If, however, you have a work history and documented figures for your prior salary and benefits, it may be possible to negotiate some of the details of your new position. For example, the starting salary, beginning date of the employment, relocation expenses, number of vacation days and sick leave, and even incentives such as bonuses or profit sharing can sometimes be negotiated. Be reasonable with your requests and flexible about your expectations when negotiating with a new employer, since you want to start your new position in a positive, optimistic context. However, don't be afraid to turn down a job offer if the salary, benefits, or other terms of employment are simply unacceptable to you at the current stage of your career.

Building a Career

In his book, *Management and the Arts*, author William Byrnes suggests a highly organized process for career development. Creating a detailed

Personal Plan can keep you focused on identifying employment opportunities that suit your interests and help you make productive job choices. Designed like a strategic plan, the Personal Plan for jobseeking follows a series of clearly defined steps:

- Develop a Personal Plan.
- Define your objectives.
- Assess your situation.
- Formulate outcome options.
- Make your choices and implement your plan.
- Continue to evaluate your choices.

"You need to put your plan in writing and remain flexible as new opportunities arise. If you follow this process you will already be far ahead of many people you will be competing with in the job market."[8]

As discussed earlier in this chapter, finding a job before becoming an arts entrepreneur can be an excellent strategy for gaining experience, developing contacts and preparing to design and launch your own business. Developing a Personal Plan like the one described above can help keep your career objectives focused on the longer-term goal of creating your own company. Working in a series of jobs or internships – even if it turns out to be only a few instances – will prepare you to become a business owner by providing insights and practical knowledge you might not find from any other source.

Like the process of building your business concept upon your personal values, beliefs, and goals, the process of becoming an employee or intern in an area that interests you can boost your confidence and sharpen your sense of purpose as you work towards the creation of your own venture.

Create a new folder called Career Development. Start new documents for your Resume, Biography, Artist Statement, (Generic) Cover Letter, Work Samples, and References. Produce additional documents if needed for Job Search, Interviewing and Negotiating. Develop a Personal Plan for job seeking and career building. Place these documents within the Career Development folder.

Future Trends in Arts Entrepreneurship

The steps involved in becoming a successful arts entrepreneur can include formal education and training in an academic environment, exposure to real-world issues and an accumulation of practical experience via internships and employment, and, eventually, the design, launch, and sustained operation of your own arts venture. To develop an awareness of the current and future possibilities for a viable arts-related organization, explore some of these areas of emerging interest in the field:

Art Entrepreneurship and Social Benefits

Artists – and business owners of all types – have a variety of motivations for establishing their own venture. These can include independent control over their income and schedule, successfully designing and delivering products and services that address the needs of their targeted consumers, acceptance and recognition of their work in the marketplace and among the media, generating employment for others, and feeling a sense of accomplishment in creating a new business.

Another key motivation for some arts entrepreneurs is the desire to improve social conditions through the development and implementation of their business concept. The initiative to produce social benefits can complement the company owner's other goals of independence, income generation and innovative product design and delivery. Some founders incorporate social benefits into the fabric of their business idea from its inception, while others integrate positive social impacts as the venture grows and its mission expands to cover a larger range of issues.

Addressing Underserved Populations

Arts entrepreneurs seeking positive social impact often focus on specific segments of society. Some programs are aimed at improving the lives of underserved populations.

Examples include:

- Working with incarcerated artists to display their work in publicly accessible galleries and keep them connected to their cultural and social environment.
- Designing programs for aging artists that allow them to continue producing creative work in their field and present it to the public. Some art practices require adaptation to the physical and mental conditions of this demographic, but the goal is to maintain a sense of purpose and creative engagement in the life's later stages.
- Promoting access to art making and display for individuals dealing with challenging physical or mental health issues. The NIAD Art Center (niadart.org) in Richmond, California, provides "a way for adults with disabilities to explore creativity, acquire new skills, and earn money from selling art."
- Arts organizations serving the needs and interests of disadvantaged youth through a variety of programs and opportunities in music, theater, visual arts, dance, and poetry – along with training to develop employable skills in everything from computer programming to welding and woodwork.
- Arts education companies working with students from school districts with underfunded – or nonexistent – arts programs. As budget cuts to public education reduce or eliminate support for arts instruction,

private companies (especially those formed as nonprofits or working through fiscal sponsors) can serve this unmet need. San Francisco's Root Division (rootdivision.org) provides visual arts instruction for students (and adults) to connect "creativity and community through a dynamic ecosystem of arts education, exhibitions, and studios."

- Community-based organizations offering training and public engagement with art forms from – and about – their immediate neighborhoods. San Francisco's Precita Eyes Muralists (precitaeyes.org) is "an inner-city, community-based, mural arts organization" that works to "enrich and beautify urban environments and educate the public about the process and history of community mural art." The Crucible in Oakland, California, (thecrucible.org) is an established "fine and industrial art center where art thrives, inspires, and is accessible."

There are arts organizations that address environmental issues, such as climate change, air and water quality, or the global challenges caused by pollution and indiscriminate consumption. Arts ventures based on recycling and creative reuse/upcycling can tap into a wealth of readily available materials and transform them into a range of unique, popular products. San Francisco's recycling and collection service (Recology) has an Artist in Residence program "to encourage people to conserve natural resources and promote new ways of thinking about art and the environment."[9]

Creative Placemaking

Another theme for arts organizations seeking positive social impact is the concept of creative placemaking. In a paper published by the National Endowment for the Arts, creative placemaking is described as follows:

> In creative placemaking, partners from public, private, non-profit, and community sectors strategically shape the physical and social character of a neighborhood, town, city, or region around arts and cultural activities. Creative placemaking animates public and private spaces, rejuvenates structures and streetscapes, improves local business viability and public safety, and brings diverse people together to celebrate, inspire, and be inspired.[10]

Developing Projects for/with Communities

In creative placemaking, arts and culture are at the core of projects designed to engage and animate communities in urban, suburban and rural settings. Some projects repurpose an existing structure – such as a former library, factory, or warehouse – and create opportunities for creative enterprise. Others propose new construction to house single or multiple art forms and attract visitors from the nearby neighborhood and overall region. The Our Town grants program (offered by the National Endowment for the Arts) features a number of case studies[11] that show a variety of projects funded for creative placemaking purposes. These include the creation of an Innovation District within an urban setting, the revitalization of a public park into a site for creativity and interaction, the launch of a downtown arts festival featuring temporary installations, and the transformation of vacant city lots into spaces for artistic production and engagement.

Creative placemaking can do the following:

- *Encourage economic growth and employment*: Because of their scope, location, and levels of support required, creative placemaking projects typically involve participation by multiple stakeholders. These can include city government departments, specialists in urban planning and architecture, contractors experienced in remodeling structures and outdoor environments, funding sources (such as foundations, government agencies, and private individuals), and entrepreneurs seeking to create programs in art and culture. In addition to reviving and reenergizing spaces and structures, creative placemaking projects often seek to inspire greater levels of economic activity in the areas where they will be located. This can be accomplished via employment from firms located in or near the creative placemaking site, from increased tax revenue realized through income generated by arts-related businesses, and from the attraction of investments that will support further development in and around the area.
- *Create opportunities for young/emerging artists, designers, makers*: For creative professionals at the beginning of their careers – especially those recently graduated from school programs in art and design— there are a number of challenges posed by the cost-of-living realities in major urban centers such as New York, Los Angeles, or San Francisco. How can one afford to live in a major city when one's income is on the lower end of the scale while you are at the beginning stages of your career? Creative placemaking projects can sometimes offer opportunities for young artists and designers to occupy an affordable space while becoming established in their field.

Artist/performer/urban developer Theaster Gates has demonstrated the possibilities for creative placemaking in his urban renewal projects focused on revitalizing neighborhoods. His efforts leading the Rebuild Foundation (rebuild-foundation.org) have produced a number of successful initiatives, including the Stony Island Arts Bank, the Black Cinema House, the Dorchester Art + Housing Collaborative, Archive House, and Listening House.

Arts Entrepreneurship and Technology

Entrepreneurship in general has benefited greatly from advances in technology, especially those businesses providing web services, communications, and social media platforms, such as Google, Facebook, Instagram, and others. Successful ventures in the "gig economy," such as Uber, Lyft, and Airbnb, would not be possible without the web-based infrastructure that allows them to attract and connect customers and service providers.

Technology can be an essential ingredient in the business concept developed and promoted by an arts entrepreneur:

- Web-based creative services – such as online galleries, platforms that connect artists with collaborators, and apps designed to connect audiences with performing arts events – have the potential to find an enthusiastic market and grow into established companies.
- Using the internet to conduct research and develop relationships with suppliers, manufacturers and distribution firms can help the founder create a business that can be managed remotely, even if these essential services are located in different states or multiple countries.
- Online services for marketing, sales, and financial management allow the owner of an arts-related business to keep the operation productive while carefully monitoring its performance.
- Skillfully promoting a business using websites, social media, email, and text campaigns can build the market for a new venture without resorting to paid advertising in traditional print media.
- Organizations focused on community development can use technology to reach out to diverse populations and promote awareness of the company's products and services.

Although the technologies available today offer an arts entrepreneur numerous opportunities to increase efficiency and build a company that leverages online communications and production capabilities, the technologies of tomorrow will no doubt provide even more possibilities for business development and growth. To keep on top of developments in technology that can influence the design of a new business – or shape the continued operation of an existing venture – follow some of the specialized tech media outlets such as wired.com, techcrunch.com, or arstechnica.com, along with the tech/business sections of traditional media sources such as nytimes.com, latimes.com, washingtonpost.com, and forbes.com.

Arts Entrepreneurship and Science

Developing a creative business that focuses on the intersection between art and science allows the owner and other stakeholders to participate in – and exert an influence on – a range of important issues such as sustainability, ecology, aging, and health. Scientific discoveries are constantly changing our understanding of the world around us and can, in certain instances, create opportunities for the arts entrepreneur to develop and launch a new business concept. For example, a company with a strong interest in environmental issues could develop its product lines, operational methods, and communication strategies in alignment with policies that reduce pollution, promote sustainability, and encourage responsible corporate behavior. Although not technically an arts-related business, the outdoor clothing and equipment company Patagonia (patagonia.com) is an excellent model of an organization dedicated to sound environmental practices in its manufacturing, marketing and activism.

Arts Entrepreneurship and Funding

Crowdfunding platforms such as Kickstarter, Indiegogo, Patreon, GoFundMe and others have allowed startups and creative entrepreneurs to attract funding in ways that were not previously possible. Many artists – along with founders of arts-related businesses – develop crowdfunding campaigns to both raise money and build support networks for their projects. Using a crowdfunding platform to experiment with a creative idea allows you to test a number of key factors for business development, such as product design and refinement, storytelling, interactions with investors and future customers, and fulfillment via efficient production and distribution methods. As the competition increases – with many crowdfunding campaigns seeking attention and resources from supporters – so the number of crowdfunding platforms are increasing for consideration as effective environments for attracting interest and financial backing. Specialty crowdfunding platforms for musicians, filmmakers, and others are expanding the range of opportunities for arts entrepreneurs looking to attract support and raise awareness about their projects.

Other forms of investment for the creative enterprise are just beginning to take shape. Like the model for socially responsible investing, impact investing in the creative economy seeks to deliver both economic returns and social benefits in the arts and cultural sectors. Organizations such as Upstart CoLab (upstartco-lab.org) are starting to develop projects that deliver profitable returns to investors while providing critical financial support for affordable artist spaces, theater renovation and sustainable fashion.

Artist and Consumer as Co-creators

In this new paradigm, the constantly evolving relationship and dialogue between the artist-entrepreneur and her audience(s) are fundamental. Thus, each becomes a co-creator within the process of generating a unique and meaningful artistic experience. While the artistic vision-project constitutes one of the artist's principal resources, this is by no means the only starting point. The artist's capacity for empathy – allowing her to engage and build with particular audiences – becomes crucial, as does her sense of civic responsibility.[12]

Many artists who produce work on commission – such as painters, sculptors, illustrators, photographers, writers, and graphic designers – are familiar with the concept of co-creation. The creator and client work together to develop a project's underlying purpose and meaning, as well as shape its final realization. A builder of musical instruments might consult and collaborate extensively with the individual who is paying for – and intending to perform with – a new musical device such as a guitar, keyboard, or custom electronic instrument. The idea of co-creation can extend beyond commissioned work and involve participation by multiple stakeholders in the generation of the aesthetic value associated with the project: "the customer plays a vital role throughout the entrepreneurial creation process: neither the entrepreneur nor the customer has the final say; rather, their embodied experiences combine with an evolving product to co-create aesthetic value.[13]

This approach differs from the individual artist or business owner deciding in advance what the product and service will be and how it will be understood and accepted by the consumer. The process shares some characteristics with Lean Startup methodology in that it involves the end-user frequently and meaningfully in the process of developing and delivering the final product. Artists may allow themselves to be influenced by both real and *imagined* customers as they develop and refine their ideas for creative work:

> Artist and customer may collaborate in the creation of art, as with some commissioned artwork; or the artist may simply envision ways to connect with future customers. Art—and, concurrently, aesthetic value—emerge as entrepreneurs process and anticipate these real or imagined customers' reactions to their work. In arts entrepreneurship, as in entrepreneurship in general, customers thus play a fundamental role in the creative process.[14]

Collaborative activities such as imagining, contemplating, and consensus building between the artist and customer can produce unique results that satisfy the interests and expectations of each participant:

> The role of customers in the entrepreneurial process goes far beyond their willingness to purchase a particular product or service; even absent customers continually enter entrepreneurs' conscious and unconscious thoughts to influence the development of entrepreneurial ideas and products.[15]

Entrepreneurial Bricolage

Bricolage is defined by the *Merriam-Webster Dictionary* as:

> construction (as of a sculpture or a structure of ideas) achieved by using whatever comes to hand
>
> also: something constructed in this way.[6]

The idea of *entrepreneurial bricolage* focuses on assembling works from materials as they are available, or as they are found through research and collection. Connected in some ways to environmental sustainability and creative reuse, this method can be applied to mixed-media visual art, as well as to innovative product design using found objects. *Conceptual bricolage* refers to using whatever ideas can be locally harvested and assembled into a viable project. For example, a theater company might invite residents of a local neighborhood to contribute suggestions for plots, characters, and settings for a series of new plays. By constraining the artwork to limited, readily available resources, the resulting product is at once highly specific to its location and affordably produced through its use of found materials.

Keeping Up with Trends in Entrepreneurship and Business

In addition to following news items in mainstream media such as the *New York Times*, the *Washington Post*, *Los Angeles Times*, the *Financial Times* and the *Wall Street Journal*, arts entrepreneurs should follow specialized publications – both in print and online – to stay informed about developing trends and find inspiration in interviews, reports, and case studies focused on innovative startups and their founders. Some examples for consideration include:

Advertising Age (adage.com)

Businessweek (businesweek.com)

Entrepreneur (enrepreneur.com)

Fast Company (fastcompany.com)

Forbes (forbes.com)

Gizmodo (gizmodo.com)

Inc. (inc.com)

Mashable (mashable.com)

TechCrunch (techcrunch.com)

Wired (wired.com)

Many of these publications offer lists of their favorite websites, blogs, social media, and other media sources that provide news and information for entrepreneurs from all fields.

Working with Other Creative Individuals, Businesses and Organizations

Although many artists and business founders work independently as they create and distribute their work, there are many benefits to developing connections with other individuals and companies that exist nearby or operate in a similar field. Musicians and bands join together to form record labels or jointly produce concerts and festivals. Visual artists collaborate on new works or coordinate their exhibitions and marketing efforts for group shows. Actors, playwrights, and directors launch theater companies to bring new works to their community. Designers, photographers, and illustrators combine their talents to form creative agencies or collectives. Owners of cafés and restaurants develop partnerships with visual artists, musicians, and poets to showcase their work and enhance the ambience of their public spaces. Architects and interior designers work closely with sound artists, sculptors, and lighting designers to produce extraordinary new spaces and dramatic environments for their clients. Composers, filmmakers, and writers develop long-term relationships as they invent, produce, and promote their collaborative projects.

Becoming a successful arts entrepreneur requires significant investments in one's time, energy, and focus in order to produce results that are financially rewarding and personally gratifying. Developing projects with partners and sharing your efforts with other creative people you know – or can discover – can bring added dimensions of quality and satisfaction to a career in the arts.

Chapter Summary

Organizational Design

Creating a detailed organizational plan helps a business identify roles and responsibilities for its management, operations, and support services. A one-person business needs to identify external consultants for legal matters, taxes, and insurance, while mid- to large-scale organizations should keep an up-to-date organizational chart that clearly defines the full range of job titles throughout the venture. Some companies use a horizontal, or flat organizational structure, with all of the positions bearing the same level of responsibility and receiving the same compensation and other rewards. Other businesses create a hierarchical, or vertical organizational structure, with the lines of internal communications and supervision starting at the top level of board members and executives then moving to progressively lower levels of managers, staff and volunteers. External communications (such as tax filings, business license renewals, bank reports, and other mandatory documents) should be managed by the venture's owner or a trusted accountant, bookkeeper or attorney. External marketing communications are the responsibility of the marketing manager or a hired marketing firm. Accurate job descriptions help the organization define positions that suit its current needs and anticipate future expansion. To encourage cooperation and efficient, effective use of everyone's time, regular meetings and status updates should be scheduled as needed – especially those that are brief and focused on resolving specific problems or leveraging opportunities. A meeting's final action items can be organized into a project management system that identifies individuals (or teams) for each deliverable and tracks their progress on a timeline. Most businesses generate a large amount of documentation, either digital or paper-based, in the process of planning and running their operations. Make sure to regularly back up digital files and follow document retention regulations for financial statements and other records. Develop a consistent human resources system for creating job descriptions and recruiting, hiring, training, and managing staff.

Career Development

Working as an employee for someone else – or serving as an intern or volunteer – can provide the prospective arts entrepreneur with a number of benefits, including the accumulation of real-world work experiences, opportunities to participate in problem-solving, developing improved communications skills with co-workers, building a network of contacts, and saving money to launch your own venture. The steps for preparing job application materials include designing a resume, writing a biography and/or Artist Statement, crafting a customized cover letter for each open position, cultivating a list of quality references, and developing a portfolio that features examples of your creative work. Job openings can be found using online services and employment platforms, or by looking directly for career opportunities with potential employers, including cultural organizations and art-related firms as well as colleges, universities and art academies. When invited to participate in a job interview, prepare by studying the job description and researching the employer (including key personnel), prepare answers to questions that may come up, develop a list of your own questions to ask when appropriate, and practice beforehand with a friend or colleague to build confidence. When offered a job, carefully consider negotiating points such as salary, benefits, and work responsibilities – but be flexible and reasonable when making specific requests for a position that is well suited to your skills and needs.

Future Trends in Arts Entrepreneurship

Arts organizations that produce social benefits are becoming increasingly popular, especially those working with underserved populations to provide opportunities for arts education, public engagement, increased job skills, and community involvement. Creative placemaking brings together artists, developers, city planners, and other partners to encourage creative reuse of buildings, neighborhoods, and districts. The results can include increased economic activity (through higher employment rates and tax revenues), improved livability and greater cultural awareness within residential/commercial/industrial zones. Technology has greatly influenced the ways arts entrepreneurs develop their business concepts and operational strategies, from online marketing and fundraising platforms to remotely controlled services for production, distribution, and financial transactions. Scientific issues and breakthroughs can create opportunities for arts-related businesses to become established and make a contribution, especially in areas such as sustainability, ecology, aging, and health. New funding possibilities – especially on crowdfunding sites – enable arts entrepreneurs to test their ideas, raise money, and build a network of supporters. Impact investing for creative ventures can provide new sources of financial support while delivering monetary returns for investors. Artists and their customers can become co-creators by entering into ongoing, mutually engaged relationships around artistic invention and production. Entrepreneurial bricolage refers to the creative use of found materials – or ideas – and making something new, locally based, and highly compelling to consumers. Arts entrepreneurs should keep themselves informed by regularly consulting traditional media outlets – they should also study websites, blogs, social media, and other sources of news, information and commentary that focus on their field. By working together with artists and business owners in similar creative disciplines – or by collaborating with others from different areas of art and enterprise – the arts entrepreneur can discover ways to increase both their financial gains and their personal satisfaction as they develop their careers and realize their goals in venture creation.

Discussion Questions

1. How does organizational design help the arts entrepreneur define positions within the company?

2. What is an organizational chart, and what does it reveal about the venture's lines of communications and supervision?

3. How do email, collaboration tools, and software development platforms support an organization's internal communications?

4. Why is it important to properly store company data and create regular back-ups?

5. When developing new positions for an organization's anticipated growth, what is the purpose of a job description?

6. Suggest some ways managers can develop productive, supportive relationships with their staff.

7. How will you design your arts organization to reflect what you have learned from your experiences as an employee?

8. How will you interact with your own employees to help your overall business succeed?

9. Why do meetings end with action items and how are they used?

10. Describe the steps for preparing to enter the job market and finding employment.

11. How do arts entrepreneurs incorporate social benefits into their business concept development and operational strategies?

12. Provide an example of an arts-related business that works with an underserved population.

Notes

1. Byrnes, William J. *Management and the arts* (Burlington, MA: Focal Press, 2015), p. 193.

2. See https://slack.com/

3. See https://github.com/

4. Byrnes, *Management and the arts*.

5. See /www.musicalartists.org/about-agma/history/

6. See www.musicalartists.org/faq-help/faq-page/

7. Byrnes, *Management and the arts*, p. 215.

8. Ibid., p. 446.

9. See www.recology.com/recology-san-francisco/artist-in-residence-program/

10. Markusen, Ann, and Anne Gadwa. *Creative placemaking* (Washington, DC: National Endowment for the Arts, 2010). Available at: www.nea.gov/pub/CreativePlacemaking-Paper.pdf

11. See www.arts.gov/exploring-our-town/showcase

12. See www.artsandhumanities.org/journal/new-approaches-to-entrepreneurship-in-the-performing-arts/

13. Elias, Sara R. S. T. A., Todd H. Chiles, Carrie M. Duncan, and Denise M. Vultee. "The aesthetics of entrepreneurship: how arts entrepreneurs and their customers co-create aesthetic value." *Organization Studies* 39 (2–3) (2017): 345–372.

14. Ibid.

15. Ibid.

16. See www.merriam-webster.com/dictionary/bricolage

Index

abstract expressionism 212
"Abundant Artist, The" 93–4
Académie Française 209
accelerators 203–4
accounting 204
accounts receivable 195
accrediting organizations 244–5
actuals 14–15, 186–7, 194, 197, 205
adaptive reuse 227
addressing customer needs 7–8
addressing underserved populations 263–4
adjusting future marketing efforts 102, 141
advertising 121
AGMA see American Guild of Musical Artists
Airbnb 266
altruism 127–8
Amazon 2
American cultural policy 211–14
American Guild of Musical Artists 251–2
Americans for the Arts 59, 75–6, 93
analytics 89–92
Andrew H. Mellon Foundation 224–5
angel networks 16, 203, 206
annual campaigns 116–17
annuities 116
anticipated financial activities 54
Apple 11
archives 205
Art of the Start, The 10
"art walk" events 28, 72
Art Works 221
articles of incorporation 172
artist and consumer as co-creators 267–70; entrepreneurial bricolage 268–9; keeping up with trends 269; working with other creatives 269–70
artist planning 35–6
artist statement 255
artists' rights under the law 154–8; contracts 157–8; copyright 154–6; patents 157; trade secrets 157; trademarks 156–7
Arts Council of Great Britain 211
arts education 219
Arts Entrepreneurship: The Business of Art 17
arts entrepreneurship in the community 24–6
arts entrepreneurship vs other types 15–28; arts entrepreneurship in the community 24–6; creating performing arts venue 23–4; experiences as business product 22–3; focus on positive social benefits 17–19; long-term commitment 15–16; nonprofit creative venture 22; online distribution 23; online platforms for fundraising 27–8; open-ended ownership 16–17; original fine art creating/selling 21–2; professional development 26–7; role of education 19–21
Artspace 231
asking network for help 259
assessment 35–66; and evaluation 55–65; see also planning
assigning responsibilities 246–52

Associated Press 228
attracting talent 31
audience education 69
audits 48, 77, 137–8; fundraising 137–8
authenticity 19
awareness raising 40

B corporation see benefit corporation
balance sheet 54, 192–4, 196–7, 201, 205–6
Bank of America 115
bank communication 244–5
banking 197–202; investments 199–200; loans 200–202
barter arrangement 246
Beaux Arts 209
being an employee 253
beliefs 40–41
Ben & Jerry's 152
benchmarks 59–60
benefit corporation 18, 52, 151–2
bequests 115–16
biography 255
board of directors 168–70
Bonin-Rodriguez, Paul 213
bookkeeping 160, 178, 204–6, 243
brainstorming 39, 42; see also SWOT analysis
brand awareness 10–11, 68–9, 85–6
break-even analysis 189–90, 195–7, 205–6
bricolage 268–9
Brown, Maren 56–7
build-measure-learn feedback loop 5, 10
building an image 68–9
building business 9–11; building brand awareness 10–11; building experienced team 9–10
building a career 261–2
building market demand 10–11
building with experience 9–10
Bureau of Educational and Cultural Affairs 218, 236
Business of Art 3
business budget 181–7, 197; vs actuals comparison 186–7, 205
business checking account 197–8
business credit card account 199
business growth planning 11–12
business idea based on values 3–5
Business Innovation Association 204
business launch design 11–15; eliminating inefficiency/waste 12–13; measuring success 13–14; planning for growth 11–12; understanding pivots 14–15
business license 174, 176, 245
business line of credit 199
business marketing 8–9; communicating product benefits 9; early-stage market research 8
business needs 107–8
business owner 165
business plans 49–50

business savings account 198
bylaws 172–3
Byrnes, William 261–2

C corporation *see* standard corporation
"cabaret license" 227
California Arts Council 215
California Lawyers for the Arts 158
call-to-action 86, 88, 95, 124
campaign cycle for crowdfunding 121–2
CAPA *see* Columbus Association for the Performing Arts
capital campaigns 47, 70, 114, 116–18
capital projects 47, 111, 113
capitalism 37
career development 253–62, 271; being an employee 253; building career 261–2; creating online profile 257–8; creating work portfolio 256–7; developing references list 257; entering job market 254–6; finding job opportunities 258–60; job interview 260–61; receiving job offer 261
cash flow projection 53–4, 181, 187–9, 195, 197, 201, 205
CBA *see* cost benefit analysis
CEMA *see* Council for the Encouragement of Music and the Arts
censorship 234–6
Center for Cultural Innovation 3
certificate of formation *see* articles of incorporation
charitable donations 223–6
Chicago Artists Resource 228
choosing appropriate language 40–42
choosing corporate form 146
Chrome 86
chronological resume 254
co-creating 267–70
coaching 140; *see also* training
Cobb, Peter 158
Coca-Cola 156
Cold War 212
collaboration 28–30, 244; with artists or owners 28–9; working with education institutions 29; working with overseas partners 29–30
collecting valuable information 103
College Art Association 228
Columbus Association for the Performing Arts 233
Comédie Française 209
commercial automobile insurance 162
commitment to company mission 252
communicating organizational structure 242–3
communicating product benefits to customers 9
communication 243–6; between management layers 243–4; with government agencies 244–5; and the marketplace 245–6; transparency 244
Communication Arts 85
Communication of Innovations 10
community building 27–8
community foundations 131
company image 245–6
company meetings 46–7, 140–41, 248
Compendium: Policies and Trends in Europe 211
competitive analysis 71–2; before the launch 71
Complete Guide to Fund-Raising Management 136
compliance 223
comprehensive record keeping 160
conceptual bricolage 269
conducting an audit 48
conducting an evaluation 60–65; assembling plan 62; assigning evaluation tasks 62; choosing indicators 61–2; defining evaluation questions 62; stating goals 61; writing outcomes 61
conducting job search 258–60; asking network for help 259; searching online for employment 258–9; universities/colleges as employer 259; using employment agency 259–60
connecting with market requirements 100–102; creating marketing plan 101–2
connecting with stakeholders 24–6, 70
Constant Contact 93–4, 124
content of crowdfunding project 119–21
contracts 52, 157–8

conventional entrepreneurship 16–17
convergence 4
ConvertKit 94
cooperative 151
copyright 154–6, 228–9
Copyright Law of the United States of America 155
corporate culture 252
corporate foundations 131
corporate inversion 234
corporate organizational structure 164–8; who does what 165–8
corporation 150–51
Corporation for Public Broadcasting 133, 222
corporations as funders 132–3
cost benefit analysis 83–5
Council for the Encouragement of Music and the Arts 211
counter-offer 158
country, cities, neighborhoods 217
create web brand 85–6
creating brand awareness 10–11
creating fine art as business model 21–2
creating fundraising plan 137–41; creating a schedule 140; developing materials 139; evaluating results 141; fundraising audit 137–8; goals/organizational needs 138; identifying funding sources 138; implementing plan 140–41; training people 140
creating marketing plan 101–2; creating schedules 102; developing materials 102; evaluating/refining 102; identifying opportunities 102; training 102
creating online job hunting profile 257–8
creating performing arts venue 23–4
creating schedule 48–9, 102, 140
Creative Capital Foundation 213
Creative Commons 156
creative destruction 2–3
creative placemaking 264
creative practice 15–16
crime and employee dishonesty protection 162
CRM software 96
cross-departmental communication 243–4
crowdfunding 118–22, 267; campaign cycle 121–2; content 119–21; elements of successful crowdfunding 119; history 119; network 121
cultivation of fundraisers 134–7
cultural diplomacy 218
cultural districts 226
cultural policy 208–239; censorship 234–6; exploring arts agencies, making connections 217–21; history in other countries 209–211; history in USA 211–14; international organizations, foreign ownership 234; labor laws 234; and the law 221–3; origins of 208–9; other government policies and regulations 226–32; outsourcing 232–4; summary 236–7; taxes, charitable donations, 501(c)(3) status 223–6; US government grants and loans 214–17
cultural tourism 220
curation 94
customer education 68–70

data management 141–2; documenting donor information 141–2
David, Jacques-Louis 209
DBA *see* doing business as statement
de Gaulle, Charles 210
decency 221, 235
define web audience 85
defining goals 48
defining market segments 73–5
defining organization vision 36–40; SWOT analysis 38–40
defining roles 242–3
defining terms 40–42
definitions of entrepreneurship 1–3
deliverables 111–12, 248
delivering digital content online 23
Department of Education 133, 219
depreciation 204
deriving benchmarks 59–60
design of business 11–15

designing company positions 250–51
determining evaluation type 57–8
developing board of directors 168–70; evolution of business and board 169–70; finding people to serve 170; initial board 168–9
developing business idea 3–8; developing unique product 7–8; evaluating/managing risk 6–7; finding business opportunity 5–6; personal and professional values 3–5
developing community projects 264–5
developing fundraising materials 108–113; goals 110; mission statement 108–9; organizational needs 111–13; organizational structure 109; strategy 110–111; target market 110; value for customers 110
developing list of references 257
developing materials 48, 102, 139
developing a unique product 7–8
developing written materials 255–6
Digital Millennium Copyright Act 228
digital rights 229
digital rights management 229
direct interaction 76
direct involvement in company mission 31
direct mail 98
directors & workers insurance 162
disability insurance 163
discovering board members 170
disruption 2–3
distribution of contents 229
DMCA see Digital Millennium Copyright Act
documentation retention 246
documenting information 141–2
doing business as statement 174, 176
"donation season" 95
donors 25
Dreeszen, Craig 56–7
DRM see digital rights management
Drucker, Peter F. 1–2
Drupal 85

early adopters 8, 10
early majority 10
early-stage market research 8
ECA see Bureau of Educational and Cultural Affairs
educating audience 68–70
educational establishments as employers 259
EFF see Electronic Frontier Foundation
efficiency 55
EIN see employer identification number
Electronic Frontier Foundation 229
eligibility of L3Cs 231
eliminating inefficiency 12–13
eliminating potential problems 65–6
email 89, 93–5, 124, 244; interesting content 94
emergency fund 180
emotional engagement 23
employer identification number 149, 174, 176, 245
employment agencies 259–60
employment practices insurance 162
encouraging participation 69–70
endowment campaigns 118
Entrepreneur Magazine 203
entrepreneurial bricolage 268–9
entrepreneurial finance 178–207; see also money management
entrepreneurs as employers 31
equity crowdfunding 203, 206, 231–2; regulations 231–2
established business marketing goals 90
evaluating choices of legal form 153–4
evaluating funding methods 114–18; annual campaign 116–17; gifts 114; grants 114–15; in-kind support 115; major gifts 117–18; planned giving 115–16
evaluating fundraising results 141
evaluating results 102, 141
evaluating risk 6–7
evaluating strategic plan 46–7, 49
evaluation 55–65; conducting the evaluation 60–65; defining type of evaluation 57–8; evaluating for whom? 57, 60; how to use information of 60; measuring effectiveness 55–6; timing the evaluation 60; using benchmarks 59–60; using outcome targets 59
evaluation data 62–5; analyzing 63–4; collecting 62–3; reporting 64–5
evaluation of marketing 82–9
events 99
evolution of board of directors 169–70
exchange model of interaction 70–71
execution of marketing 82–9
existing markets 10–11
exit strategy 16–17
experiences as business product 22–3
exploring arts agencies 217–21; arts education 219; cultural diplomacy 218; federally funded cultural institutions 218; humanities grants 220; other government programs 220–21; preserving US cultural heritage 218
export duties/fees 232
external opportunities 78
external threats 38–9, 78
extra-governmental cultural policy 225

Facebook 2, 28, 86, 89–91, 121, 124, 231, 259, 265
fair use 156, 228
Fairey, Shephard 228
family foundations 131
FAP see Federal Arts Project
FCC see Federal Communications Commission
federal arts programs 133, 214–15, 221–2
Federal Arts Project 212
Federal Communications Commission 229
federally funded cultural institutions 218
FedEx 156
fictitious business name 149, 174, 176, 245
Fifth Republic 210
FileMaker Pro 83
filing documents 205
financial effectiveness 55–6
financial plan 53–4
financial reporting 197
financial risk 7
Financial Times 269
financial vision 179
finding business opportunities 5–6, 258–60
finding employment 254–6
fine art 21–2
FireFox 86
First Amendment 229, 235
Fiscal Sponsor Directory 148
fiscal sponsors 148, 153
Fisher, Rod 211
501(c)(3) status 18, 146–8, 151–3, 168, 174, 216, 223–6, 231, 237
focus groups 76
focus on positive social benefits 17–19
Forbes 203
Ford Foundation 231
foreign ownership 234
Foundation Center 131–4, 139
Foundation Directory Online 132–4
foundations as funders 130–32; communication with 244–5
Fractured Atlas 148, 163, 224
fraud 162
Free Software Foundation 229
Freeculture 229
French cultural policy 209–211
French Revolution 209
"friends of friends" network 129
FSF see Free Software Foundation
Fulbright Fellowships 218
functional resume 254–5
Fundamentals of Arts Management 56–7
fundraising 27, 106–144; creating/implementing plan 137–41; crowdfunding 118–22; data management 141–2; developing materials 108–113; evaluating methods 114–18; importance for nonprofit organizations 106–8; researching sources 128–34; special events 126–7; strategy 134–7; summary

142–3; understanding why people give 127–8; use of digital media 123–6
fundraising audit 137–8
future employment 36–7
future trends 262–7, 271–2; funding and arts entrepreneurship 267; science and arts entrepreneurship 266–7; social benefits of arts entrepreneurship 263–5; technology and arts entrepreneurship 265–6

Gates, Theaster 265
general liability insurance 162
general small business loan 200
gifts 114, 117–18; major 117–18
gig economy 266
GitHub 244
Giving USA 134
goals of organization 36–40, 58, 79, 110, 138
GoFundMe 27, 267
Google 2, 86–7, 89, 93, 102, 265
government agency communication 244–5
government arts agencies 217–18
government loans 214–17
governments as funders 133–4
grant writing 139
Grantmakers in the Arts 75
grants 114–15
GrantSpace 132–4
Great Depression 212, 236
Green, Clark A. 17
growing new business 73–6
growing your business 13–14, 56
Guggenheim, Solomon R. 212
Guillebeau, Chris 4, 6
Gust 203

harvesting 16
helping one another 28–9
high culture 210
history of crowdfunding 119
history of cultural policy 209–214; French cultural policy 209–211; UK cultural policy 211; US cultural policy 211–14
homepages 87
Hootsuite 93
How 85
How the United States Funds the Arts 107, 134–5, 220
Huff, Cory 93–4
humanities grants 220

identification of individuals for specific deliverables 248
identify web goals 84
identifying funding 48, 138
identifying marketing opportunities 102
identifying potential problems 65–6
identity system 85–6
IM 125–6
implementing evaluation 62–4; analyzing data 63–4; data collection 62–3; reporting results 64
implementing fundraising plan 137–41
implementing strategic plan 46–7, 49
import duties/fees 232
importance of fundraising 106–8; for nonprofits 106–8
improving your website 87
in-kind support 115, 125–7, 133, 218
increasing effectiveness 55
incubators 203–4
indeed.com 257–9
Indiegogo 27, 118–20, 122, 267
individual software programs 82–3
individuals as funders 128–30
infrastructure 113
infringement of copyright 156
initial board of directors 168–9
innovators 10
inspire visitors to website 88–9
inspiring productivity 252

Instagram 28, 86, 90, 92–3, 121, 124, 259, 265
Instant Messaging see IM
Institute of Museum and Library Services 133, 222
institutional memory 170
insurance 162–3; management 161–4
integrated digital marketing 90–99; CRM software 96; direct mail 98; email 93–5; events 99; print advertising 96–7; radio 97; social media 90–93; television 98; text/SMS 95
integrity of documentation 249
intellectual property 52, 175, 228–9
inter-departmental communication 243–4
interacting with government arts agencies 217–18
internal databases 82–9; individual software programs 82–3; marketing management systems 82; websites 83–9
Internal Revenue Service 18, 22, 146–8, 174, 181–3, 190, 224, 231, 246
internal strengths 78
internal weaknesses 38, 78
international organizations 234
internships 259
interpretations of "entrepreneurship" 1–34; arts entrepreneurship 15–28; building the business 9–11; collaboration 28–30; definitions 1–3; design of business launch 11–15; developing a business idea 3–8; launching a new business 30–31; marketing the business 8–9; summary 31–3
Intersection for the Arts 148
interview for job 260–61
intra-management communications 243–4
Intuit Payroll 204
Investing in Creativity 213
investment regulations 230–32; Equity Crowdfunding Regulations 231–2; Program Related Investment Rules 231
investment of time 142–3
investments 199–200
investor communication 244–5
investors 25
inviting participation 68–70
iPhone 11
IRA 200
IRS see Internal Revenue Service
iteration of product attributes 8

James Irvine Foundation 114
jazz 212
job satisfaction 31
John F. Kennedy Center for the Performing Arts 218, 222, 236
Johnson, L.B. 212–13

K-12 schools 219
Kawasaki, Gary 10
keeping business on track 194–7; financial reports for lenders 197
keeping up with trends 269, 271–2
Kennedy, Jacqueline 212
Kennedy, John 212
key elements of business plan 50–55; appendix 54–5; executive summary 51; financial plan 53–4; market analysis/plan 52–3; mission statement 51–2; operations plan 5; organization overview 52; table of contents 51; title page 50–51
Kickstarter 27, 118–20, 122, 231, 267
Korza, Pam 56–7

L3C corporation see low-profit, limited liability corporation
labor laws 234
labor unions 251–2
laggards 10
Lang, Jack 210–211
late majority 10
launching new business 11–15, 30–31; managing growth 30–31; providing training 31
law and cultural policy 221–3; federal programs 221–2; state and local laws 222–3
Lean Startup, The 5, 15, 268
legal issues 145–77; articles of incorporation 172; artists' rights 154–8; bylaws, operating agreements, MOUs 172–3; choosing corporate form 146; corporate organizational structure 164–8; developing board of directors 168–70; evaluating choice of

legal forms 153–4; legal structures for for-profits 148–53; legal structures for nonprofits 146–8; limiting liability 161–4; other business requirements 173–4; structure, management, resource allocation 170–72; summary 174–6; tax planning 159–61
legal risk 7
legal structures for for-profits 148–53; benefit corporation 151–2; cooperatives 151; corporation 150–51; L3C corporation 153; limited liability company 151; limited partnership 149–50; partnership 149; sole proprietorship 148–9
legal structures for not-for-profits 146–8; fiscal sponsors 148
Lessig, Lawrence 229
Library of Congress 222
life and group health insurance 163
life insurance 116
limited liability company 52, 146, 148, 151, 172–3, 175, 204
limited partnership 149–50
limiting liability 161–4; insurance 162–3; risk minimization 163–4
LinkedIn 93, 121, 204, 250, 257–9
LLC see limited liability company
loans 200–202
local arts agencies 133
local U.S. laws 222–3
long-term commitment to creative practice 15–16
Los Angeles Times 269
Louis XIV 209
low-profit, limited liability corporation 18, 153, 231; eligibility of 231

McCarthy era 212
Mailchimp 93–4, 124
maintaining communications 249
maisons de la culture 210
major gifts 117–18
making connections 217–21
Malraux, André 210
Management and the Arts 261–2
management of insurance 161–4
management layers communication 243–4
managerial hierarchy 165–8
managing employees 247
managing growth 30–31
managing people 246–52; company meetings 248; creating corporate culture 252; designing staff positions 250–51; labor unions 251–2; maintaining integrity 249; managing employees 247; proposals/reports/working documents 248–9; scheduling/project management 248; termination 251
managing risk 6–7
managing use of funds information 141–2
Marillion 119
market analysis 52–3
market research 71–2
market segmentation 73–5
marketing 27, 67–105; connecting with market requirements 100–102; exchange model of interaction 70–71; integrated digital marketing 90–99; internal databases 82–9; market research, competitive analysis 71–2; promoting/growing new business 73–6; shaping your image 68–70; strategic marketing plans 77–82; summary 103
marketing landscape 71–2
marketing management systems 82
marketing planning 82–9
marketing policies 81–2, 101
marketplace and communication 245–6
Marks, Charles C. 211
measuring organizational effectiveness 55–6
measuring product success 13–14
media coverage 73
media regulations 229
memorandum of understanding 172–3
mentorship 213
merchandise sell-through 75, 106–7
merchant services account 198–9
Merriam-Webster Dictionary 1
Method 152
methods 40–42

Metropolitan Museum of Art 230
Microsoft Excel 82–3, 180, 205
Miller v. California 235
minimization of risk 163–4
minimum viable product 5, 13, 24, 32
mission statement 17, 36–8, 44, 51–2, 108–9
Mitterand, François 210
moderate to complex tax planning 160–61
money management 178–207; banking 197–202; bookkeeping, accounting, taxes 204; business budget 181–6; financial vision, goals 179; keeping business on track 194–7; other financial documents 186–94; other forms of financing 202–4; personal budget 179–81; personal expenses 179; record-keeping, archives 205; summary 205–6
motivations 17
MOU see memorandum of understanding
Musée du Quai Branly 211

Napoleon 209
National Council of Nonprofits 126
National Endowment for the Arts 5, 29, 59, 107, 114–15, 133–5, 211–22, 235–6, 264–5
National Endowment for the Arts v. Finley 221, 235
National Endowment for the Humanities 133, 220, 222
National Gallery of Art 218, 236
Nazi Occupation 210
NEA see National Endowment for the Arts
needs assessment 57
negotiating employment details 261
NEH see National Endowment for the Humanities
Net 85
Netflix 2
new business launch 30–31
new business marketing goals 90
New Deal 212
New York Foundation for the Arts 93
New York Times 269
NIAD Art Center 263
Nike 156
nonprofit creative ventures 22
nonprofit fundraising 106–8; different needs of different business 107–8; organizational mission 108

Obama, Hope 228
objectives 58
obscenity 235
Oculus Rift project 231
$100 Startup, The 4, 6
one-person organization 165–6
online distribution 22
online fundraising platforms 37–8
online identity 90–91
online profile for job hunting 257–8
open-ended dialogue 43–4
open-ended ownership 16–17
operating agreement 172–3
operating foundations 131
operational effectiveness 55–6
operational needs 112–13
operations 118
operations plan 53
opportunities 5–6, 38–9, 78, 258–60; external 78
organization mission 36–40, 108
organization planning 35–6
organizational chart 109–110, 243
organizational design 240–42, 270–71
organizational effectiveness 55–6
organizational goals 36–40, 79, 110, 138
organizational needs 79, 111, 138; programmatic needs 111–12
organizational structure 109
original fine art 21–2
Origins of the Arts Council Movement 211
origins of cultural policy 208–9
Ormston, Andrew 211
Orrin G. Hatch–Bob Goodlatte Music Modernization Act 228

other areas of interest 240–73; artist/consumer as co-creators 267–70; assigning responsibility 246–52; career development 253–62; communication 243–6; defining roles and communicating organizational structure 242–3; documentation/records retention 246; future trends 262–7; organizational design 240–42; summary 270–72
other business requirements 173–4
other financial documents 186–94; balance sheet 192–4; break-even analysis 189–90; business budget vs actuals comparison 186–7; cash flow projection 187–9; profit and loss statement 190–92
other forms of financing 202–4
other government arts programs 220–21
other resources for future work 48
Our Town 114–15, 221, 264
outcome evaluation 57–8
outcome targets 59
outsourcing 232–4
overlay district 227
overseas partners 29–30
owner's draw 181, 183, 186, 190–91
ownership of cultural property 230

P&L statement see profit and loss statement
Pandora 23
participation 68–70
partnership 24–5, 149, 165–7
passion 4–5
Patagonia 152, 267
patents 175
Patreon 267
patrons 25
percent-for-art 226
performance interruption and non-appearance insurance 162
Performing Policy 213
personal budget 179–81
personal expenses 179
personal values based business idea 3–5
Photoshop 256
Pinterest 93
pivots 14–15, 30
Pixar 11
planned giving 115–16
planning 35–66; for artists and arts organizations 35–6; defining vision, mission, goals 36–40; evaluation, assessment 55–65; strategic planning 40–55; summary 65–6
planning for business growth 11–12
planning strategically 42–6
planning for succession 30–31
polices and regulations that impact the arts 226–32; import/export duties 232; intellectual property, copyright 228–9; investment regulations 230–32; media regulations 229; ownership of cultural property 230; zoning 226–7
pornography 235
portfolio featuring creative work 256–7
positive social benefits 17–19
pre-launch research 72–3
Precita Eye Muralists 264
preparing to enter job market 254–6; creating a resume 254–5; other written materials 255–6
preserving cultural heritage 218
PRI see program related investment
print advertising 96–7
private good 128
pro forma statements 53–4
process evaluation 57
producer–consumer interaction 70–71
product attributes 8
professional development 26–7
professional values based business idea 3–5
profit and loss statement 54, 181, 186, 190–92, 196–7, 201, 205–6
program related investment 153, 231, 237; Rules 231
programmatic effectiveness 55–6
programmatic needs 111–12
project management 248

promoting new business 73–6; defining/reaching market segments 73–5; established organization 75–6; working with the media 73
property taxes 225
proposals 248–9
public access to company information 244
public communication 243–4
public domain 156
public good 127–8, 224

quality control 21
QuickBooks 190, 204

radio 97
raising awareness 40
rapport 136
re-energizing fundraising 60
reaching audiences 79–82; for established business 80; marketing policies 82; for new business 80
reaching broader audience 13–14
reaching market segments 73–5
real estate 116
real-time financial activity see actuals
Rebuild Foundation 265
receiving job offer 261
Recology 264
record-keeping 205
records retention 246
recruiting staff 250–51
refining business operations 12–13
refining fundraising efforts 141
refining your website 87
refreshing your website 87
regional arts organizations 133, 215–16
relationship marketing 128
Renaissance 209
repatriation of foreign art 230
reporting for funders 141–2, 248–9
reputational risk 7
resale license 174, 176, 245
research post-establishment 75–6
researching funding sources 128–34; corporations 132–3; foundations 130–32; government 133–4; individuals 128–30
resource allocation 170–72
responsibility for company image 245–6
restrictions on import/export 232
results 41
resumes 254–5
return on investment 82, 128, 202
revenue 224
Ries, Eric 5, 15
risk management 2–3, 161–4
Roberts, Joseph S. 17
Rogers, Everett M. 10
ROI see return on investment
role of education 19–21
role of marketing 68–70; educating audiences 69; inviting participation 70
Roosevelt, Franklin D. 212
Root Division 264
Roth IRA 200

Safari 86
safety training 163
sales taxes 225–6
SBA see Small Business Administration
Schedule C form 181–3, 190, 205
scheduling 48–9, 140, 248
Schumpeter, Joseph 2
science 266–7
search engine optimization 82, 89
searchable financial history 205
searching online for employment 258–9
SEC see Securities and Exchange Commission
Securities and Exchange Commission 231–2

selling fine art as business model 21–2
SEO *see* search engine optimization
serial entrepreneurship 16
Serra, Richard 235
Serra v. General Services Administration 235
service marks *see* trademarks
service to address customer needs 7–8
shaping image 68–70
sharing responsibility 174–6
Shoemaker, F. Floyd 10
Short Message Service *see* SMS
simple tax planning 159–60
skill transformation 4
Slack 244
Small Business Administration 149, 161, 166, 174, 200–202, 206
Smithsonian Institution 218, 222
SMS 95
Snapchat 93
social benefits of arts entrepreneurship 17–20, 147, 224, 263–5;
      addressing underserved populations 263–4; creative
      placemaking 264; developing community projects 264–5
social exchange 128
social media 89–93, 124–5, 129, 257–8, 265–6; Facebook 90–91;
      helpful tips 93; Instagram 92–3; Twitter 92; underlying
      concepts 90
Société Républicaine des Arts 209
software 82–9
sole proprietorship 52, 148–9
solicitation of fundraisers 134–7
soliciting crowdfunding donations 121
SoundCloud 88
special events 126–7, 163
special projects 118
special use districts 227
specific project for strategic planning 47–9
sponsorships 117–18, 148
Squarespace 85
standard corporation 150–51, 153, 160, 204
start-up launch platforms 203
startups.co 203
state arts agencies 133, 215
state laws 222–3
statement of activities 54, 190; *see also* profit and loss statement
statement of financial position 54, 192–3; *see also* balance sheet
Stellar Sounds Music Festival 201
stewardship of fundraisers 134–7
strategic marketing plans 77–82; audit 77; goals/organizational
      needs 79; marketing SWOT analysis 77–9; reaching audiences
      79–82
strategic planning 40–55; business plans 49–50; defining terms
      40–42; evaluating plan 47; implementing plan 46–7; key
      elements of business plan 50–55; process of 42–6; for specific
      projects 47–9
strategy for fundraising 110, 134–7; solicitation and stewardship
      134–7
strengths 38–9, 78; internal 78
studying arts entrepreneurship 31–3
successful crowdfunding 119
succession 30–31
suppliers 25, 29–30; overseas 29–30
supporters 25
surveymonkey.com 76
surveys 76
sustainability 113, 267
SWOT analysis 38–40, 77–9, 101, 103; marketing 77–9

target market 110
targeting evaluation 57
Tax Cuts and Jobs Act 2018 126
tax laws providing benefits to arts organizations 225–6
tax planning 159–61, 175; moderate to complex 160–61; simple
      159–60
tax-exempt status 146–7
taxes 204, 223–6; compliance 223; revenue 224–5; tax laws providing
      financial benefits 225–6

technology 265–6
television 98
telling daily stories 94
termination 251
testing your website 86–7
text 95, 125–6
text-to-give campaigns 125–6
theatrical property and real property insurance 162
Third Republic 209
threats 38–9, 78; external 38–9, 78
timing for evaluation 60
tips for social media use 93
tools and techniques 82–9
tour insurance 163
tourism taxes 225
trade secrets 157, 175
trademarks 156–7, 175
training 49, 102, 140, 213, 250–51
transparency 244, 247
trusts 116
Tumblr 93
Twitter 86, 89–90, 92, 121, 124
types of organization 165–8

UK cultural policy 211
underlying concepts of social media 90
understanding customers 71–2
understanding pivots 14–15
understanding reasons for giving 127–8
UNESCO 211, 218, 232
Uniform Trade Secrets Act 157
Universal Declaration of Human Rights 210
Upchurch, Anna Rosser 211
Upstart CoLab 267
Urban Institute 213–14
U.S. Copyright Office 155
U.S. Department of State 218
U.S. government grants 214–17; country, cities, neighborhoods 217;
      federal arts programs 214–15; interacting with government
      arts agencies 217–18; regional arts organizations 215–16; state
      arts agencies 215
U.S. Patent and Trademark Office 157
use cases 42
using evaluation information 60
using experienced advisors 9–10
using financial reports 194–7
using graphics on website 87–8
using outcome targets 59
USPTO *see* U.S. Patent and Trademark Office

validated learning 5
value for consumer 110
value of strategic planning 46–7
venture capital 16, 128
venture philanthropy 128, 213
Vichy regime 209–210
Vimeo 88
virtual methods of fundraising 123–6; email 124; social media 124–5;
      text/instant messaging 125–6; websites 123–4
voice of the company 245–6

Wall Street Journal 203, 269
Wallace Foundation 75
Washington Post 269
waste elimination 12–13
weaknesses 38–9, 78; internal 38, 78
websites 83–9, 123–4; creating brand/image 85–6; defining audience
      85; design decisions based on goals 86; identifying goals
      84; inspiring visitors to act 88–9; interesting homepage 87;
      refreshing, improving 87; testing 86–7; updating content 87;
      using graphics 87–8
Weinstein, Stanley 136
when to use pivots 14–15
Wireframe 86
Wix 85

WordPress 885
work in progress 94
workers compensation insurance 162
working documents 248–9
working with education institutions 29
working with the media 73
working with other creatives 269–70
Works Progress Administration 212

World War I 224
World War II 210–211, 236
WPA *see* Works Progress Administration
written materials for job prospects 255–6

YouTube 88–9, 93, 124

zoning 226–7, 237

Made in United States
Orlando, FL
14 August 2022

21021769R00163